PMP® In Depth:

Project Management Professional Study Guide for PMP® and CAPM® Exams

Dr. Paul Sanghera

THOMSON
™
COURSE TECHNOLOGY
Professional ■ Technical ■ Reference

ISBN: 1-59863-177-2

Library of Congress Catalog Card Number: 2006923222

Printed in the United States of America

06 07 08 09 10 PH 10 9 8 7 6 5 4 3 2 1

Publisher and General Manager, Thomson Course Technology PTR:
Stacy L. Hiquet

Associate Director of Marketing:
Sarah O'Donnell

Manager of Editorial Services:
Heather Talbot

Marketing Manager:
Heather Hurley

Acquisitions Editor:
Mitzi Koontz

Project Editor/Copy Editor:
Cathleen D. Snyder

Technical Reviewers:
Paul Gneco and Anil Punjabi

PTR Editorial Services Coordinator:
Elizabeth Furbish

Interior Layout Tech:
Bill Hartman

Cover Designer:
Mike Tanamachi

Indexer:
Katherine Stimson

Proofreader:
Heather Urschel

THOMSON

COURSE TECHNOLOGY

Professional ■ Technical ■ Reference

Thomson Course Technology PTR, a division of Thomson Learning Inc.
25 Thomson Place ■ Boston, MA 02210 ■ http://www.courseptr.com

To life

Whose every day is a project

That I run from the time's shoulders.

To my friends,

the key stakeholders:

Gurmail Kandola, John Serri, and Kulwinder

Baldev Khullar, Ruth Gordon, and Bhupinder

Stanley Wong and Srilatha are a few to name.

With friends, I can see clearly

Through storm and rain.

Friends without whom

Every path is just a trail of dust.

With whom I'm like the first man

Walking on the planet Earth.

Acknowledgments

Each time I get a book published, I re-learn a lesson that transforming an idea into a finished book takes a project (it produces a unique product—that is, the book—and it has a beginning and an end) and a project team. As they say (well, if they don't anymore, they should), first thing first. Let me begin by thanking Mitzi Koontz for initiating this project. With two thumbs up, thanks to Cathleen Snyder for managing this project from the planning stage through the executing stage, the monitoring/controlling stage, and all the way to the closing stage.

It's my pleasure to acknowledge the hard work of other members of the team as well: Bill Hartman for layout, Heather Urschel for proofreading, and Katherine Stimson for indexing. My special thanks to Paul Gneco and Anil Punjabi, the technical editors of this book, for carefully reviewing all the chapters and offering valuable feedback.

In some ways, writing this book is an expression of the project manager and educator inside me. I thank some great minds from whom I directly or indirectly learned about management during my journey in the computer industry from Novell to Dream Logic: Chuck Castleton at Novell, Delon Dotson at Netscape and MP3.com, Kate Peterson at Weborder, and Dr. John Serri at Dream Logic. I also thank my colleagues and seniors in the field of education for helping me in so many ways to become a better educator. Here are a few to mention: Dr. Gerald Pauler (Brooks College), Professor David Hayes (San Jose State University), Professor Michael Burke (San Jose State University), and Dr. John Serri (University of Phoenix).

Last, but not least, my appreciation (along with my heart) goes to my wife, Renee, and my son, Adam, for not only peacefully coexisting with my projects, but also for supporting them.

About the Author

Dr. Paul Sanghera is an educator, technologist, and an entrepreneur living in Silicon Valley, California. With a master's degree in Computer Science from Cornell University and a Ph.D. in Physics from Carleton University, he has authored and co-authored more than 100 technical papers published in well-reputed European and American research journals. He has more than 10 years of project management experience in the computer industry and at research labs at CERN and Cornell. Having worked in various roles, including director of project management at companies such as MP3.com and Dream Logic, director of software development, and software developer, he has a broader view of project management. He has earned several industry certifications, including CompTIA Project+, Network+, Linux+, Sun Certified Java Programmer, and Sun Certified Business Component Developer. Dr. Sanghera has contributed to building world-class technologies such as Netscape Communicator and Novell's NDS. He has taught technology courses at various institutes, including San Jose State University and Brooks College. As an engineering manager, he has been on the ground floor of several startups. He has also authored three technology books published by Apress, Manning, and McGraw-Hill.

Contents

Chapter 5   Planning the Project Schedule 113

Introduction

"'Begin at the beginning, and go on till you come to the end: then stop.'"

—Alice in Wonderland by Lewis Carroll

The primary purpose of this book is to help you pass the Project Management Professional (PMP) exam and the Certified Associate in Project Management (CAPM) exam, both administered by the Project Management Institute (PMI). Because the book has a laser-sharp focus on the exam objectives, expert project managers who want to pass any of these exams can use this book to ensure that they do not miss any objective. Yet this is not an exam-cram book. The chapters and the sections within each chapter are presented in a logical learning sequence: A topic and a chapter only depend upon the previously covered topics and chapters, and there is no hopping from topic to topic. The concepts and topics, both simple and complex, are clearly explained when they appear for the first time. No prior knowledge of project management is assumed. This facilitates stepwise learning, prevents confusion, and makes this book useful also for beginners who want to get up to speed quickly to pass the CAPM exam, even if they are new to the discipline of project management.

Who This Book Is For

With a focus on the PMP and CAPM exam topics, this book is designed to serve the following audiences:

- ◆ Project management practitioners who want to prepare for the PMP exam.
- ◆ Entry-level project managers and project team members who want to prepare for the CAPM exam.
- ◆ Beginners who want to join the field of project management.
- ◆ Project managers who want a book to use as a quick and easy reference to the discipline of project management.
- ◆ Instructors and trainers who want a textbook for a course on project management. Instructional resource materials related to this book are available from the publisher.

How the Book Is Organized

This book tells the story of project management in a cohesive, concise, yet comprehensive fashion. This book is written to the most current version of the PMP and CAPM exams based on the third edition of *A Guide to the Project Management Body of Knowledge* (PMBOK) by PMI. The discipline of project management, according to PMBOK, contains nine knowledge areas, such as cost management and quality management, and five process groups: initiating, planning, executing, controlling, and closing. The PMBOK and almost all project management exam books are organized along the knowledge areas. However, the exam objectives published by PMI are organized in order of the process groups. This poses a problem for the reader preparing for the exam based on exam objectives. For example, one of these books refers to 11 chapters for one exam objective in its exam readiness checklist. This book solves this problem by presenting the material in order of process groups: initiating, planning, executing, controlling, and closing. This order of presentation is also consistent with the lifecycle of a project, and therefore facilitates natural learning by connecting to real-world experience.

How Each Chapter Is Organized

With the exception of Chapter 1, on project management framework, each chapter begins with a list of exam objectives on which the chapter is focused. These objectives are officially called *tasks* by PMI, and these tasks are organized into domains, which are essentially the process groups, except the last domain. We have exactly followed the order of the domains published by PMI, but have shuffled around a few objectives to keep the topics and the subject matter in line with sequential learning and to avoid hopping from topic to topic.

The first section in each chapter is an introduction in which we establish three concepts or topics that will be explored in the chapter. Each chapter has the following features:

- ◆ **Exam Objectives.** Each exam objective covered in the chapter is fully explained at the beginning of the chapter.
- ◆ **Summary.** The Summary section of each chapter provides the big, unified picture while reviewing the important concepts in the chapter.
- ◆ **Exam's Eye View.** The Exam's Eye View section highlights the important points in the chapter from the perspective of the exam: the things that you must comprehend, the things that you should watch out for because they might not seem to fit in with the ordinary order of things, and the facts that you should memorize for the exam.
- ◆ **Key Terms.** This section lists the important terms and concepts introduced in the chapter along with their definitions.
- ◆ **Review Questions.** Each chapter ends with a Review Questions section that has a two-pronged purpose: to help you test your knowledge about the material presented in the chapter, and to help you evaluate your ability to answer the exam questions based on the exam objectives covered in the chapter. The answers to the review questions are presented in Appendix A.

> **NOTE**
>
> Notes present helpful material related to the topic being described.

> **TIP**
>
> Tips provide additional real-world insight into the topic being discussed.

About the PMP and CAPM Exams

This book covers the material for the following two exams:

- ◆ **PMP Exam.** Passing this exam is necessary to obtain PMP certification.
- ◆ **CAPM Exam.** Passing this exam is necessary to obtain CAPM certification.

To be eligible to take any of these exams, you must meet a set of minimum requirements. These requirements and other details for the PMP and CAPM exams are listed in the following table.

The Details of the PMP and CAPM Exams

Exam Detail	PMP	CAPM
Number of questions	Scoreable: 175 Pretest: 25	Scoreable: 135 Pretest: 15
Maximum time allowed	Four hours	Three hours
Question types	Multiple choice	Multiple choice
Minimum educational background	Category 1: Bachelor's degree Category 2: High school diploma	High school diploma, associate degree, or equivalent
Minimum project management experience	Category 1: 4,500 hours Category 2: 7,500 hours	1500 hours of work on a project team, or 23 contact hours of formal project management education
Minimum formal project management education	Category 1: 35 contact hours Category 2: 35 contact hours	N/A
Exam Fee (Given in U.S. dollars. May vary by country.)	Member: $405 Nonmember: $555	Member: $225 Nonmember: $300
Sign code of professional conduct	Yes	Yes

As mentioned previously, the PMP and CAPM exam objectives are organized along the process groups (stages of the project lifecycle, as we call them in this book). These process groups and the topics of professional and social responsibility are called the *domains*. The relative weight given to these domains in the PMP exam is listed in the following table.

Proportion of Questions from Each Domain

Domain #	Domain Name	Approximate Percentage Coverage in the Exam
1	Initiating the Project	11
2	Planning the Project	23
3	Executing the Project	27
4	Monitoring and Controlling the Project	21
5	Closing the Project	9
6	Professional and Social Responsibility	9
	Total	100

The relative weight given to these domains in the CAPM exam is approximately the same. The main difference between the questions in the two exams is that the PMP exam will have situational questions that assume you have been working in the project management field.

The following points are common to both the exams:

◆ Pretest questions are randomly placed throughout the examination. Your score does not depend on these questions.

◆ Computer-based exams are preceded by a 15-minute computer tutorial, which is not part of the allotted exam time.

◆ The passing score is determined by an approach called the *Modified Angoff Technique*, which relies on the collective judgment of groups of CAPM certificants from around the globe. The final passing score for the examination is based on this pooled judgment and the calculation of the standard error on the mean. Finally, item analysis and reliability indices are calculated for each question.

These credential examinations are offered via computer at locations in North America and in other countries around the world. For a complete list of computer-based testing locations, please visit http://www.2test.com.

For the most up-to-date information regarding these examinations, please visit the certification section of the PMI Web site at http://www.pmi.org.

Following are a few tips that you can use during the exam:

◆ The questions in the PMP exam can be wordy and might include unnecessary information to distract you from the relevant facts. So, you need to read the questions carefully and patiently and figure out what counts and what does not.

◆ Get comfortable with the idea that there will be some questions that you will not be able to answer correctly. Don't let it bother you, and leave these questions for a possible review later if you have time. Move on without getting frustrated.

◆ There will be tricky questions to weed out candidates who might have project management experience, but who do not have an in-depth understanding of the discipline of project management from the perspective of PMI, as covered in this book.

◆ There will be questions for which you will need to choose between an innocent way of skipping the formal process to save time and following the formal project management process. In almost all the cases, the correct answer will be to follow the process.

◆ There will be questions for which you will need to choose between facing the problem head-on or taking an easy way out, such as dodging a thorny issue, ignoring a challenging problem, or postponing a difficult decision. Almost always, the correct answer is to meet the problem head-on.

◆ To answer some questions correctly, understand that in the world of project management as seen from the perspective of PMI, project managers communicate directly and clearly and do not say things between the lines. For example, if you have a problem with a team member, you talk to the team member face to face rather than going to the member's manager, which you might need to do eventually if you can't solve the problem by directly dealing with the team member.

◆ Understand clearly the roles of the key stakeholders, such as the project manger, project sponsor, and customer. Especially understand your responsibilities as a project manager. You need to be proactive to make decisions and manage the project, influence the factors that contribute to changes rather than waiting for the changes, and have up-to-date information about the project.

Best wishes for the exam; go for it!

Exam Readiness Checklist

Exam Objective	Chapter #
1. Initiating the Project	
1.1 Conduct Project Selection Methods	2
1.2 Define Scope	
1.3 Document Project Risks, Assumptions, and Constraints	4
1.4 Identify and Perform Stakeholder Analysis	2
1.5 Develop a Project Charter	
1.6 Obtain Project Charter Approval	
2. Planning the Project	
2.1 Define and Record Requirements, Constraints, and Assumptions	3
2.2 Identify Project Team and Define Roles and Responsibilities	3, 5
2.3 Create the WBS	
2.4 Develop Change Management Plan	7
2.5 Identify Risks and Define Risk Strategies	4
2.6 Obtain Plan Approval	5
2.7 Conduct Kick-Off Meeting	6
3. Executing the Project	
3.1 Execute Tasks Defined in the Project Plan	6
3.2 Ensure Common Understanding and Set Expectations	
3.3 Implement the Procurement of Project Resources	
3.4 Manage Resource Allocation	5
3.5 Implement a Quality Management Plan	6
3.6 Implement Approved Changes	
3.7 Implement Approved Actions and Workarounds	
3.8 Improve Team Performance	

Exam Readiness Checklist

Exam Objective	Chapter #
4. Monitoring and Controlling the Project	
4.1 Measure Project Performance	7
4.2 Verify and Manage Changes to the Project	
4.3 Ensure Project Deliverables Conform to Quality Standards	
4.4 Monitor All Risks	
5. Closing the Project	
5.1 Obtain Final Acceptance for the Project	8
5.2 Obtain Financial, Legal, and Administrative Closure	
5.3 Release Project Resources	
5.4 Identify, Document, and Communicate Lessons Learned	
5.5 Create and Distribute Final Project Report	
5.6 Archive and Retain Project Records	
5.7 Measure Customer Satisfaction	
6. Professional and Social Responsibility	9
6.1 Ensure Individual Integrity	
6.2 Contribute to the Project Management Knowledge Base	
6.3 Enhance Personal Professional Competence	
6.4 Promote Interaction among Stakeholders	

Chapter 1

Project Management Framework

Learning Objectives

- Basic concepts of project management

- The project lifecycle: process groups

- Project management knowledge areas

- Project stakeholders

- Influence of organizational structure on project management

Introduction

What do the Taj Mahal, the Internet, and this book have in common? Projects! All three of them are products of projects. Even given all the required material and the knowledge, how do people really build immense and complex structures or systems, such as the Taj Mahal of Agra, the Eiffel Tower of Paris, or the World Wide Web of the Information Age? The answer is again projects. Through projects, it is possible to build small and big, and simple and complex things in an effective and efficient manner. All projects need to be managed. A so-called unmanaged project is simply a poorly managed project that is destined to fail. Therefore, the importance of project management cannot be overstated.

Managing a project means managing the lifecycle of the project, starting from the beginning (initiating) and going to the end (closing); this is accomplished using processes, which constitute what are called *project management knowledge areas*. Although you use your knowledge in terms of processes to manage the projects, the management will be greatly influenced by the structure of the organization in which the project is being performed.

The goal of this chapter is to walk you through the framework of project management. To that end, we will explore three avenues: the project lifecycle, project management knowledge areas, and the influence of the organizational structure on the project management.

Basic Concepts

Each discipline of knowledge builds upon some basic concepts. The terms that refer to or define these concepts make up the language of the discipline. The very basic terms in project management are described briefly in the following list:

- ◆ **Project.** A project is a work effort made over a finite period of time with a start and a finish to create a unique product, service, or result. Because a project has a start and an end, it is also called a *temporary effort or endeavor*.
- ◆ **Organization.** An organization is a group of individuals organized to work for some purpose or mission. Computer companies, energy companies (to whom you pay your electric bills), and cable companies are examples of organizations. An organization might offer products, such as books and donuts, or services, such as Internet access or online banking. A project is usually performed inside an organization.

◆ **Project stakeholder.** A project stakeholder is an individual or an organization that can be positively or negatively affected by the project execution. A project can have a wide spectrum of stakeholders, from the project sponsor, to an environmental organization, to an ordinary citizen.

◆ **Process.** A process is a set of related tasks performed to manage a certain aspect of a project, such as cost. Each process belongs to a knowledge area.

◆ **Knowledge area.** A knowledge area in project management is defined by its knowledge requirements related to managing a specific aspect of a project, such as cost, by using a set of processes. PMI recognizes a total of nine knowledge areas, such as cost management and human resource management.

◆ **Performing organization.** The performing organization is the organization that is performing the project.

◆ **Project management.** Project management is the usage of knowledge, skills, and tools to manage a project from start to finish with the goal of meeting the project requirements. It involves using the appropriate processes.

◆ **Program.** A program is a set of related projects managed in a coordinated fashion to improve overall efficiency and effectiveness. For example, a program could be delivering a product (or service) that consists of sub-products (or service components) delivered by the constituent projects. Also, a program might include related work that is not included in the scope of the constituent projects.

◆ **Program management.** Program management is the centralized, coordinated management of a specific program to achieve its strategic goals, objectives, and benefits.

◆ **Program management office (PMO).** Program management office (or project management office) refers to an entity in an organization who is responsible for providing centralized coordinated management for programs—that is, projects in the organization.

This is a minimal set of terms that you need to understand before you can start the exploration of the world of project management. More terms will be introduced as you continue exploring the discipline of project management in this book.

Now that you understand these basic terms, you can ask a very basic question: What does it mean to manage a project? In other words, what's involved in managing a project?

Managing Projects

At any organization there are many activities being executed every day. Most of these activities are organized into groups of interrelated activities. These groups fall into two categories: projects and operations. An operation is an ongoing and repetitive set of tasks, whereas a project has a lifecycle—a beginning and an end.

Understanding a Project

A project is a work effort made over a finite period of time with a start and a finish to create a unique product, service, or result. Because a project has a start and a finish, it is also called a *temporary effort or endeavor*. In other words, a project is a temporary endeavor taken to create a unique product, service, or result. So, a project has two defining characteristics: It is temporary and it creates a unique product. Let's explore further these two defining concepts: temporary and unique.

Temporary. The temporary nature of projects refers to the fact that each project has a definite beginning and a definite end. A project can reach its end in one of two possible ways:

◆ The project has met its objectives—that is, the planned unique product has been created.

◆ The project has been terminated before its successful completion for whatever reason.

The temporary nature of projects can also apply to two other aspects:

◆ The opportunity to market the product that the project will produce is temporary—that is, the product needs to be produced in a limited timeframe; otherwise, it will be too late.

◆ A project team is temporary—that is, the project team is disbanded after the project ends, and the team members may be individually assigned to other projects.

However, remember that the temporary nature of a project does not refer to the product it creates. The projects can create lasting products, such as the Taj Mahal, the Eiffel Tower, or the Internet. The second defining characteristic of a project is that it must create a unique product.

Unique product. The outcome of a project must be a unique product, service, or result. How do a product, service, and result differ from each other?

◆ **Product.** This is a tangible, quantifiable artifact that is either the end item or a component of it. The big-screen television set in your living room, the Swiss watch on your wrist, and the wine bottle on your table are some examples of products.

◆ **Service.** Actually, when we say a project can create a service, we really mean the capability to perform a service. For example, a project that creates a Web site for a bank to offer online banking has created the capability to offer the online banking service.

◆ **Result.** This is usually the knowledge-related outcome of a project—for example, the results of an analysis performed in a research project.

Quite often we will refer to product, service, or result as just "product" for brevity.

Projects are organized to execute a set of activities that cannot be addressed within the limits of the organization's ongoing normal operations. To clearly identify whether an undertaking is a project, you must understand the difference between a project and an operation.

Distinguishing Projects from Operations

An organization executes a multitude of activities as part of the work to achieve objectives. Some of these activities are to support projects and others are to support what are called *operations*. An operation is a set of tasks that does not qualify to be a project. In other words, an operation is a function that performs ongoing tasks: It does not produce a unique (new) product or it does not have a beginning and an end—or both. For example, to put a data center together is a project, but after you put it together, keeping it up and running is an operation.

It is important to understand that projects and operations share some characteristics, such as the following:

◆ Both require resources, including human resources (people).
◆ Both are constrained to limited, as opposed to unlimited, resources.
◆ Both are managed—that is, planned, executed, and controlled.
◆ Both have objectives.

The distinctions between projects and operations can be made by sticking to the definition of a project—that it is temporary and unique. Operations are generally ongoing and repetitive. Although both projects and operations have objectives, a project ends when its objectives are met, whereas an operation continues toward attaining a new set of objectives when the current set of objectives has been attained.

Projects can be performed at various levels of an organization; they vary in size, and accordingly can involve just one person or a team. Table 1.1 presents some examples of projects.

Table 1.1 Examples of Projects

Project	Outcome (Product, Service, or Result)
Constructing Eiffel Tower	Product
Running presidential election campaign	Results: win or lose; Products: documents
Developing a Web site to offer online education	Service
Setting up a computer network in one building	Service
Moving a computer network from one building to another	Result: network is moved
Study the genes of members of Congress	Results (of the research); Product: research paper

A project can result in a product (or service) that is sustained by an operation. For example, constructing the Eiffel Tower is a project, whereas managing it for the tourists visiting it every day is an operation.

Where do projects originally come from? In other words, how do you come up with a project? Sure, you have an idea, a concept of some final product, but how exactly you write it down and declare it a project? A project is born and brought up through a procedure called *progressive elaboration*.

Understanding Progressive Elaboration

As the saying goes: Rome was not built in a day. Rest aside, the product of a project—even the project plan—is not built in a day either. Usually there is a concept first, and a broad vision for the end product—that is, the outcome of the project. The clearer vision you have of the unique product that you want from the project, the more accurate the project plan will be. So, you move toward the project plan in incremental steps as the ideas about the final product are refined and as you get more and more information about the requirements in a progressive fashion. This procedure of defining (or planning) a project is called *progressive elaboration*.

Here is an example of progressive elaboration. You wake up one morning with an idea to close the digital gap in your community. Now, you have a concept of the final product (result) of your project: Close the digital gap in your community. But what do you really mean by that? It might include many things—building computers in an economic way and providing them at low prices to those who don't have them, raising awareness of the necessity of computer literacy, offering classes, and the like. Now you are really working to refine your idea of the final product. The second question is, how are you going to do this? Here you are referring to the project plan. You can see that the project plan and its accuracy and details depend upon how refined the idea of the final product is. The final product or objectives and the plan to achieve them will be elaborated further in steps.

> **TIP**
>
> Uncontrolled changes that make it into the project without being properly processed are called *scope creep*. Do not confuse progressive elaboration with scope creep.

Progressive elaboration, in general, means developing something in incremental steps. The project plan will be broadly defined to start, and will get more accurate, detailed, and explicit in an incremental fashion as better understanding about the project deliverables and objectives develops.

Even after you have an approved final project plan and the project starts executing, progressive elaboration continues to some extent. For example, you will see later in this chapter that execution and planning stages of the project interact with each other. Each stage of a project is managed by performing a set of processes.

Understanding a Process

Processes are the heart of project management. If you want to think of project management like a project management professional, think in terms of processes. Almost everything in the world of project management is done through processes.

What is a process, anyway? Back up a little and look around you; you will see processes everywhere, not only in project management. For example, when you make coffee in the morning, you go through a process. The water, the coffee filter, and the roasted hazelnut coffee made by grinding golden-colored beans are the input items to this process. The coffeemaker is the tool, and how you made the coffee is the technique. A cup of freshly brewed hazelnut coffee is an output item from this process. So, a process is a set of interrelated activities performed to obtain a specified set of products, results, or services. A process, as explained in the example and in Figure 1.1, consists of three elements: input, tools and techniques, and output.

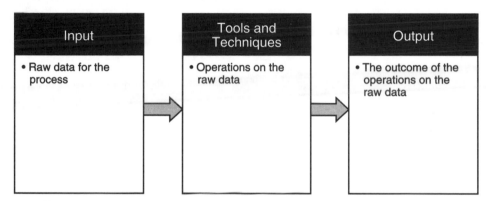

FIGURE 1.1 *Three elements of a process*

Of course, you can come up with other examples of processes that you have been using in your life without realizing it. In project management, you use processes to accomplish things, such as developing a project schedule, directing and managing the project execution, and developing and managing the project team.

Each process consists of three elements, described in the following list:

◆ **Input.** The input to a process consists of the raw data that is needed to start the process. For example, the list of activities that need to be scheduled is one of several input items to the process that will be used to develop the schedule of a project.

◆ **Tools and techniques.** Tools and techniques are the methods used to operate on the input to transform it into output. For example, project management software that helps to develop a schedule is a tool used in the schedule development process.

◆ **Output.** The output is the outcome or the result of a process. Each process contains at least one output item; otherwise, there would be no point in performing a process. For example, an output item of the schedule development process is, well, the project schedule.

Now that you understand what a process is, you likely realize that you will be using different processes at the different stages of a project, such as planning and execution. Actually, the whole lifecycle of a project can be understood in terms of five stages, with each stage corresponding to a group of processes.

Understanding the Project Lifecycle

From authorization to completion, a project goes through a whole lifecycle that includes defining the project objectives, planning the work to achieve those objectives, performing the work, monitoring the progress, and closing the project after receiving the product acceptance. Figure 1.2 shows the different stages of the project lifecycle; the arrows indicate the flow of information.

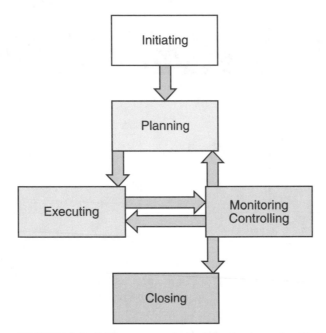

FIGURE 1.2 *Different stages in the lifecycle of a project. Each of these stages represents a process group.*

The five stages, called *process groups*, of a project lifecycle are described in the following list.

Initiating. This stage defines and authorizes the project. The project manager is named and the project is officially launched through a signed document called the *project charter*, which contains items such as the purpose of the project, a high-level product description, assumptions and constraints, a summary of the milestone schedule, and a business case for the project. Another outcome of this stage is a document called the *preliminary scope statement*, which describes the characteristics and boundaries of the project. The processes used to perform this stage fall into a group called the *initiating process group*.

> **◆ NOTE**
>
> In the discipline of project management, like in many other disciplines, the term *high-level* means lacking details or not referring to details. Keep this meaning in mind when you read the terms in this book, such as high-level product description, high-level plan, and the like.

Planning. In this stage, you, the project manger, along with the project management team, refine the project objectives and requirements and develop the project management plan, which is a collection of several plans that constitute a course of actions required to achieve the objectives and meet the requirements of the project. The project scope is finalized with the project scope statement. The project management plan, the outcome of this stage, contains subsidiary plans, such as a project scope management plan, a schedule management plan, and a quality management plan. The processes used to perform this stage fall into a group called the *planning process group*.

Executing. In this stage you, the project manager, implement the project management plan, and the project team performs the work scheduled in the planning stage. You coordinate all the activities being performed to achieve the project objectives and meet the project requirements. Of course, the main output of this project is the project deliverables. Approved changes, recommendations, and defect repairs are also implemented in this stage. But where do these changes and recommendations come from? They arise from monitoring and controlling the project. The stakeholders can also suggest changes, which must go through an approval process before implementation. The project execution is performed using the processes that fall into a group called the *executing process group*.

Monitoring and controlling. You monitor and control the project through its lifecycle, including the executing stage. Monitoring and controlling includes defending the project against scope creep (unapproved changes to the project scope), monitoring the project progress and performance to identify variance from the plan, and recommending preventive and corrective actions to bring the project in line with the planned expectations. Requests for changes, such as change to the project scope, are also included in this stage; they can come from you or from any other project stakeholder. The changes must go through an approval process, and only the approved changes are implemented. The processes used in this stage fall into a group called the *monitoring and controlling process group*.

Closing. In this stage, you manage the formal acceptance of the project product, close any contracts involved, and bring the project to an end by disbanding the project team. Closing the project includes conducting a project review for lessons learned, and possibly turning over the outcome of the project to another group, such as the maintenance or operations group. Don't forget the last, but not the least, task of the closing stage: celebration. Terminated projects (that is, projects cancelled before completion) should also go through the closing stage. The processes used to perform the closing stage fall into the group called the *closing process group*.

> **NOTE**
>
> What we refer to as project stages here are not actually the project phases. A project phase is part of the whole project in which certain milestones or project deliverables are completed. All these stages can be applied to any phase of a project that is divided into multiple phases.

Table 1.2 presents a summary of the project lifecycle. The initiating stage authorizes a project by naming the project manager, the planning stage further defines the project objectives and plans the work to meet those objectives, the execution stage executes the work, the monitoring and controlling stage monitors the progress of the project and controls it to keep it in line with the plan, and the closing stage formally closes the project by obtaining the product acceptance. Each of these stages is performed by using a group of processes. Thereby, these stages are called *process groups*.

Table 1.2 The Stages of a Project Lifecycle: The Project Process Groups

Stage (Process Group)	Main Goal	Main Output
Initiating	Authorize the project	Project charter and preliminary project scope statement
Planning	Plan and schedule the work to perform the project	Project management plan that contains subsidiary plans, such as scope management plan and schedule management plan
Executing	Perform the project work	Project deliverables: product, service, results
Monitoring and controlling	Monitor the progress of the project to identify the variance from the plan and to correct it	Change requests and recommendations for preventive and corrective actions
Closing	Close the project formally	Product acceptance and contract closure

The stages of a project lifecycle determine when a process is executed, whereas the processes themselves belong to certain knowledge areas of project management.

Understanding Project Management Knowledge Areas

Managing projects is applying knowledge, skills, and tools and techniques to project activities in order to meet the project objectives. You do this by performing some processes at various stages of the project, discussed in the previous section. That means processes are part of the knowledge required to manage projects. Each aspect of a project is managed by using the corresponding knowledge area. For example, each project has a scope that needs to be managed, and the knowledge required to manage scope is in the knowledge area called *project scope management*. To perform the project work within the project scope, you need human resources, which need to be managed; the knowledge used to manage human resources is called *human resource management*. You get the idea. Each process belongs to one of the nine knowledge areas discussed in the following list.

Project scope management. The primary purpose of the project scope management is to ensure that all the required work (and only the required work) is performed to complete the project successfully. This is accomplished by defining and controlling what is included in the project and what is not. To be specific, the project scope management includes the following:

- ◆ **Scope plan.** Develop the project scope management plan, which describes how the project scope will be defined and controlled, and how all the work within the scope will be verified as complete at the end of the project.
- ◆ **Scope definition.** Develop the detailed project scope statement, which is the basis for the project scope.
- ◆ **Work breakdown structure (WBS).** Decompose the project deliverables into smaller, more manageable work components. The outcome of this exercise is called the *work breakdown structure*.
- ◆ **Scope control.** Control changes to the project scope—only the approved changes to the scope should be implemented.
- ◆ **Scope verification.** Plan how the completed deliverables of the project will be accepted.

Obviously, these components are performed by using the corresponding processes. So, the project scope management, in part, defines the work required to complete the project. It's a finite amount of work and will require a finite amount of time, which needs to be managed as well.

Project time management. The primary purpose of the project time management is to develop and control the project schedule. This is accomplished by performing the following components:

- ◆ **Activity definition.** Identify all the work activities that need to be scheduled to produce the project deliverables.
- ◆ **Activity sequencing.** Identify the dependencies among the activities that need to be scheduled (that is, the schedule activity) so that they can be scheduled in the right order.
- ◆ **Activity resource estimating.** For each schedule activity, estimate the types of resources needed and the quantity for each type.

◆ **Activity duration.** Estimate the time needed to complete each schedule activity.

◆ **Schedule development.** Analyze the data created in the previous steps to develop the schedule.

◆ **Schedule control.** Control changes to the project schedule.

You perform these tasks by using the corresponding processes. It will cost you to get the activities in the schedule completed, and the cost needs to be managed too.

Project cost management. The primary goal of the project cost management is to estimate the cost and to complete the project within the approved budget. Accordingly, cost management includes the following components:

◆ **Cost estimate.** Develop the cost of the resources needed to complete the project, which includes schedule activities and outsourced work.

◆ **Cost budgeting.** Aggregate the costs of individual activities to establish a cost baseline.

◆ **Cost control.** Monitor and control the cost variance in the project execution—that is, the difference between the planned cost and actual cost during execution, as well as changes to the project budget.

You will use the appropriate processes to accomplish these tasks. The resources needed to complete the project activities include human resources, which need to be managed as well.

Project human resource management. The primary purpose of the project human resource management is to obtain, develop, and manage the project team that will perform the project work. To be specific, the project human resource management includes the following components:

◆ **Planning human resources.** Identify project roles, responsibilities for each role, and reporting relationships among the roles. Also, create the staff management plan that describes when and how the resource requirements will be met.

◆ **Acquiring the project team.** Obtain the human resources.

◆ **Developing the project team.** Improve the competencies of the team members and the interaction among members to optimize the team performance.

◆ **Managing the project team.** Track the performance of team members, provide them with feedback, and resolve issues and conflicts. This should all be done with the goal to enhance performance—that is, to complete the project on time and within the planned cost and scope.

These components are performed by using the corresponding processes. There will be situations in which your organization does not have the expertise to perform certain schedule activities in-house. For this or other reasons, you might want to acquire some items or services from an outside vendor. This kind of acquisition is called *procurement*, which also needs to be managed.

Project procurement management. The primary purpose of the procurement management is to manage acquiring products (that is products, services, or results) from outside the project team in order to complete the project. The external vendor who offers the service is called the *seller*. The procurement management includes planning acquisitions, planning contracts with sellers, selecting sellers, administering contracts with sellers, and closing contracts. You use the corresponding processes to accomplish these tasks.

Be it the procured or the in-house work, there are always some uncertainties that give rise to project risks, which need to be managed.

Project risk management. A project risk is an event that, if it occurs, has a positive or negative effect on meeting the project objectives. The primary purpose of project risk management is to identify the risks and respond to them should they occur. To be specific, the project risk management includes the following:

- ◆ Plan the risk management—that is, determine how to plan and execute the risk management tasks.
- ◆ Identify the risks.
- ◆ Perform risk analysis.
- ◆ Develop a risk response plan—that is, what action to take should a risk occur.
- ◆ Monitor and control risks—that is, track the identified risks, identify new risks, and implement the risk response plan.

These tasks related to risk management are performed by using the corresponding processes. The goal of the risk management is to help meet the project objectives. The degree to which the project objectives and requirements are met is called *quality*, which needs to be managed.

Project quality management. Project quality is defined as the degree to which a project satisfies its objectives and requirements. For example, a high-quality project is a project that is completed on time and with all the work in the project scope completed within the planned budget. The project quality management includes the following:

- ◆ Perform quality planning—that is, determine which quality standards are relevant to the project at hand and how to apply them.
- ◆ Perform quality assurance—that is, ensure the planned quality standards are applied.
- ◆ Perform quality control—that is, monitor specific project results to ensure they comply with the planned quality standards, and recommend actions to eliminate the causes of unsatisfactory progress.

These tasks of project quality management are performed by using the corresponding processes. In order to unify different pieces into a whole project, the different project management activities need to be integrated.

Project integration management. The project is planned and executed in pieces, and all those pieces are related to each other and need to come together. That is where integration management comes in. For example, integrating different subsidiary plans into the project management plan needs to be managed. The project integration management includes developing the project management plan, directing and managing project execution, monitoring and controlling the project work, and closing the project.

So, while managing all the aspects of the project, you, the project manager, will need to coordinate different activities and groups, and for that you need to communicate.

Project communication management. It is absolutely imperative for the success of the project that the project information is generated and distributed in a timely fashion. Some would say communication is the most important aspect of a project and the most important skill for a project manager to have. But without a doubt, it is certainly a critically important component of project management. The communication management includes the following:

◆ Plan communication—that is, determine the information and communication needs of the project at hand.

◆ Distribute needed information to the project stakeholders in a timely fashion.

◆ Report the project performance, including the project status.

◆ Communicate to resolve issues among the stakeholders.

As you have seen, managing a project largely means performing a set of processes at various stages of the project, such as initiating and planning. Accordingly, processes are grouped corresponding to these stages, and the groups are called *process groups*. Processes are part of the knowledge required to manage projects. Each of these processes belongs to one of the nine knowledge areas identified in the PMBOK. So a process has a dual membership—one in a process group, indicating at what stage of the project the process is performed, and the other in a knowledge area, indicating what aspect of the project is managed by using the process. Table 1.3 shows this membership for all the processes identified in the PMBOK.

NOTE

Not all the processes are used in all the projects. The project management team decides which processes need to be used in a given project.

Figure 1.3 shows the big picture of project management in terms of the project, processes, project lifecycle, and project aspects managed by different knowledge areas.

Each project is performed by individuals, and it can affect individuals or organizations even if they are not directly (officially) involved in the project. Now we are talking about the project stakeholders.

Table 1.3 Mapping of the Project Management Processes to Process Groups and Knowledge Areas

Knowledge Areas	Process Groups				
	Initiating Process Group	Planning Process Group	Executing Process Group	Monitoring and Controlling Process Group	Closing Process Group
Communications Management	n/a	Communications planning	Information distribution	1. Performance reporting 2. Managing stakeholders	n/a
Cost Management	n/a	1. Cost estimating 2. Cost budgeting	n/a	Cost control	n/a
Human Resource Management	n/a	Human resource planning	1. Acquire project team 2. Develop project team	Manage project team	n/a
Integration Management	1. Develop project charter 2. Develop preliminary project scope statement	Develop project management plan	Direct and manage project execution	1. Monitor and control project work 2. Integrated change control	Close project
Procurement Management	n/a	1. Plan purchases and acquisitions 2. Plan contracting	1. Request seller responses 2. Select sellers	Contract administration	Contract closure
Quality Management	n/a	Quality planning	Program quality assurance	Perform quality control	n/a
Risk Management	n/a	1. Risk management planning 2. Risk identification 3. Qualitative risk analysis 4. Risk response planning	n/a	Risk monitoring and control	n/a
Scope Management	n/a	1. Scope planning 2. Scope definition 3. Create WBS	n/a	1. Scope verification 2. Scope control	n/a
Time Management	n/a	1. Activity definition 2. Sequencing 3. Activity resource estimating 4. Activity duration estimating 5. Schedule development	n/a	Schedule control	n/a

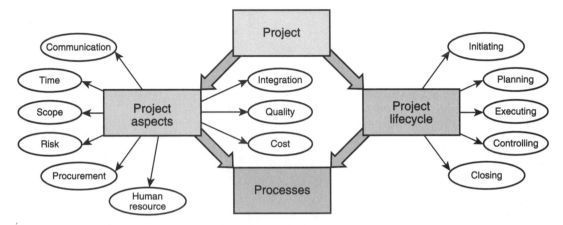

FIGURE 1.3 *The big picture of project management—the aspects of a project that need to be managed at different stages of the project lifecycle by using the processes*

Introducing Project Stakeholders

Right from the day you assume responsibility for managing a project, you start meeting a very special class of people called *project stakeholders*. It is very important for the success of the project that you identify these individuals and communicate with them effectively throughout the project.

Identifying Project Stakeholders

Project stakeholders are individuals and organizations whose interests are affected (positively or negatively) by the project execution and completion. In other words, a project stakeholder has something to gain from the project or lose to the project. Accordingly, the stakeholders fall into two categories—positive stakeholders who will normally benefit from the success of the project and negative stakeholders who see some kind of disadvantage coming from the project. The implications obviously are that the positive stakeholders would like to see the project succeed and the negative stakeholders' interests would be better served if the project was delayed or cancelled altogether. For example, your city mayor might be a positive stakeholder in a project to open a Wal-Mart store in your neighborhood because it brings business to the city, whereas some local business leaders might look at it as a threat to the local businesses and thereby may act as negative stakeholders.

Negative stakeholders are often overlooked by the project manager and the project team, which increases the project risk. Ignoring positive or negative project stakeholders will have a damaging impact on the project. Therefore, it's important that you, the project manager, start identifying the project stakeholders early on in the project. The different project stakeholders can have different and conflicting expectations, which you need to analyze and manage.

Identifying all the project stakeholders might be a difficult task, but the following are the obvious stakeholders, starting with you:

◆ **Project manager.** Include yourself, the project manager, in the list of the stakeholders to start with.

◆ **Project management office (PMO).** If your organization has a PMO and it is directly or indirectly responsible for the outcome of a project, then the PMO is a stakeholder in that project.

◆ **Project management team.** These are the members of the project team involved in the project management tasks.

◆ **Project team members.** The members of the project team who are actually performing the project work are also project stakeholders.

◆ **Performing organization.** The organization whose employees are doing the project work is a stakeholder organization.

◆ **Customer/user.** This includes the individuals or the organizations for whom the project is being performed and the users who will use the product that will result from successful completion of the project.

◆ **Project sponsor.** This is the individual or group that provides financial resources for the project.

◆ **Influencers.** These are the individuals or groups who are not direct customers or users of the product or service that will come from the project, but who can influence the course of the project due to their positions in the customer organization or performing organization. The influence can be positive or negative—that is, for or against the project.

In addition to these key stakeholders, who are easy to identify, there can be a number of other stakeholders, who might be more difficult to identify, inside and outside of your organization. Depending upon the project, these might include investors, sellers, contractors, family members of the project team members, government agencies, media outlets, lobbying organizations, individual citizens, and society at large. Have I left anyone out?

So, the stakeholders not only are affected positively and negatively by the project, but the project can also be impacted positively or negatively by them. It is critical for the success of the project that you identify positive and negative stakeholders early on in the project, understand and analyze their varying and conflicting expectations, and manage those expectations throughout the project

Identifying the Stakeholder Within

You, the project manager, are a very special project stakeholder yourself. The job (role) of a project manager is extremely challenging and thereby exciting. With the help of your team, it is your responsibility to bring all the pieces together and make the project happen. You do it by using a multitude of skills, described here.

Communication. The importance of communication in project management cannot be overemphasized. Even a well-scheduled and well-funded project can fail in the hands of a hard-working team of experts due to the lack of proper communication. As a project manager, you might be dealing with a wide functional variety of individuals, ranging from executives, to marketing personnel, to technologists. You should be able to wear different communication hats depending upon whom you are communicating with. For example, you will not be using technical jargon to talk to executives or marketing folks, and you will not speak marketing lingo to the software developers. You will be speaking to different stakeholders in their language, while filling the language gap between different functional groups and eliminating misunderstandings due to miscommunication. The key point is that you put on the appropriate communication hat depending on which individual you are communicating with. Be able to switch communication hats quickly and avoid technical jargon and acronyms that are not understood by the person or group with whom you are communicating. The goal is clarity of the language to convey the message accurately.

You will be communicating throughout the project. So, for a given project, you must develop a communication strategy that addresses the following issues:

◆ What needs to be communicated?

◆ With whom do you want to communicate? You might need to communicate different items to different individuals or groups.

◆ How do you want to communicate—that is, what is the medium of communication? Again, this might differ depending on whom you are communicating with.

◆ What is the outcome of your communication? You need to monitor your communication and its results to see what works and what does not, so you can improve communication.

Communication is an ingredient for many other skills, such as negotiation and problem-solving.

Negotiation. A negotiation is give-and-take, with the goal of generating a win-win outcome for both parties. You might need to negotiate at any stage of the project lifecycle. Here are some examples of negotiations:

◆ Negotiating with the stakeholders regarding the expectations during the project planning. For example, the suggested deadline for the project schedule might not be practical, or you might need a certain type or quantity of resources to make it happen.

◆ Negotiating with the functional managers for obtaining human resources, such as software developers.

◆ Negotiating with the team members for specific job assignments and possibly during conflict resolution among the team members.

◆ Negotiating the changes to the project schedule, budget, or both because a stakeholder proposed changes to the project objectives.

◆ Negotiating with the external vendors in procurement. However, in contract negotiations, representatives from the legal department might be involved.

Sometimes you will be negotiating to solve a problem.

Problem-solving. Project-related problems might occur among the stakeholders (including team members) or with the projects. Either way, they are there to damage the project. Your task is twofold—identify the problem early enough and solve it. Here is the general technique for accomplishing this:

- ◆ Look for early warning signs by paying close attention to the formal progress reports and to what the team members say and do regarding the project.
- ◆ Once you identify a potential problem, do your homework. Understand and identify the problem clearly by collecting more information without passing judgment.
- ◆ Once the problem and its causes are clearly identified, work with the appropriate stake-holders, such as project team members, to explore multiple (alternative) solutions.
- ◆ Evaluate the multiple solutions and choose the one you will implement.

The key point throughout the problem-solving process is to focus on the problem, not on the individuals, with the goal of finding the solution in order to help the project succeed. There should be no finger-pointing.

Sometimes, in choosing and implementing the correct solution, you will need to exercise your influencing skill.

Influencing. Influencing means getting individuals or groups to do what you want them to do without necessarily having a formal authority to mandate an outcome from them. This is increasingly becoming an essential management skill in today's information economy. To exercise influence, you must understand the formal and informal structure of your organization. Again, you might need to use influencing when you are dealing with any aspect of the project—for example, controlling the changes to the project, negotiating schedule or resource assignments, resolving conflicts, and the like.

Leadership. In the traditional organizational structure, project managers do not have formal authority over the project team members who perform the team work. So you have no other choice than managing by leadership and not by authority (power). The good news is that managing by leadership is overall more effective and productive than managing by authority anyway. A project team is generally a group of individuals coming together for the lifetime of the project from different functional groups with different skills and experience. They need a leader to show them the vision, and to excite, inspire, and motivate them toward the goals and the objectives of the project. You, the project manager, are that leader.

Different organizations have different attitudes and policies toward project management. The structure of the performing organization has a big influence on your job as a project manager.

Organizational Influences on Projects

A project is typically performed inside an organization called the *performing organization*. Therefore, projects are influenced by many characteristics of the performing organizations, such as culture, style, organizational structure, and maturity of the organization.

From the perspective of a project, there are two kinds of organizations: project-based and non-project-based. The project-based organizations fall into two subcategories—those that derive their revenue primarily from performing projects for others, and those that do in-house projects to deliver products or services for customers. Project-based organizations are well aware of the importance of project management and generally have systems to support project management. Non-project-based organizations generally have a low appreciation and understanding of the importance of project management and often lack systems to support project management.

To do your job efficiently and effectively, you must figure out what kind of organization you are in. Another huge factor that greatly influences the projects and the management is the organizational structure. From the perspective of structure, organizations fall into three categories—functional organizations, projectized organizations, matrix organizations.

Functional Organization

Functional organization has a traditional organizational structure in which each functional department, such as engineering, marketing, and sales, is a separate entity. As shown in Figure 1.4, the members of each department (staff) report to the functional manager of that department, and the functional manager in turn reports to an executive, such as the chief executive officer (CEO). Depending on the size of the organization, there could be a hierarchy within the functional managers—for example, directors of engineering, QA, and IT operations reporting to the vice president (VP) of engineering, who in turn reports to the CEO.

The scope of a project in a functional organization is usually limited to the boundaries of the functional department. Therefore, each department runs its projects largely independent of other departments. When a communication needs to occur between two departments, it is carried through the hierarchy of functional managers.

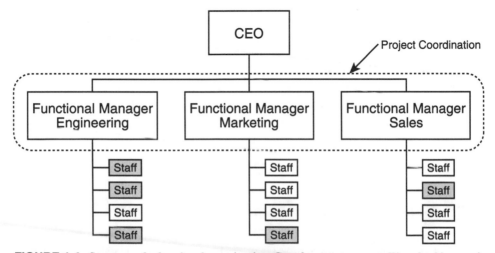

FIGURE 1.4 *Structure of a functional organization. Gray boxes represent staff involved in a project.*

All the managerial power (authority) in a functional organization is vested in the functional managers, who control the team members' performance evaluations, salary, bonus, hiring, and firing. Project managers are held responsible for the project results even though they have little say over resource assignments and holding team members accountable for their work. As a result, project managers in a functional organization are often frustrated. Their work is, at best, challenging. You, as a project manager in a functional organization, can benefit greatly from your good relationships with functional managers and team members. Networking and leadership are the key points to your success in a functional organization.

A project manager in a functional organization has the following attributes:

◆ The project manager's role and project team are part-time.

◆ There is little or no authority over anything: resource assignments, team members, and the like.

◆ The project manager reports directly to a functional manager.

◆ There is little or no administrative staff to help with the project.

NOTE

In functional organizations, project management might be conducted under other names, such as project coordinator or team leader.

On the other end of the spectrum is the projectized organization.

Projectized Organization

A projectized organization's structure is organized around projects. Most of the organization's resources are devoted to the projects. As shown in Figure 1.5, the project team members report directly to the project manager, who has a great deal of independence and authority. Along with responsibility comes the high level of autonomy over the projects. The project managers are happy campers in a projectized organization. A functional organization and a projectized organization are on the opposite ends of the spectrum of a project manager's authority.

A project manager in a projectized organization has the following attributes:

◆ The project manager is full-time.

◆ The project manager has full authority over the project team.

◆ There is full-time administrative staff to help with the project.

In the middle of the spectrum are the matrix organizations.

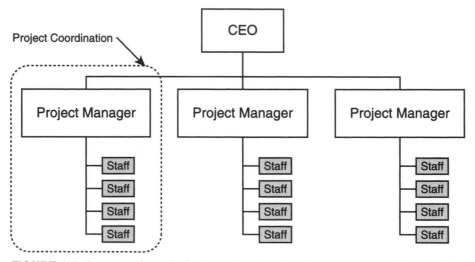

FIGURE 1.5 _Structure of a projectized organization. Gray boxes represent staff involved in a project under a given project manager._

Matrix Organization

A matrix organization is organized into functional departments, but a project is run by a project team, with members coming from different functional departments, as shown in Figure 1.6. On the spectrum of a project manager's authority, matrix organizations are in the middle of two extremes: functional and projectized organizations. The matrix organizations are generally categorized into a strong matrix, which is closer to projectized structure; a weak matrix, which is closer to functional structure; and a balanced matrix, which is in the middle of strong and weak.

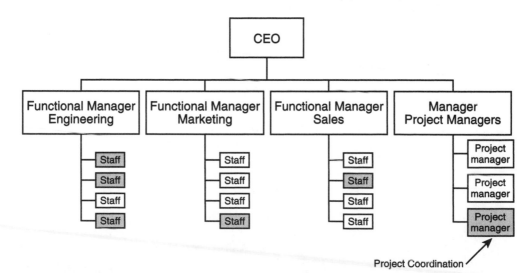

FIGURE 1.6 _Structure of a matrix organization. Gray boxes represent staff involved in a project._

Table 1.4 summarizes the influences of the different organizational structures on the projects.

Table 1.4 Influences of the Organizational Structures on Projects

Organization Structure	Project Characteristic		
	Functional	Matrix	Projectized
Project manager's authority	None to low	Low to high	High to full
Project manager's role	Part-time	Part-time to full-time	Full-time
Project management administrative staff	None to part-time	Part-time to full-time	Full-time
Project budget controlled by	Functional manager	Functional manager, project manager, or both	Project manager
Resource availability	Low	Limited to high	High to full

You have learned how the five process groups (the different stages in the project lifecycle) and nine project management knowledge areas constitute the project management framework. The actual implementation of project management is greatly influenced by the facts on the ground—the organizational structure, for example. Throughout the book, you will be exploring the details of project management, and getting introduced to some advanced concepts up front will make that journey more pleasant and smoother.

Advanced Concepts

Throughout this book, you will be encountering concepts such as probability, baseline, project team, and project management team. Those concepts are introduced in the following sections.

Probability

The theory of probability has its early seventeenth-century roots in the investigations of games of chance, such as roulette and cards. Since then, a multitude of mathematicians and scientists have contributed to the development of the theory of probability. Today, the concepts of probability appear in almost every discipline, ranging from physics to project management. In the modern age, probability has already entered into the folk psyche through phrases such as, "What are the odds that this will happen?"

Probability. Probability is defined as a chance that something will happen. For example, when you play the lottery and you wonder what the odds are that you will win, you are thinking of probability. The simplest example of probability is tossing a coin. The question is, when you toss a coin, what is the probability that the coin will land heads-up? When you toss a coin, there are only two possibilities: It will land either heads-up or tails-up. Each possibility is equally likely if you are not cheating. Therefore, the probability that the coin will land heads-up is 1 out of 2, or 50 percent, or 0.5. In general, if there are n possible outcomes of an event and each outcome is equally likely, then the probability of a specific outcome is $1/n$.

Random variable. A random variable can acquire any value within a given range or out of a set of values. For example, you can use a random variable to represent the results of rolling a fair die, which has six sides numbered by dots from 1 to 6. The possible outcome of rolling a die could be any number from the set of outcomes: {1, 2, 3, 4, 5, 6}.

Expected value. This is the expected value of an outcome. As an example, assume you get into a bet that you will win $10 if a coin toss results in heads, and you will lose $5 if it results in tails. Given that the probability for heads or tails is 0.5 for each, the expected value for the money that you will win is $10 * 0.5 = $5, and the expected value for the money that you will lose is $5 * 0.5 = $2.5.

Variance. The variance of a random variable is the deviation from the expected value. It is computed as the average squared deviation of each number from its mean. For example, assume that the values of a random variable are 2, 4, 5, 7, and 2 in five measurements. The mean value for these measurements is

$$(2 + 4 + 5 + 7 + 2) / 5 = 4$$

The variance of the spread of these values is

$$V = \theta^2 = [(2–4)^2 + (4–4)^2 + (7–4)^2 + (2–4)^2] / 5 = 3.4$$

Standard deviation. This is the square root of the variance—that is, θ.

Project Team and Project Management Team

To avoid confusion, make sure you can distinguish the project team from the project management team. The project management team consists of the individuals who perform the project management activities for the project. The project team consists of all the individuals directly involved in the project—the individuals who perform the schedule activities; the members of the project management team; and perhaps some other stakeholders, such as the project sponsor.

Baseline

The project baseline is defined as the approved plan for the cost, schedule, and scope of the project. The project performance is measured against this baseline. The project baseline is also referred to in terms of its components—cost baseline, schedule baseline, and scope baseline. How do you know how the project is performing? You compare the performance against the baseline. Approved changes in cost, schedule, and scope will also change the baseline.

In this chapter, you have learned how project management is performed by applying knowledge and skills to project activities in order to meet the project objectives. Applying knowledge boils down to performing processes.

The three most important takeaways from this chapter are as follows:

◆ The project lifecycle consists of five stages: initiating, planning, executing, monitoring/controlling, and closing. Each of these stages is called a *process group* due to the set of processes that is performed in the stage.

◆ The project processes that are performed to manage projects constitute nine project management knowledge areas: communication management, cost management, human resource management, integration management, procurement management, quality management, risk management, scope management, and time management.

◆ A project manager has none to low authority in a functional organization, low to high authority in a matrix organization, and high to full authority in a projectized organization.

Summary

The activities inside an organization are generally organized into groups, which fall into two categories—operations and projects. Operations usually consist of ongoing routine work, whereas a project has a goal to generate a unique product, service, or result in a finite time—that is, it has a planned beginning and a planned end. Organizations launch projects for different reasons, such as to meet a business or legal requirement, or to take on an opportunity offered by the market. A project, like anything else in an organization, needs to be managed. The project management is the application of knowledge and skills to project activities in order to meet the project objectives. It involves performing a set of processes that constitute nine knowledge areas of project management: communication management, cost management, human resource management, integration management, procurement management, quality management, risk management, scope management, and time management. Each process is part of a knowledge area and has a membership in one of five process groups: initiating, planning, executing, monitoring/controlling, and closing. The process groups represent different stages of a project lifecycle.

Each project has a set of individuals or organizations that it influences positively or negatively, and these individuals and organizations are accordingly called *positive* and *negative stakeholders*. Some of these stakeholders may influence the project. Therefore, you must identify all the project stakeholders, positive and negative. The different project stakeholders might have different and conflicting expectations, which you need to analyze and manage.

Another big influence factor for the project management is the structure of the performing organization, which could be functional, projectized, or matrix. On one end of the spectrum, a project manager is usually part-time and has little or no authority in a functional organization. On the other end, the project manager is full-time and has high to full authority in a projectized organization. In the middle of the spectrum are the matrix organizations, in which a project manger has low to high authority.

As you learned in this chapter, the first stage of the project lifecycle is initiating. You will start your journey of project management by exploring the initiating stage in the next chapter.

Exam's Eye View

Comprehend

◆ The way PMI views it, the discipline of project management is composed of nine knowledge areas, such as project cost management, project scope management, and project human resource management.

◆ Depending upon in which stage of the project lifecycle they are executed, the processes are grouped into five process groups, such as the initiating group and the planning group.

◆ The project manager's authority is none to low in a functional organization, low to high in a matrix organization, and high to full in a projectized organization.

Look Out

◆ For a work effort to be qualified as a project, it must be temporary (that is, have a start and a finish), and the outcome must be a unique product, result, or a service. Routine, ongoing work is an operation, not a project.

◆ Any individual or organization that is positively or negatively affected by a project is a project stakeholder. Stakeholders can exist outside of the performing organization.

◆ You must identify both positive and negative stakeholders of your project, and you must not ignore the negative stakeholders.

◆ Regardless of the structure of the performing organizations, project managers are responsible for the project results.

Memorize

◆ The lifecycle of a project has five stages, called *process groups*: initiating, planning, executing, monitoring/controlling, and closing.

◆ All the processes that are executed at different stages of a project belong to nine knowledge areas: communication management, cost management, human resource management, integration management, procurement management, quality management, risk management, scope management, and time management. A given process belongs to only one knowledge area.

Key Terms

- **knowledge area.** A knowledge area in project management is defined by its knowledge requirements related to managing a specific aspect of a project, such as cost, by using a set of processes. PMI recognizes a total of nine knowledge areas, such as cost management and human resource management.

- **organization.** A group of individuals organized to work for some purpose or mission.

- **performing organization.** The organization that is performing the project.

- **process.** A set of interrelated activities performed to obtain a specified set of products, results, or services.

- **program.** A set of related projects managed in a coordinated fashion to improve the overall efficiency and effectiveness.

- **program management.** The centralized coordinated management of a specific program to achieve its strategic goals, objectives, and benefits.

- **program management office (PMO).** Program management office (or project management office) refers to an entity in an organization that is responsible for providing centralized coordinated management for programs—that is, projects in the organization.

- **project.** A work effort made over a finite period of time, with a start and a finish, to create a unique product, service, or result. A process consists of three elements: input, tools and techniques, and output.

- **project management.** Application of knowledge, skills, and tools and techniques to project activities in order to meet project objectives. You do this by performing some processes at various stages of the project.

- **project stakeholder.** An individual or an organization that is positively or negatively affected by the project.

Review Questions

1. Which two of the following are the essential characteristics that make a group of activities a project? (Choose two.)

    A. It takes multiple individuals to perform these activities.

    B. The work is managed by a project manager.

    C. The group has a budget.

    D. The group has a start date and a finish date.

    E. The group's outcome will be a new product.

2. Which of the following is a project?
   - **A.** Running a donut shop
   - **B.** Building another library in your area
   - **C.** Keeping a network up and running in a university department
   - **D.** Running a warehouse

3. Which of the following is not a process group?
   - **A.** Initiating
   - **B.** Planning
   - **C.** Implementing
   - **D.** Controlling
   - **E.** Closing

4. Which of the following is not a project management knowledge area?
   - **A.** Project procurement management
   - **B.** Project risk management
   - **C.** Project quality management
   - **D.** Project team management
   - **E.** Project time management

5. Which of the following is the best definition of progressive elaboration?
   - **A.** Taking the project from concept to project management plan
   - **B.** Taking the project from conception to completion
   - **C.** Taking the project from initiating to closing
   - **D.** Decomposing the project objectives into smaller, more manageable work pieces

6. In which of the following organizational structures does the project manager have the greatest authority?
   - **A.** Functional
   - **B.** Projectized
   - **C.** Matrix
   - **D.** Leveled

7. In which of the following organizational structures does the project manager have the least authority?
   - **A.** Functional
   - **B.** Projectized
   - **C.** Matrix
   - **D.** Leveled

Chapter 2

Initiating the Project

PMP Exam Objectives

Objective	*What It Really Means*
1.1 Conduct Project Selection Methods	You must know the project selection methods, such as benefit measurement methods and expert judgment.
1.2 Define Scope	You must know how to define the project scope based on the business need with the purpose of meeting customer expectations. Understand the process of developing a preliminary project scope statement.
1.4 Identify and Perform Stakeholder Analysis	Understand how to identify both the negative and positive stakeholders. You must know the key stakeholders in any project, such as the project manager, sponsor, and project team members.
1.5 Develop a Project Charter	Understand the develop project charter process. You must know that the project charter names and authorizes the project manager.
1.6 Obtain Project Charter Approval	Understand that the project charter approval process depends upon the project and the performing organization. You must know that the project charter approval officially starts a project.

Introduction

As you learned in the previous chapter, you manage projects through processes. A process is composed of input, tools and techniques, and output. You use the tools and techniques on the input of a process to generate its output. You manage the initiation of a project through a process group called the *initiating process group*, which consists of two processes: developing a project charter and developing a preliminary project scope statement. Before you can initiate a project, it must originate from somewhere.

So the central question in this chapter is, how is a project initiated? In search of the answer, you will explore three avenues with me: the origins of projects, the project charter, and the preliminary project scope statement.

Origins of Projects

Before you can begin the project initiation process, someone must request the project. So where do the projects originally come from? Projects are often originated from sources external to the project management office—for example, internally, by some department of the company, or externally, by an enterprise or a government agency. A project may originate as a result of one or more of the following categories of reasons.

♦ **Business requirements.** This category includes projects based on a business need or a legal requirement. For example, perhaps a Web design company authorizes a project to automate certain aspects of maintaining Web sites to increase efficiency and revenue. As another example, consider a building owner authorizing a project to make the building accessible to physically disabled persons in order to meet the legal requirements for using the building for a specific business.

♦ **Opportunities.** The projects that fall into this category might include those based on a customer request, a market demand, or a breakthrough in technology. For example, several electronics companies authorized projects to manufacture MP3 players following the invention and popularity of MP3 technology.

♦ **Problems.** Projects are also authorized to offer solutions to certain problems in a company or a country, or to address social needs in a society. For example, the government might start a project to help the victims of a natural disaster, such as a hurricane. A company might authorize a project to analyze the problem of low employee productivity and to design a solution for this problem.

The sources of the project requests can vary widely in different organizations. Depending upon your organization, the origins of projects might be inside the organization, outside the organization, or both.

So a project can originate from multiple possible sources. Not all requested projects are authorized by the organization, however. How does an organization decide which projects to select?

Understanding Project Selection

A project can be selected by using one or more project selection methods that fall into three categories: benefit measurement methods, constrained optimization methods, and expert judgment.

Benefit Measurement Methods

These methods use comparative approaches to compare the benefits obtained from the candidate projects so that the project with the maximum benefit will be selected. These methods fall into three categories: scoring models, benefit contributions, and economic models.

Scoring Models

A scoring model evaluates projects by using a set of criteria with a weight (score) assigned to each criterion. You can assign different weights to different criteria to represent the varied degree of importance given to various criteria. All projects are evaluated (scored) against this set of criteria, and the project with the maximum score is selected. The set of criteria can include both objective and subjective criteria, such as financial data, organizational expertise, market value, innovation, and fit with the corporate culture. The advantage of a scoring model is that you have the freedom to assign different weights to different criteria in order to select projects consistent with the goals, mission, and vision of your corporation. This freedom, however, is also a disadvantage because your selection is only as good as the criteria with larger weights. Furthermore, developing a good scoring model is a difficult task that requires unbiased cross-departmental feedback from different levels of the organization.

Benefit Contributions

These methods are based on comparing the benefit contributions from different projects. These contributions can be estimated by performing a cost benefit analysis, which typically calculates the projected cost, revenue, and savings of a project. This method favors the projects that create profit in the shortest time and ignores the long-term benefits of projects that might not be tangible at the current time, such as innovation and strategic values.

Economic Models

An economic model is used to estimate the economic efficiency of a project, and it involves a set of calculations to provide overall financial data about the project. The common terms involved in economic models are explained in the following list.

◆ **Benefit Cost Ratio (BCR).** This is the value obtained by dividing the benefit by the cost. The greater the value, the more attractive the project is. For example, if the projected cost of producing a product is $20,000, and you expect to sell it for $60,000, then the BCR is equal to $60,000/$20,000, which is equal to 3. For the benefit to exceed cost, the BCR must be greater than 1.

◆ **Cash flow.** Whereas cash refers to money, cash flow refers to both the money coming in and the money going out of an organization. Positive cash flow means more money coming in than going out. Cash inflow is benefit (income), and cash outflow is cost (expenses).

◆ **Internal Return Rate (IRR).** This is just another way of interpreting the benefit from the project. It looks at the cost of the project as the capital investment and translates the profit into the interest rate over the life of that investment. Calculations for IRR are out of the scope of this book. Just understand that the greater the value for IRR, the more beneficial the project is.

◆ **Present Value (PV) and Net Present Value (NPV).** To understand these two concepts, understand that one dollar today can buy you more than what one dollar next year can buy. (Think about inflation and return.) The issue arises because it takes time to complete a project, and even when a project is completed its benefits are reaped over a period of time, not immediately. In other words, the project is costing you today but will benefit you tomorrow. So, to make an accurate calculation for the profit, the cost and benefits must be converted to the same point in time. The NPV of a project is the present value of the future cash inflows (benefits) minus the present value of the current and future cash outflows (cost). For a project to be worthwhile economically, the NPV must be positive. As an example, assume you invest $300,000 today to build a house, which will be completed and sold after three years for $500,000. Also assume that real estate that is worth $400,000 today will be worth $500,000 after three years. So the present value of the cash inflow on your house is $400,000, and hence the NPV is the present value of the cash inflow minus the present value of the cash outflow, which equals $400,000–$300,000, which equals $100,000.

◆ **Opportunity cost.** This refers to selecting a project over another due to the scarcity of resources. In other words, by spending this dollar on this project, you are passing on the opportunity to spend this dollar on another project. How big an opportunity are you missing? The smaller the opportunity cost, the better it is.

♦ **Discounted Cash Flow (DCF).** The discounted cash flow refers to the amount that someone is willing to pay today in anticipation of receiving the cash flow in the future. DCF is calculated by taking the amount that you anticipate receiving in the future and discounting (converting) it back to today on the time scale. This conversion factors in the interest rate and opportunity cost between now (when you are spending cash) and the time when you will receive the cash back.

♦ **Return on Investment (ROI).** The ROI is the percentage profit from the project. For example, if you spend $400,000 on the project, and the benefit for the first year is $500,000, then ROI equals ($500,000–$400,000)/$400,000, which equals 25%.

The details and calculations for these quantities are out of the scope of this book. Just understand the basic concepts and whether a larger or a smaller value for a given quantity favors the project selection.

As the name suggests, all the benefit measurement methods are based on calculating some kind of benefit from the given project. However, the benefit will never be realized if the project fails. This concern has given rise to methods based on calculating the success of the projects; these methods are called *constrained optimization methods*.

Constrained Optimization Methods

Constrained optimization methods are concerned with predicting the success of the project. These methods are based on complex mathematical models that use formulae and algorithms to predict the success of a project. These models use the following kinds of algorithms:

♦ Linear

♦ Nonlinear

♦ Dynamic

♦ Integer

♦ Multiple objective programming

TIP

For the exam, you need to know two things about constrained optimization methods: the names of the types of the algorithms and that these methods are only used for complex projects, and therefore are not typically used for most projects.

The details of these models are out of the scope of this book.

Either in conjunction with other methods or in absence of them, organizations often rely on expert judgment in making selection decisions.

Expert Judgment

Expert judgment is one of the techniques used in project management to accomplish various tasks, including project selection. It refers to making a decision by relying on expert advice from one or more of the following sources:

♦ An appropriate unit within the organization

♦ The project stakeholders, including customers and sponsors

♦ Consultants

♦ Professional and technical associations

♦ Industry groups

The use of expert judgment is not limited to the project selection; it can be used in many processes, such as developing a project charter. Keep in mind that expert judgment can be very subjective at times and might include political influence. An excellent salesperson or an executive with great influence can exploit this method successfully.

An organization might use multiple selection methods to make a decision. During the project selection process, you might start interacting with a very important group of people called *project stakeholders*.

Identifying the Project Stakeholders

Project stakeholders are individuals and organizations whose interests are affected (positively or negatively) by the project's execution and completion. In other words, a project stakeholder has something to gain from the project or something to lose to the project. Accordingly, the stakeholders fall into two categories: positive stakeholders, who will normally benefit from the success of the project, and negative stakeholders, who see some kind of disadvantage coming from the project. The implications obviously are that the positive stakeholders would like to see the project succeed and the negative stakeholders' interests will be better served if the project is delayed or cancelled altogether. For example your city mayor might be a positive stakeholder in a project to open a Wal-Mart store in your neighborhood because it brings business to the city, whereas some local business leaders might look at it as a threat to the local businesses and thereby may act as negative stakeholders.

Negative stakeholders are often overlooked by the project manager and the project team, which increases the project risk. Ignoring positive or negative project stakeholders will have a damaging impact on the project. Therefore, it's important that you, as a project manager, start identifying the project stakeholders early on in the project. The different project stakeholders might have different and conflicting expectations that you need to analyze and manage.

Identifying all the project stakeholders might be a difficult task, but the following are the obvious ones:

- ◆ **Project manager.** Include yourself, the project manager, in the list of the stakeholders.
- ◆ **Project Management Office (PMO).** If your organization has PMO that is directly or indirectly responsible for the outcome of a project, then the PMO is a stakeholder in that project.
- ◆ **Project management team.** These are the members of the project team involved in the project management tasks.
- ◆ **Project team members.** The members of the project team that are actually performing the work are also the project stakeholders.
- ◆ **Performing organization.** The organization whose employees are doing the project work is a stakeholder organization.
- ◆ **Customer/user.** Customer/users include the individual or the organization for whom the project is being performed and the users who will use the product that will result from successful completion of the project.
- ◆ **Project sponsor.** The sponsor is the individual or group that provides financial resources for the project.
- ◆ **Influencers.** These are the individuals or groups who are not direct customers or users of the product or service that will come from the project, but who can influence the course of the project due to their positions in the customer or performing organization. The influence can be positive or negative—that is, for or against the project.

In addition to these key stakeholders, which are obvious to identify, there can be a number of other less obvious stakeholders inside and outside of your organization. Depending upon the project, these might include investors, sellers, contractors, family members of the project team members, government agencies, media outlets, lobbying organizations, individual citizens, and society at large.

It is critical for the success of the project that you identify positive and negative stakeholders early on in the project, understand and analyze their varying and conflicting expectations, and manage those expectations throughout the project.

The project initiation process group includes two processes: developing a project charter and developing a preliminary project scope statement.

Developing a Project Charter

The single most important task for the develop project charter process is to authorize a project. To accomplish that, it is necessary to document the business needs and the new product or service that the project will launch to satisfy those needs. This way, the project charter links the proposed project to the ongoing work in the organization and clears the way to authorize the project.

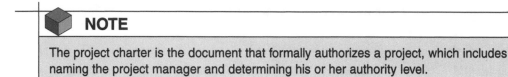

NOTE

The project charter is the document that formally authorizes a project, which includes naming the project manager and determining his or her authority level.

The output of the develop project charter process is of course the project charter, and this output is generated by applying the tools and techniques to the input of this process, as shown in Figure 2.1.

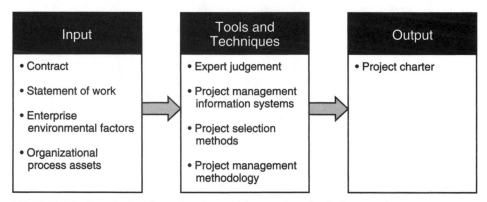

Input	Tools and Techniques	Output
• Contract • Statement of work • Enterprise environmental factors • Organizational process assets	• Expert judgement • Project management information systems • Project selection methods • Project management methodology	• Project charter

FIGURE 2.1 *Developing the project charter: input, tools and techniques, and output*

Input to Developing the Project Charter

Like any other process, the develop project charter process also has input. The input comes from the origin of the project and from within the organization that will perform the project. The possible input items for the process of developing a project charter are the following:

Contract. A project for a customer who is external to the performing organization is usually done based on a contract.

Statement of Work (SOW). The statement of work describes the products or services that will be delivered by the project. For an internal project the SOW is provided by the project initiator or the project sponsor, whereas for an external project the SOW is received from the customer as part of a bid document, such as a request for proposals, a request for bids, or a contract. The SOW includes business needs that the project will satisfy, the product scope, and a strategic plan.

Enterprise environmental factors. During the development of the project charter, you must consider the performing organization's environmental factors, which include the following:

◆ Commercial databases, such as standardized cost estimating data and risk databases

◆ The culture and structure of the performing organization

◆ Government and industry standards, such as legal requirements, product standards, and quality standards relevant to the project

◆ Human resources currently available in the organization, such as skills and expertise

◆ Infrastructure, such as facilities and equipment to do the project

◆ Marketplace conditions relevant to the project

◆ Personnel administration information, such as guidelines for hiring, firing, and performance reviews

◆ Project management information systems, such as software tools for scheduling tasks and meetings

◆ Risk tolerances of the project stakeholders

◆ Work authorization system of the organization, because the project needs to be authorized

Note that the environmental factors can be internal to the performing organization, such as the organization's culture, or external to the organization, such as market conditions.

Organizational process assets. The organizational process assets are typically grouped into two categories: processes and procedures for conducting work, and a corporate knowledge base for storing and retrieving information. For example, the performing organization might have its own guidelines, policies, and procedures, whose effect on the project must be considered while developing the project charter and other project documents that will follow. Another example of an organization's process assets are the knowledge and learning base acquired from the previous projects. Here are some specific examples from the organizational process assets:

◆ Project closure guidelines and requirements

◆ Templates to support some project management tasks, such as risk, project schedule network diagrams, and work breakdown structure

◆ Procedures for defect management

◆ Procedures for issuing work authorizations

◆ Defect management database systems that allow one to enter a defect and monitor its status

You take the available input and apply the relevant tools and techniques to develop the project charter.

Tools and Techniques for Developing the Project Charter

Like any other process, the develop project charter process requires that some tools and techniques be applied to the input to produce output. Exactly which tools and techniques will be used depends upon the specific project at hand. Following is a list of types of tools and techniques that can be used to develop the charter.

◆ **Project selection methods.** These methods were discussed previously in this chapter.

◆ **Project management methodology.** A project management methodology defines a set of project management process groups and the processes in each group. These processes can be the standard formal processes or informal techniques in your organization. This methodology must be kept in mind in preparing the project charter.

◆ **Project management information systems.** This is a set of project management tools organized into an integrated system that automates some tasks of developing the project charter, such as facilitating feedback, refining the project charter document, controlling changes to the document, and releasing the approved document.

◆ **Expert judgment.** Expert judgment, a method used to evaluate the input to developing the project charter, was discussed previously in this chapter.

These tools and techniques are used on the input to develop the project charter.

Output of Developing the Project Charter

The output of the develop project charter process is a formal document called the *project charter*. It is a high-level document that summarizes the business needs, the understanding of customer requirements, and how the new product or service will satisfy these requirements. To be specific, the project charter should include the following information.

◆ The project justification, which includes the purpose of the project and the business case for the project, which in turn may include return on investment

◆ A project description that includes the business needs that the project addresses and the high-level product requirements

◆ Project requirements based on the needs of the customer, the sponsor, and other stakeholders

◆ A list of participating functional departments of the organization and their roles in the project

◆ Organizational, environmental, and external assumptions and constraints

◆ A summary of the high-level schedule, including milestones

◆ A budget summary

◆ An assigned project manager, a specified authority level for that project manager, and defined stakeholder influences

An *assumption* is a factor that you consider to be true without any proof or verification. For example, an obvious assumption that you might make during planning for an in-house project could be the availability of the required skill set to perform the project.

It's important to document assumptions clearly and validate them at various stages of the project because assumptions carry a certain degree of uncertainty with them, and uncertainty means risk. Assumptions can appear in both the input and the output of various processes.

A *constraint* is a restriction (or a limitation) that can affect the performance of the project. It can appear both in the input and the output of various processes. For example, there could be a schedule constraint that the project must be completed by a predetermined date. Similarly, a cost constraint would limit the budget available for the project.

The project charter provides the project manager with the authority to use organizational resources to run the project. Remember that formally speaking, project charters are prepared external to project management by an individual or a committee in the organization. In other words, project management starts where the project charter ends. However, practically, the would-be project manager might actually be involved in writing the project charter or a part of it. The project approval and funding will still be external to the project management boundaries.

NOTE

Some organizations might perform a feasibility study or its equivalent to justify the project before developing the project charter and initiating the project. The feasibility study may itself become a project.

Once you have the project charter, you know the high-level product (or service) requirements that the project will satisfy. However, a high-level requirement written in a certain way might mean different things to different stakeholders. So after you get the project charter, your first task is to develop a common understanding of the project among the project stakeholders. You accomplish this by drawing boundaries around the project—that is, what is included and what is not—thereby spelling out what exactly the deliverables are. By doing this, you are determining the scope of the project.

NOTE

If a project includes multiple phases, the initiation process may be performed at the beginning of each phase to validate the assumptions made during the previous phases.

Developing a Preliminary Project Scope Statement

Project scope is defined as the work that must be performed to deliver a product, service, or results with specified features and functions. The scope specifies what is included and what is not. It is equivalent to drawing boundaries around the project and its products and services. You accomplish this as part of the initiation process group by writing a formal document called a *preliminary project scope statement*, which is the output of the process called develop preliminary project scope statement, as shown in Figure 2.2.

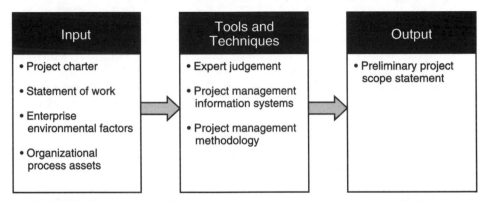

Input	Tools and Techniques	Output
• Project charter	• Expert judgement	• Preliminary project scope statement
• Statement of work	• Project management information systems	
• Enterprise environmental factors	• Project management methodology	
• Organizational process assets		

FIGURE 2.2 *Developing a preliminary project scope statement: input, tools and techniques, and output*

The project charter is one of the items that act as input to the develop a preliminary project scope statement process.

Input to Developing the Preliminary Project Scope Statement

The following items are the input to the develop a preliminary project scope statement process.

◆ The project charter
◆ The statement of work
◆ The enterprise environment factors
◆ The organizational process assets

All these items were discussed previously in this chapter. Note that the statement of work, the enterprise environment factors, and the organizational process assets are input items to both developing the project charter and developing the preliminary project scope statement.

To develop the scope statement, you apply the tools and techniques discussed in the next section to this input.

Tools and Techniques for Developing the Preliminary Project Scope Statement

The tools and techniques used to develop the scope statement are listed here.

◆ Project management methodology, discussed earlier, defines a process that helps in developing a preliminary project scope statement and controlling changes to it.

◆ Project management information systems, discussed earlier, help to accomplish the following:

◆ Generate the scope statement document.

◆ Facilitate feedback to refine the document.

◆ Control changes to the document.

◆ Release the final approved document.

◆ Expert judgment, discussed earlier, can be applied to technical and management details included in the scope statement.

Note that project management methodology, project management information systems, and expert judgment can be applied to both developing the project charter and developing the preliminary project scope statement. You apply these tools and techniques to produce a formal document called the *preliminary project scope statement*.

The Preliminary Project Scope Statement

The preliminary project scope statement is naturally the output of the develop a preliminary project scope statement process: one of the two processes in the initiating process group. The main purpose of the scope statement is to define the scope of the project. Accordingly, the two main elements included in the scope statement but not in the project charter are the project scope and the scope change control. To be specific, the following items are included in the preliminary scope statement:

◆ Objectives of the project and the product (or service) that the project will deliver.

◆ Project assumptions and constraints.

◆ Requirements and characteristics of the product or service that the project will deliver, and the specific project deliverables.

◆ Product (or service) acceptance criteria.

◆ Project boundaries: what is included and what is not.

◆ Initial work breakdown structure (WBS), which will be discussed in the following chapter.

◆ Scheduled milestones.

◆ Initial project team.

◆ Initial defined risks.

◆ Project configuration management requirements. The configuration management includes formal documented procedures in the organization, the change control system, and an auditing system that can be used to audit the products, services, or components to verify their conformance to requirements.

◆ Cost estimate in order of magnitude.

■ NOTE

An order of magnitude estimate is an approximation rounded to the nearest power of 10. For example, with an accuracy of one order of magnitude, the exact value for the number 300 could be anywhere between 250 and 350, and the exact value for the number 3,000 could be anywhere between 2,500 and 3,500.

A project with a poorly defined scope is an ill-defined project on the path to failure. The preliminary project scope statement, in addition to the project charter, accomplishes the following three things:

◆ Defining the project scope

◆ Defining the project change control

◆ Developing a common understanding of the project among all the stakeholders by defining the project scope and the project change control

Remember that the project scope statement at this stage is a preliminary statement that will be refined in the scope definition process discussed in Chapter 3.

So, the project charter and the preliminary project statement are the two important documents of the project initiating stage. However, the project does not initiate until the project charter is approved.

Obtaining Project Charter Approval

The single most important outcome of the project initiation process group is the project charter approval. In other words, a project is initiated through an approval of the project charter by an appropriate person in the performing organization. Who this person is depends on the organization and the project. This person, for example, could be the CEO of the company, the project sponsor, or a representative of the project selection committee.

Issuing an approved project charter and developing a preliminary project scope statement moves the project from the initiation stage into the planning stage.

The three most important takeaways from this chapter are as follows:

◆ A project can originate inside the performing organization or outside of it, in order to meet business requirements, take on an opportunity, or offer a solution to a problem.

◆ The project charter names the project manager and determines authority level of the project manager.

◆ The preliminary project scope statement takes the project understanding to the next level by specifying the project scope and the project change control, and thereby helps to get the stakeholders on the same page.

Summary

Organizations start projects for different reasons, such as to meet a business or legal requirement, to take on a business opportunity, or to develop a solution for a problem. Three categories of methods are available to select from the proposed projects. The first type of method is the benefit measurement method, which evaluates the benefits from the projects. Constrained optimization methods focus on the probability of completing the projects successfully, and expert judgment relies on expert advice. As a project manager, you need to identify each stakeholder: an individual or an organization that is going to gain or lose from the successful completion of the project.

The two output items of the initiation process group are the project charter, which names and authorizes the project manager, and the preliminary scope statement, which outlines the scope of the project. The project charter also includes project justification based on the business needs and a high-level description of the product or service that the project will offer to meet those business needs. The preliminary project scope statement takes the project understanding to the next level by specifying project scope and project change control, which helps to get the stakeholders on the same page.

Issuing an approved project charter and developing a preliminary project scope statement move the project from the initiation stage into the planning stage, which is composed of a number of processes collectively called the *planning process group*. I will discuss the processes related to scope planning in the next chapter.

Exam's Eye View

Comprehend

◆ The project manager and project sponsor are also project stakeholders.

◆ A contract can be an input item for developing the project charter, but not for developing the preliminary project scope statement.

◆ The project charter is an input item to developing the preliminary scope statement, not vice versa.

◆ The initial assumptions and constraints about a project are listed in the project charter.

Look Out

◆ The statement of work can be an input item to both the project charter and the preliminary scope statement.

◆ A project stakeholder is an individual or organization that has anything to gain or lose from the successful completion of the project. It could be anyone from the CEO of the performing organization to an ordinary citizen.

Memorize

◆ Project stakeholders are individuals and organizations whose interests are affected (positively or negatively) by the project execution and completion.

◆ The project charter is the document that formally authorizes a project, which includes naming a project manager.

◆ Constrained optimization methods used for project selection use these kinds of algorithms: linear, nonlinear, dynamic, integer, and multiple objective programming.

◆ These tools and techniques are used in developing both the project charter and the preliminary project scope statement: expert judgment, project management information systems, and project management methodology.

◆ These input items are used to develop both the project charter and the preliminary project scope statement: statement of work, enterprise environmental factors, and organizational process assets.

Key Terms

◆ **assumption.** A factor that you consider to be true without any proof or verification. Assumptions can appear in both the input and the output of various processes.

◆ **constraint.** A restriction (or a limitation) that can affect the performance of the project. Assumptions can appear in both the input and the output of various processes.

◆ **enterprise environmental factors.** The environmental factors internal or external to the performing organization that can influence the project's success, such as the organization's culture, infrastructure, existing skill set, market conditions, and project management software. These are input to both the project charter and the preliminary project scope statement.

◆ **initiating process group.** A process group that contains two processes: develop project charter and develop preliminary project scope statement.

◆ **methodology.** A system of practices, procedures, rules, and techniques used in a specific discipline.

◆ **organizational process assets.** The assets that can be used to perform the project successfully, such as templates, guidelines, knowledge base, and policies and procedures.

◆ **preliminary project scope statement.** The document that specifies the project scope during the initiation stage.

◆ **project charter.** A document issued by the project initiator or the project sponsor that, when signed by an appropriate person in the performing organization, authorizes the project by naming the project manager and specifying the authority level of the project manager.

◆ **Project Management Information System (PMIS).** An information system that consists of tools used to store, integrate, and retrieve the outputs of the project management processes. This can be used to support all stages of the project from initiating to closing.

◆ **project scope.** The work that must be performed to deliver a product, service, or results with the specified features. The project scope draws the boundaries around the project: what is included and what is not.

◆ **Statement of Work (SOW).** A document that describes the products or services to be delivered by the project. It is an input to developing the project charter and the preliminary project scope statement.

Review Questions

1. Which of the following issues the project charter document?
   - **A.** The performing organization's higher management
   - **B.** Any stakeholder
   - **C.** The customer
   - **D.** The project manager

2. What document is the result of the project initiation process group?
   - **A.** Statement of work
   - **B.** Project charter
   - **C.** Scope plan document
   - **D.** Preliminary scope statement

3. The project charter is important for which of the following reasons?
   - **A.** It authorizes the sponsor.
   - **B.** It names the project manager.
   - **C.** It authorizes the project manager to use the organization's resources.
   - **D.** It identifies all the stakeholders.
   - **E.** It identifies the project team members.

4. Which of the following is not included in the project charter?
   - **A.** The purpose of the project
   - **B.** High-level product requirements
   - **C.** A summary of the high-level schedule
   - **D.** Initial defined risks
   - **E.** The budget summary

5. Which of the following is not included in the preliminary scope statement?
   - **A.** Project objectives
   - **B.** The product requirements
   - **C.** Project deliverables
   - **D.** Initial defined risks
   - **E.** Initial project team
   - **F.** Statement of work

6. Which of the following lists the documents in the order they are written?

   A. Statement of work, project charter, preliminary project scope statement

   B. Project charter, statement of work, preliminary project scope statement

   C. Preliminary project scope statement, project charter, statement of work

   D. Statement of work, preliminary project scope statement, project charter

7. You have been named the project manager for a project in your company codenamed Thank You Mr. Glad. The project must complete before Thanksgiving Day this year. This represents which of the following project characteristics?

   A. Assumption

   B. Constraint

   C. Schedule

   D. Crashing

8. Which of the following is true about assumptions in the project planning?

   A. Because assumptions are a part of the project charter that you did not write, you don't need to validate them. Just assume the assumptions are true, and if the project fails, it's not your fault.

   B. Because assumptions represent risk, you must validate them at various stages of the project.

   C. An assumption is a condition that has been verified to be true, so you don't need to validate it.

   D. You must not start a project until all the assumptions have been proven to be true.

9. Which of the following is not an example of a project selection method?

   A. Expert judgment

   B. Scoring models

   C. Benefit cost ratio

   D. Constrained optimization methods

   E. Enterprise environmental factors

10. Your company runs a Web site that makes digital music downloads available to end users. You have been assigned a project that involves adding parental guidance warnings to various downloads. This project originated due to which of the following?

    A. Business requirements that include legal requirements

    B. Opportunity

    C. Problems

    D. Internal business needs

Chapter 3

Planning the Project Scope

PMP Exam Objectives

Objective	What It Really Means
1.2 Define Scope	You must know how to define the project scope based on the business need with the purpose of meeting the customer expectations. Understand how to develop the detailed project scope statement by using the scope definition process.
2.1 Define and Record Requirements, Constraints, and Assumptions	Understand the elements of the detailed project scope statement, such as project requirements, assumptions and constraints, product description, and initial risk identification.
2.3 Create the WBS	Understand the process of creating the WBS. You must know that the WBS is used in many other processes, such as cost estimating, human resource planning, schedule development, and risk management planning.

Introduction

After the project has been initiated, as discussed in the previous chapter, you need to develop a project management plan, which becomes the primary source of information for how the project at hand will be planned, executed, controlled, and closed. One component of the project management plan is planning the project scope, which you will explore in this chapter. The primary purpose of project scope management is to ensure that the required work (and *only* the required work) is performed to complete the project successfully. If changes in the work requirements are made, they must be controlled—that is, the scope must be controlled.

Before you start defining the scope, you need to know how to do so. In other words, you need to develop a scope management plan. Once you have defined the scope, it needs to be broken down into concrete, manageable tasks that can be assigned and performed. This is accomplished through what is called the *work breakdown structure* (WBS).

The central issue in this chapter is planning for the project scope. To be able to put your arms around this issue, you will explore three avenues: project scope management plan, scope definition, and WBS. The scope management plan is the part of the project management plan I will introduce first.

Creating the Project Management Plan

Once the project has been initiated, it is time to do some planning. Project planning starts with the process of developing a project management plan, which defines, prepares, coordinates, and integrates all subsidiary plans, such as scope and risk management plans, into one plan called the *project management plan*. The goal here is to develop a source of information that will work as a guideline for how the project will be planned, executed, controlled, and closed.

One reason why it is important to develop a project management plan is that not all the projects need all the planning processes, and to the same degree. Therefore, the content of the project management plan will depend upon a specific project. As the project goes through different stages, the project management plan may be updated and revised through the change control process. Following is an incomplete list of issues that a project management plan addresses.

◆ Which project management processes will be used for this process, what the level of implementation for each of these processes will be, and what the inputs and tools and techniques for these processes are

◆ How the changes will be monitored and controlled

◆ What the needs and techniques for communication among the stakeholders are

◆ How the project lifecycle looks, including the project phases if the project is a multi-phase project

Depending upon the complexity of the project, the project management plan can be either a summary or a collection of subsidiary plans and components, which might include the following:

◆ Standard plans from the project planning process group, such as the cost management plan, communication management plan, process scope management plan, and risk management plan.

◆ Other components, such as the milestones list, resource calendar, and baselines for schedule, cost, and quality. A baseline is a reference plan against which all the performance deviations are measured. This reference plan can be the original or the updated plan.

The process of developing the project management plan falls in the knowledge area of integration management because it coordinates the various processes and activities. Therefore, project management processes, in addition to the preliminary project scope statement, are the obvious inputs to this process. The other inputs are enterprise environmental factors and organizational process assets. To develop the project management plan, you apply the following tools and techniques to this input: expert judgment, project management information systems, and project management methodology.

One of the crucial parts of managing any project is scope management, which is discussed next.

Managing Scope

The *scope* of a project is defined as the work that must be performed to deliver the required results (products or services) of a project. It is about both what is included in the project and what is not. In other words, scoping a project means drawing boundaries around it. The importance of managing the project scope cannot be overemphasized because it has a profound impact on the overall success of the project.

The major goal of scope management is to ensure that the required work (and only the required work) is included and performed in the project. This is accomplished by using the processes shown in Figure 3.1 and discussed as follows:

◆ **Scope planning.** This is used to determine the *how* of the scope management: how to define, control, and verify the project scope, and how to define and create a work breakdown structure (WBS).

◆ **Scope definition.** This is used to develop the detailed project scope statement.

◆ **Create WBS.** This is used to break down the project deliverables into manageable tasks that can be assigned to team members. These tasks are called *work packages*.

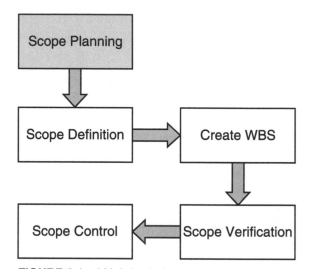

FIGURE 3.1 *A high-level view of process interactions and data flow between the processes included in scope management*

◆ **Scope verification.** This is used to formalize the acceptance of the completed project deliverables.

◆ **Scope control.** This is used to control changes to the project scope.

The scope control and scope verification processes are parts of the monitoring and controlling process group; therefore, they are covered in Chapter 7, "Monitoring and Controlling Projects." The other three processes are explored in this chapter.

Before you can define, control, and verify the scope, you need to determine how to do it for the project at hand. This is accomplished by developing the project scope management plan.

Developing the Project Scope Management Plan

By now you have three documents—two from the initiating stage, namely the project charter and the preliminary scope statement, and one from the planning stage, namely the project management plan. You use these three documents as input to develop the project scope management plan.

The process for developing the project scope management plan is shown in Figure 3.2.

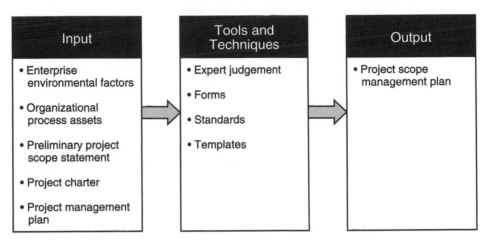

FIGURE 3.2 *The scope planning process: input, tools and techniques, and output*

Input for Scope Planning

The project charter and preliminary project scope statement developed in the initiation stage, along with the project management plan developed in the beginning of the planning stage, work as input to the scope planning process.

The enterprise environment factors, discussed in Chapter 2, should also be considered when developing the project scope management plan. The performing organization's culture, availability of human resources and tools, infrastructure, personnel policies, and market conditions can have an impact on how project scope will be managed.

Furthermore, the organizational process assets, discussed in Chapter 2, can also influence how the project scope will be managed. The following process assets are of special interest to the scope planning:

- ◆ The relevant historical information in the knowledge base of the organization to make use of the lessons learned from the scope planning of previous projects
- ◆ Organizational policies related to scope planning and scope management
- ◆ Organizational procedures related to scope planning and scope management

You use some tools and techniques on this input to hammer out the project scope management plan.

Tools and Techniques for Scope Planning

While planning the scope, expert judgment can be used based on how the scope was planned and managed in similar projects performed in the past.

The following tools can also be useful:

◆ Templates, such as scope management plan templates and WBS templates.

◆ Project scope change control forms. You can select which of the existing forms to use for the given project or you can develop new ones.

◆ Standards that the organization follows regarding scope planning and scope management. You can determine which of these standards applies to the given project.

You use these tools and techniques on the input to iron out the project scope management plan—in other words, the output of the scope planning process.

Output of Scope Planning

The purpose of the scope planning is to develop a project scope management plan that will provide guidance on how to define, verify, and control the project scope. Accordingly, the output of the scope planning provides the answers to the three questions described here:

◆ **How can you define the scope?** To answer this question, the scope management plan includes the following:

◆ A process to prepare a detailed project scope statement based on the preliminary project scope statement.

◆ A process that will enable the creation of the work breakdown structure (WBS) from the detailed project scope statement and will establish how the WBS will be maintained and approved.

◆ **How can you verify the scope?** The scope management plan answers this question by including a process that describes how the formal verification and acceptance of the completed project deliverables will be obtained.

◆ **How can you control the scope?** The scope management plan answers this question by including a process that specifies how the requests for changes to the detailed project scope statement (which we also refer to as the *scope statement*) will be processed.

The project scope management plan becomes part of the project management plan.

TIP

Whether the project scope management plan is informal and high-level (without too much detail) or formal and detailed depends upon the size, complexity, and needs of the project.

So the project scope management plan specifies how to define, verify, and control the project. With this plan in place, you are ready to define the scope.

Defining the Project Scope

Recall that the preliminary project scope statement that you developed in the project initiation stage contained the major deliverables, assumptions, and constraints. You build on these elements to develop the detailed project scope statement, one component of the scope definition. Now that the project is in the planning stage, you have more information than you had in the initiation stage. Therefore, you are in a better position to analyze the needs and expectations related to the project and convert them into requirements. Furthermore, the assumptions and constraints can be revisited and analyzed at greater length, and additional assumptions and constraints can be identified. This will help to define the project scope with more clarity and specificity.

Figure 3.3 presents the process of defining scope. You apply tools and techniques to the input to develop the output of the scope definition process.

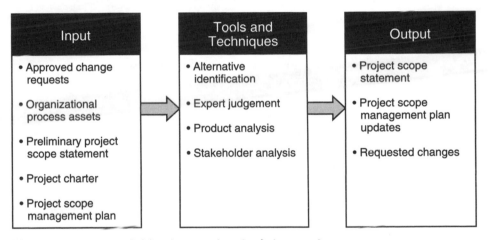

FIGURE 3.3 *Scope definition: input, tools and techniques, and output*

Input to Scope Definition

The project scope management plan will guide you on how to develop the project scope definition, while the project charter and the preliminary project scope statement will provide the initial content for the scope definition. You should also consider the organizational process assets, such as standards and policies of the performing organization, relevant to defining the project scope.

Another important input to defining the project scope is the approved change request. When the project is being performed, any change request to it will need to go through an approval process. When a change request has been approved, it is your responsibility to document the change in the project scope due to the approved change request.

Once you have input for the scope definition, you apply the tools and techniques discussed next to define (or redefine) the project scope.

Tools and Techniques for Scope Definition

This section discusses tools and techniques used in the scope definition process.

◆ **Identification of alternatives.** This is a technique used to apply nonstandard approaches to perform project work, in this case to define the project scope. A host of general management techniques can be used in this category; the most common ones are brainstorming and lateral thinking. Brainstorming is a creative technique generally used in a group environment to gather ideas as candidates for a solution to a problem or an issue. The evaluation and analysis of these ideas happens later. Lateral thinking is synonymous with thinking outside the box. The idea is to think beyond the realm of your experience to search for new solutions and methods, not just better uses of the current ones.

◆ **Expert judgment.** You can use help from relevant experts in the organization to develop parts of the detailed project scope.

◆ **Product analysis.** To hammer out the details of the project scope, you might need to perform product analysis, which might include techniques such as product breakdown and system analysis. The goal is to translate the project objectives to tangible deliverables and requirements. Each application area has different product analysis methods to accomplish this.

◆ **Stakeholder analysis.** This includes identifying the needs, wants, and expectations of the various stakeholders and prioritizing them according to the stakeholders' influence. The goal here is to quantify the interests of the stakeholders into concrete requirements. For example, what does customer satisfaction mean? Unless you quantify it into a feature or a deliverable, it is a vague and uncertain concept, and with uncertainty comes risk.

You apply one of these tools or techniques to the input to hammer out the output of the scope definition process.

Output of Scope Definition

Depending on the input, the scope definition process can generate two kinds of output: the detailed project scope statement that contains the original scope definition, and approved changes and updates. The project scope statement is a component of the baseline used to manage the change requests to the project.

Changes and Updates to Scope

The requested changes that impact the scope become part of the scope definition after they are approved through the change control process. After a change request has been approved, you should also evaluate its impact on the scope management plan and document the resulting changes to the plan.

Project Scope Statement

The key output item of the project definition process is the detailed project scope statement, which we also refer to as the *project scope statement* or the *scope statement*. The scope statement basically states what needs to be accomplished by the project. It provides a documented basis for the following:

◆ Developing a common understanding among the stakeholders about the project scope

◆ Making project decisions throughout the lifecycle of the project

◆ Measuring performance deviations from the scope

The specific elements of the project are discussed in the following sections.

Project assumptions and constraints. Assumptions and constraints are initially included in the project charter. However, at this stage, you have more information about the project and therefore you can revisit the initial assumptions and constraints and you might be able to identify more assumptions and constraints. You should document the specific assumptions related to the project scope and also analyze their impact in case they turn out to be false. Due to the uncertainty built into them, the assumptions are potential sources of risk.

The constraints related to the project scope must also be documented in the scope statement. Because the constraints limit the team's options, the constraints' impact on the project must be evaluated. The constraints can come from various sources, such as a predetermined deadline (also called a *hard deadline*) for the completion of the project or a milestone, limits on the funds available for the project, and contractual provisions. However, the following are common constraints to consider across all projects:

◆ Quality

◆ Resources

◆ Scope

◆ Time (or schedule)

I will discuss the details about these constraints in Chapter 7.

Project objectives. A project might include a variety of objectives, such as business, schedule, technical, and quality objectives. A project objective might have attributes assigned to it, such as cost. The objectives might also include how to measure the success of the project. Success criteria must be measurable. For example, customer satisfaction and substantial increase in revenue are not measurable criteria, whereas a three-percent increase in revenue is measurable.

Project deliverables. A deliverable is a unique and verifiable product, a capability to provide a service, or a result that must be produced to complete a project, a process, or a phase of the project. The deliverables can include project management reports and documents.

Project requirements. The requirements include the conditions that the project items must satisfy, the capabilities that the project items must possess, or both. These requirements fall into the following categories:

◆ **Requirements on deliverables.** These are the requirements imposed on deliverables that might stem from a contract, standard, or specification, or from an analysis of stakeholders' needs, wants, and expectations. The scope statement lists the specification documents to which the project must conform.

◆ **Approval requirements.** The scope statement also identifies the approval requirements that will be applied to specific items, such as objectives, documents, deliverables, and work.

◆ **Configuration management requirements.** Configuration management refers to controlling the characteristics of a product, service, or result of a project. It includes documenting the features of a product or a service, controlling and documenting changes to the features, and providing support for auditing the products for conformance to requirements. The project scope statement specifies the level of configuration management requirements, including change controls to be implemented during the project execution.

> **TIP**
>
> You must be able to make a distinction between objectives, deliverables, and requirements. For example, in a project to launch a Web site, the Web site is a deliverable. That the Web site must print a warning message at the login time is a requirement, and that the Web site should increase the company revenue by three percent is an objective.

Project boundaries. This involves drawing boundaries around the project by specifying what is included and what is not, especially focusing on the gray areas where the stakeholders can make their own assumptions, different from each other.

Product description. The scope statement must describe the product scope and the product acceptance criteria:

◆ **Product scope description.** Product scope is defined as features and functions that characterize a product, service, or result to be delivered by the project. Do not confuse the *product* scope with the *project* scope, which is the scope of the whole project and is defined as the entire work required to create the project deliverables. Product scope and project scope, although related, are different concepts.

◆ **Product acceptance criteria.** This defines the process and criteria for accepting the completed products that the project will deliver.

Initial project team. The scope statement identifies the project team members and the stakeholders. The identification of the team members might be at a high level and incomplete at this stage.

Scheduled milestones. Although the detailed schedule is not in place yet, the customer or the performing organization can identify milestones and assign deadlines to them. This will, of course, impose schedule constraints on the project.

Cost estimate. Although an exact cost of the project cannot be calculated at this stage, you can make a cost estimate and document it. Any fund limitations should also be documented as a constraint.

Initial risk identification. Although a detailed risk analysis will be performed later, the risks that can be identified at this stage should be recorded in the scope statement.

> **NOTE**
>
> It is important to understand the difference between the project scope and the product scope. As an example, consider the project to launch a Web site. The functional Web site with predetermined features is the product scope. The project scope is the work that needs to be done to produce this product scope, which includes writing software, testing software, putting all the software pieces together on a Web server, and making the Web site live.

The project scope statement serves the following purposes:

◆ It serves as a component to the baseline that will be used to evaluate whether the request for a change or additional work falls within or beyond the scope of the project.

◆ By providing a common understanding of the project scope, the scope statement helps bring the stakeholders onto the same page in their expectations.

◆ Because the scope statement describes the deliverables and the work required to create those deliverables, it is used to create a WBS, which helps in scheduling the project.

◆ It serves as a guide for the project team to do more detailed planning, if necessary, and to perform work during project execution.

So the project scope statement specifies the scope of the project in terms of the products, services, or results with specified features to be delivered by the project. From the perspective of actually performing the work, the scope statement is still a high-level document. To be able to schedule the project, identify and assign resources, and manage the project successfully, these deliverables need to be broken down into manageable tasks. This is accomplished by creating an entity called the *work breakdown structure* (WBS).

Creating a Work Breakdown Structure (WBS)

What is the secret behind accomplishing seemingly impossible tasks in any area? The answer is to break down the required work into smaller, manageable pieces. This is also a very important process in project management. To be able to actually execute the project, the project scope is broken down into manageable tasks by creating a work breakdown structure (WBS). In other words, a WBS is a deliverable-oriented hierarchy of the work that must be performed to accomplish the objectives of and create the deliverables for the project.

Figure 3.4 shows the input, tools and techniques, and output of creating the WBS. The project scope statement contains the list of deliverables and objectives, which are the basis for creating the WBS. The project scope management plan can provide guidelines on how to create the WBS for the project, and you should always consider organizational process assets while going through this and several other processes. The approved change requests must also go through this process before they become parts of the changes to the WBS.

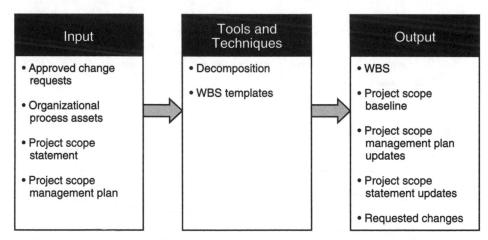

FIGURE 3.4 *Creating the WBS: input, tools and techniques, and output*

Even though each project is unique, there are similarities among sets of projects in an organization. These similarities can be used to prepare templates that will be used as a starting point for the WBS, to avoid the duplication of work. With or without templates, you will need to go through breaking down the deliverables, a very important step in creating the WBS.

Decomposition

Decomposition is a technique for subdividing the project deliverables into smaller, manageable tasks called *work packages*. The WBS is a hierarchical structure with work packages at the lowest level of each branch. Based on their complexity, different deliverables can have different levels of decomposition, as shown in the examples presented in Figure 3.5.

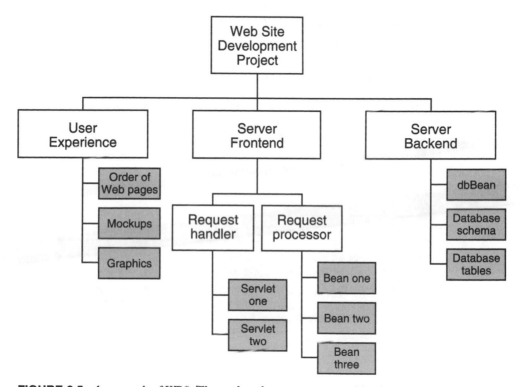

FIGURE 3.5 *An example of WBS. The work packages are represented by the dark boxes at the end of each branch. Servlet and Bean refer to the programs that will need to be written.*

You decompose the project work by executing the following steps:

1. Identify the deliverables and the work involved by analyzing the project scope statement.

2. Structure and organize the first level (just below the root of the hierarchical tree) of the WBS hierarchy. Based on the project at hand, you can use one of the following approaches:
   - Use the deliverables as the components in the first level.
   - Use the phases of the project as the components in the first level.

♦ Use the subprojects as components in the first level. A subproject is a part of the project that is independent enough of the rest of the project that it can be performed by another project team. This approach is useful when you want to outsource parts of the project.

♦ Use different approaches within each branch of WBS—for example, a subproject and deliverables in the first level.

3. Decompose the upper level into more detailed components for the lower level.

4. Keep decomposing to lower levels until necessary and sufficient decomposition has been achieved.

5. Assign identification codes to the WBS components.

As the work is decomposed to lower levels of details, work components become more concrete and manageable. However, you should avoid excessive decomposition because it will lead to a large number of work packages and it will not be possible to manage all of them effectively. In other words, excessive decomposition leads to inefficient use of management and other resources. Necessary and sufficient decomposition is the key.

TIP

During decomposition, the components are defined in terms of how the project work will actually be executed and controlled. You must verify the correctness of the decomposition at each level by requiring that the lower-level components are necessary and sufficient to the completion of the corresponding higher-level deliverables.

The WBS document is the key item of the create WBS process, but there are some other output items as well.

Output of Creating WBS

The output of the create WBS process consists of the items discussed in the following list.

Work breakdown structure. The project manager creates this document with the help of the project team. Following are some important characteristics of the WBS:

♦ Each component in the WBS hierarchy, including work packages, is assigned a unique identifier called a *code of account* identifier. These identifiers can then be used in estimating costs, scheduling, and assigning resources.

♦ The WBS embraces the full scope of the project. If a task is not included in the WBS, it will not be done as a part of the project.

♦ Because the project manager creates the WBS with the help of the project team, it is also the beginning of the team-building process on the part of the project manager.

◆ The WBS decomposes the project work into manageable pieces (work packages) that can be assigned to individuals. This helps define the responsibilities for the team members and is the starting point for building the schedule.

◆ Throughout the project, the WBS works as a reference for communication regarding what is included in the project and what is not.

WBS dictionary. This is a supporting document for the main WBS document to provide details about the components of the WBS. The details about a component might include a code of account identifier, a statement of work, a list of milestones schedule, and the organization responsible for this component.

Updates. During the create WBS process, the project team might realize that something out of the existing scope must be included in order to accomplish something in the scope. This will give rise to a change request, which might also come from other stakeholders during or after the first creation of the WBS. After the change request has been approved, not only the WBS will be changed—the scope statement must also be updated accordingly. The impact of the approved change request on the project scope management plan must be evaluated, and the plan must be updated accordingly.

Scope baseline. This is not a different item in itself. The scope statement, the WBS document, and the WBS dictionary combined constitute the scope baseline against which all the change requests will be evaluated.

NOTE

Do not confuse the WBS with other information breakdown structures, such as the organizational breakdown structure (OBS), which provides a hierarchy of the performing organization and can be used to identify organizational units for assigning the WBS work packages. Remember, the end goal of the WBS is to specify the project scope in terms of work packages; this is what distinguishes the WBS from other information breakdown structures.

You might wonder who creates the WBS. Well, it is your responsibility, and you perform it with the help of the team. Which team? The work packages do not exist before the WBS is complete; therefore, no assignments have been made yet. Yes, you are right—depending upon the project, the final project team might not even exist yet. However, recall that one of the components of the project scope statement identifies the initial team members and the stakeholders. This is the team you will use to create the WBS.

Before and After the WBS

From the initiating process group until now, I have discussed quite a few documents created in various processes. Some of these documents become input into another process that creates some other document. It is important to understand the order in which these documents are created and which document is an input to creating which other document. This is shown in Figure 3.6.

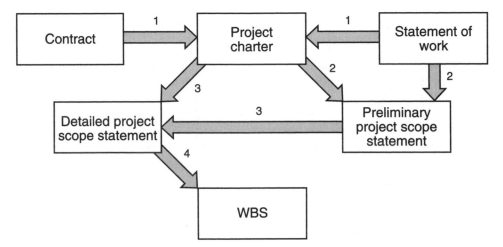

FIGURE 3.6 *A number of documents are created during the initiation and scope planning processes. An arrow shows the documents that are input to creating other documents, and the numbers indicate the order in which these documents are created.*

Table 3.1 presents some items that are input to processes. Note that organizational process assets are input into all the listed processes, approved changes are input into all the scope-related processes, and enterprise environment factors are an input into initiating and scope planning.

Table 3.1 Input Items for Various Processes*

	Process			
Input item	**Initiation (Develop project charter)**	**Scope planning**	**Scope definition**	**Create WBS**
Approved change requests	No	No	Yes	Yes
Contract	Yes	No	No	No
Enterprise environmental factors	Yes	Yes	No	No
Organizational process assets	Yes	Yes	Yes	Yes
Statement of work	Yes	No	No	No

*"Yes" means the item is included in the input list of the corresponding process.

The WBS is at the heart of project management. It affects directly or indirectly almost all the processes that are performed after its creation. Figure 3.7 shows some of the processes that are based on the WBS.

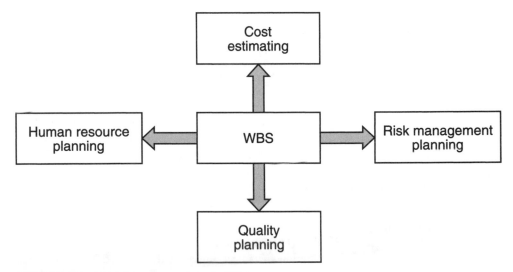

FIGURE 3.7 *Some processes based on the WBS*

The three most important takeaways from this chapter are as follows:

◆ The scope management plan is the part of the project management plan that specifies how to define, control, and verify the project scope.

◆ The scope management plan, along with the project charter and the preliminary project scope statement from the initiation stage, becomes the input to developing the detailed project scope statement, which is a document that states what needs to be accomplished by the project.

◆ The project scope statement is an input item to create the work breakdown structure (WBS), which is a breakdown of project deliverables into manageable pieces called *work packages*. The WBS is supported by another document called the *WBS dictionary*, which offers details for the WBS components.

Summary

After a project has been initiated, the project management plan is developed to specify how the project at hand will be planned, executed, controlled, and closed. The project management plan can contain subsidiary plans, such as a quality management plan, a risk management plan, and a project scope management plan. The scope management plan specifies how to define, control, and verify the scope. The scope management plan, along with the project charter and the preliminary project scope statement from the initiation stage, becomes the input to developing the detailed project scope statement, also referred to as the *scope statement*.

The project scope statement is a document that defines the scope of a project by stating what needs to be accomplished by the project. It includes project objectives, deliverables, a product description, and requirements. The project scope statement is an input item to creating the work breakdown structure (WBS), which is a breakdown of project deliverables into manageable pieces called *work packages*, which in turn are used to develop the project schedule. The WBS is supported by another document called the *WBS dictionary*, which offers details for the WBS components.

The scope statement, the WBS document, and the WBS dictionary combined constitute the scope baseline against which all change requests are evaluated. One advantage of project planning is that it identifies and addresses uncertainties in the project. The uncertainties are bad because they are a source of risks. Risk management planning, along with quality planning, is discussed in the next chapter.

Exam's Eye View

Comprehend
◆ The project charter and the preliminary project scope statement are input items to the scope definition process that is used to develop the detailed project scope statement.
◆ The detailed project scope statement is an input item to creating the WBS.
◆ The scope statement, the WBS document, and the WBS dictionary combined constitute the scope baseline against which all change requests are evaluated.

Look Out
◆ Do not confuse project scope with product scope. The product scope consists of the features and functions that characterize a product, service, or result to be delivered by the project, whereas the project scope is composed of the work that must be performed (and only that work) to deliver products, services, or results with specified features.
◆ The project scope management plan is an input item to both the scope definition and the WBS creation processes, but these processes can also update the project scope management plan.

Memorize

◆ The project scope statement includes these elements: project objectives, project deliverables, project requirements, product description, assumptions and constraints, cost estimates, scheduled milestones, initial risk identification, and the initial project team.

◆ Quality, resources, scope, and time are the common constraints you should consider across all projects.

◆ The success criteria stated in the scope statement of a project must be measurable, such as a three-percent increase in revenue, not vague, such as a substantial increase in revenue.

◆ The project scope management plan is a part of the project management plan.

Key Terms

◆ **alternatives identification.** A technique used to apply nonstandard approaches, such as brainstorming and lateral thinking, to perform project work.

◆ **baseline.** A reference plan for components, such as schedule, scope, and cost, against which performance deviations are measured. The reference plan can be the original or the modified plan.

◆ **brainstorming.** A creative technique generally used in a group environment to gather ideas as candidates for a solution to a problem or an issue without any immediate evaluation of these ideas. The evaluation and analysis of these ideas happens later.

◆ **configuration management.** Refers to controlling the characteristics of a product, a service, or a result of a project. It includes documenting the features of a product or a service, controlling and documenting changes to the features, and providing support for auditing the products for conformance to requirements.

◆ **decomposition.** A planning technique to subdivide the project scope, including deliverables, into smaller, manageable tasks called *work packages*.

◆ **deliverable.** A unique and verifiable product, a capability to provide a service, or a result that must be produced to complete a project or a process or phase of the project.

◆ **lateral thinking.** Thinking outside the box, beyond the realm of your experience, to search for new solutions and methods, rather than only better uses of the current solutions and methods.

◆ **product scope.** Features and functions that characterize a product, service, or result to be delivered by the project.

◆ **project scope.** The work that must be performed (and only that work) to deliver products, services, or results with specified features that were promised by the project. The project scope draws the boundaries around the project: what is included and what is not.

◆ **project scope statement.** A document that defines the scope of a project by stating what needs to be accomplished by the project.

◆ **scope baseline.** The reference scope against which all the scope deviations are measured. It consists of the scope statement, the WBS document, and the WBS dictionary.

◆ **scope definition.** The process used to develop the detailed project scope statement.

◆ **scope planning.** The process of developing the project scope management plan.

◆ **subprojects.** Parts of the main projects that are independent enough that each can be performed by separate project teams.

◆ **work breakdown structure (WBS).** A deliverable-oriented hierarchical decomposition of the work that must be performed to accomplish the objectives and create the deliverables of the project.

◆ **work package.** A deliverable or a task at the lowest level of each branch of the WBS.

Review Questions

1. Which of the following is a false statement about the WBS?

   A. Each item in the WBS (not just the work packages) is assigned a unique identifier called a *code of account* identifier.

   B. You should keep decomposing WBS components to lower levels until necessary and sufficient decomposition has been achieved.

   C. Each work component appears in the WBS once and only once.

   D. The work packages should appear from left to right in the order in which the work will be performed.

2. Which of the following is done first?

   A. Creating the scope statement

   B. Creating the WBS

   C. Creating the preliminary project scope statement

   D. Creating the project charter

3. The WBS is the output of which of the following processes?
   - **A.** The create WBS process
   - **B.** The scope definition process
   - **C.** Creating the project scope
   - **D.** Project initiation

4. The project scope statement is the output of which of the following processes?
   - **A.** The create WBS process
   - **B.** The scope definition process
   - **C.** Creating the project scope
   - **D.** Project initiation

5. Which of the following is a false statement about the project scope management plan?
   - **A.** It describes how to verify the scope.
   - **B.** It describes how to control the scope.
   - **C.** It serves as the baseline for the project scope.
   - **D.** It describes how to create the WBS.

6. What are the components in the lowest level of the WBS hierarchy collectively called?
   - **A.** Work packages
   - **B.** Milestones
   - **C.** Phases
   - **D.** Features

7. Which of the following is not a constraint common to all the projects?
   - **A.** Resources
   - **B.** Scope
   - **C.** Time
   - **D.** Quality
   - **E.** Skill set

8. Which of the following constitutes the project scope baseline?
    A. The preliminary scope statement and the detailed scope statement
    B. The detailed scope statement
    C. The WBS document
    D. The WBS, the WBS dictionary, and the detailed scope statement
    E. The WBS document and the WBS dictionary

9. Who creates the WBS?
    A. The project manager alone
    B. The project manager and the project sponsor
    C. The customer
    D. The project manger with help from the project team
    E. The upper management in the performing organization

10. Which of the following is not included in the project scope statement?
    A. Project assumptions and constraints
    B. The WBS
    C. Project objectives
    D. Project deliverables
    E. Product descriptions

Chapter 4

Planning Quality and Risk Management

PMP Exam Objectives

Objective	*What It Really Means*
1.3 Document Project Risks, Assumptions, and Constraints	You must know the relationship of assumptions and constraints to risks. Understand the risk management planning process.
2.5 Identify Risks and Define Risk Strategies	You must know that uncertainties in a project are sources of risk. You also must know that there can be both positive and negative risks and that negative risks pose threats, whereas positive risks offer opportunities. Understand the processes for risk identification, risk analysis, and risk response planning.

Introduction

Quality and risk are two important interrelated aspects of any project that need to be managed. While quality refers to the degree to which a set of characteristics of project deliverables and objectives fulfill the project requirements, risk refers to an uncertain event or condition that, if it occurs, has a positive or negative effect on meeting the project objectives. After you have planned the project scope to the WBS level, as discussed in the previous chapter, you are ready to plan the quality and risk management. After the project starts executing, you will not have enough time to plan a response to a risk if it occurs, so you need to plan risk responses before the project starts executing. To do that, you need to identify the risks and analyze them.

The core question in this chapter is: How do you plan for quality and risk management? In search of an answer, we will explore three avenues: planning quality, identifying and analyzing risks, and planning risk responses.

Managing Quality

Quality refers to the degree to which a set of characteristics of project deliverables and objectives fulfills the project requirements. In other words, it is the sum of project and product characteristics that help fulfill the requirements. The broader goal of quality management is to ensure that a given project will satisfy the needs for which it was undertaken. Quality management has two components: project quality management and product quality management. Whereas product quality management techniques depend upon the specific product that the project is going to produce, project quality management applies to all projects independent of the nature of the products. The performing organization might have its own quality policy and procedures in addition to the three quality management processes shown in Figure 4.1 and explained in the following list.

- ◆ **Quality planning.** This process is used to identify which quality standards are relevant to the project at hand and to determine how to meet these standards.
- ◆ **Perform quality assurance.** This process is used to apply the planned systematic quality activities to ensure that the project employs all the planned processes needed to meet all the project requirements.
- ◆ **Quality control.** This process monitors the project results to ensure that they meet the agreed-upon quality standards and identifies ways to eliminate the factors that keep the project results from meeting standards.

The quality assurance and quality control processes are used during the project execution and control stages and are therefore discussed in Chapters 6 and 7, respectively. The quality planning process is used during the project planning stage and is discussed next.

FIGURE 4.1 *Processes used in quality management*

Planning Quality

According to PMBOK, quality is defined as the degree to which a set of characteristics of project deliverables and objectives fulfill the project requirements. Therefore, any characteristic that influences the satisfaction of the stakeholders is included in determining the quality. The project quality management processes include performing quality planning, quality assurance, and quality control. Quality planning is the quality process that is performed during the planning phase to accomplish the following goals.

◆ Identify which quality standards are relevant to the project at hand

◆ Determine how to satisfy these standards

Figure 4.2 depicts the quality planning process.

The project scope statement is the key input to the quality planning process, in addition to other input items discussed next.

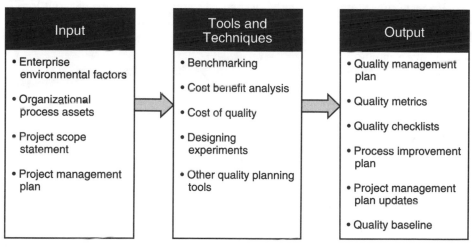

FIGURE 4.2 *Quality planning: input, tools and techniques, and output*

Input to Quality Planning

This section details the items that can be used as input into the quality planning process.

Enterprise environment factors. Guidelines, regulations from a government agency, rules, and standards relevant to the project at hand are examples of enterprise environment factors that must be considered during quality planning.

Organizational process assets. The following organizational process assets can affect the project from the perspective of quality planning:

◆ Information from the previous projects and lessons learned

◆ An organizational quality policy, which is composed of overall intentions and high-level direction of an organization with respect to quality, established by the management at executive level

◆ Procedures relevant to the application area of this project

If the performing organization lacks a quality policy, the project team will need to develop a quality policy for the project. Once a quality policy is in place, it is your responsibility to ensure that the project stakeholders are aware of it and are on the same page.

Project management plan. The project management plan includes which processes will be implemented and to what level. It also includes which tools and techniques will be used to implement these processes. This information provides useful input to quality planning.

Project scope statement. The project scope statement is the major input into quality planning. Before you can plan quality, you need to understand what quality means for this project. Therefore, the following components of the project scope statement are especially relevant to quality planning:

◆ Project deliverables.

◆ Project objectives.

◆ Project requirements.

◆ A product scope description that may contain the details of technical issues and other quality-related concerns.

◆ Product acceptance criteria. The definition of acceptance criteria has an impact on the quality cost.

With the input items in place, you use some tools and techniques to perform quality planning, as discussed in the following section.

Tools and Techniques Used for Quality Planning

The tools and techniques used for quality planning include benchmarking, cost/benefit analysis, experiment design, and brainstorming.

Benchmarking. Benchmarking is comparing practices, products, or services of a project with those of some reference projects for the purpose of learning, improving, and creating the basis for measuring performance. These reference projects might be the previous projects performed inside or outside of the performing organization. Improvement and performance are of course quality-related factors. For example, you might have a similar project performed in the past that accepted no more than two defects in each feature. You might use that as a quality criterion—a benchmark—for your project.

Cost of quality and cost/benefit analysis. The cost of quality is the total cost incurred in implementing conformance to the requirements, reworking due to the defects resulting from failure to meet the requirements, and updating the product or service to meet the requirements. During quality planning, you must consider the tradeoff between the cost and the benefit of quality and strike the appropriate balance for a given project. Implementing quality has its costs, including quality management and fulfilling quality requirements. The benefits of meeting quality requirements include less rework, resulting in overall higher productivity; lower costs of maintaining the product or service; and higher customer satisfaction.

Experiment design. This is a statistical method that can be used to identify the factors that might influence a set of specific variables for a product or a process under development or in production. By using the results from these experiments, you can optimize the products and processes.

Other quality planning tools. Other tools that you can use in quality planning, depending upon the project, include brainstorming and flowcharting.

You can use one or more of these techniques to generate the output of quality planning.

Output of Quality Planning

A major output of the quality planning process is the quality management plan. This section discusses the quality management plan and other output items.

Quality management plan. The quality management plan describes how the quality policy for this project will be implemented by the project management team. It also addresses quality assurance and quality control, as explained in the previous section. This plan becomes a component of the overall project management plan.

> ◆ **TIP**
>
> Whether the quality management plan is informal and high-level or formal and detailed depends upon the size, complexity, and needs of the project.

Quality metrics. This is an operational criterion that defines in specific terms what something (such as a characteristic or a feature) is and how the quality control process measures it. For example, it is not specific enough to say the defects in the product will be minimized. Rather, specifying something such as that no feature will have more than two defects is a measurable criterion and hence a metric. The metrics that you set during quality planning will be used in quality assurance and quality control.

Quality checklist. A checklist is a structured tool used to verify that a predetermined set of required steps has been performed. The checklists can come in imperative form ("to do" lists) or in interrogative form ("have you done this" lists). Checklists are prepared (or identified if they already exist in the organization) in quality planning and used in quality control.

Process improvement plan. This plan describes how to improve some of the processes that will be used in the project. For example, one purpose of improvement is to prevent activities in the processes which are not needed for this project. This is accomplished by describing the purpose, start, and end of a given process, the input to the process, and the output of the process.

Quality baseline. The quality baseline specifies the quality objectives for the project and thereby makes the basis for measuring and reporting the quality performance. This becomes a part of the performance measurement baseline for the project, which is an integrated plan for the project specifying some parameters for the performance measurements, such as scope, schedule, and cost. The performance of the project is measured against this baseline. For example, a project that is finished on time, with everything delivered in scope, and that stayed within its cost is a project with high performance.

Project management plan updates. Although the project management plan is an input item to quality planning, quality planning updates the project management plan. The biggest update is that the quality management plan becomes part of the project management plan.

Quality assurance is the process of ensuring that the quality plan is implemented. Because it is part of the execution process group, it is explored in Chapter 6, "Executing the Project." Quality control is the process of monitoring the project results to ensure that they conform to the planned quality. This process is part of the control process group and therefore is explored in Chapter 7, "Monitoring and Controlling Projects."

Note that quality planning might influence other planning processes. For example, implementing the identified quality standards will impact the cost and the schedule. Furthermore, the implementation of a quality characteristic might require a risk analysis of the problem that the quality characteristic addresses.

Managing Risks

To most of us, risk means danger—if it happens, it will result in negative, undesired consequences. However, according to PMI, risk is an uncertain event or condition that, if it occurs, has a positive or negative effect on meeting the project objectives related to components such as schedule (time), cost, scope, or quality. For example, one of the obvious schedule objectives for a project is to complete the project by the scheduled deadline. If a risk related to the schedule occurs, it can delay the completion of the project, or it can make it possible to finish the project earlier. The two characteristics of a risk in project management are the following:

♦ It stems from the elements of uncertainty.

♦ It might have negative or positive effects on meeting the project objectives.

The process of risk management includes planning risk management, identifying and analyzing the risks, preparing the response plan, monitoring the risk, and implementing the risk response if the risk occurs. Figure 4.3 shows the corresponding processes used to accomplish these tasks, which are also explained in the following list:

♦ **Risk management planning.** Used to determine the *how* of the risk management— how to plan and execute the risk management activities for the given project.

♦ **Risk identification.** Used to identify and document the risks that might occur for a given project.

♦ **Qualitative risk analysis.** Used to estimate the overall probability for risks to occur and their impact, and to prioritize them accordingly for further analysis.

♦ **Quantitative risk analysis.** Used to analyze numerically the effect of identified risks on meeting the project objectives.

♦ **Risk response planning.** Used to prepare a risk response plan to increase the positive impact and decrease the negative impact of each identified risk.

♦ **Risk monitoring and control.** Used to track identified risks, identify new risks, execute risk response plans, and evaluate the effectiveness of executing response throughout the lifecycle of the project.

TIP

The data flow between the different processes shown in Figure 4.3 is true in general. However, note that depending upon the project and the experience of the risk management team, shortcuts can be taken. For example, you can go directly from risk identification to quantitative risk analysis, or even to risk response planning.

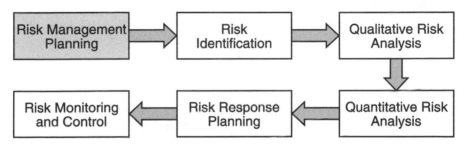

FIGURE 4.3 *Processes used in risk management*

The risk monitoring and control process is part of the control process group; therefore, we will discuss this process in Chapter 7. The other five processes are discussed in the following sections, starting with risk management planning.

Planning Risk Management

Risk management planning is the process used to decide how the risk management activities for the project at hand will be performed. The major goals for planning the risk management are threefold: Ensure that the type, level, and visibility of risk management are proportionate with the actual risk involved in the project and the importance of the project to the organization; secure sufficient resources, including time for risk management activities; and set up an agreed-upon basis for evaluating risks. To be specific, you use the risk management planning process to determine the following:

◆ How to approach the risk management activities for this project

◆ How to plan the risk management activities

◆ How to execute the risk management activities

Figure 4.4 shows the risk management planning process.

The input to risk management planning is identical to that of quality planning.

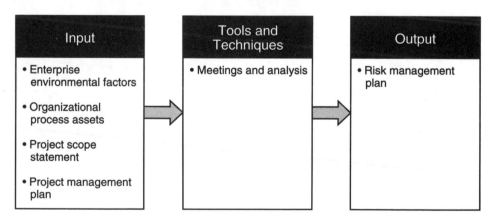

Input	Tools and Techniques	Output
• Enterprise environmental factors • Organizational process assets • Project scope statement • Project management plan	• Meetings and analysis	• Risk management plan

FIGURE 4.4 *The risk management planning process: input, tools and techniques, and output*

Input to Risk Management Planning

As Figures 4.2 and 4.4 suggest, the lists of input items to quality planning and risk management planning are identical. The enterprise environment factors include the organizational attitude toward risks and the risk tolerance level of the organization. This information can be found from the policy statements of the organization and from actual experience with previous projects.

The organization process assets include organizational approaches toward risk management, definitions of concepts and terms used within the organization, standard risk templates you can use, a roles and responsibilities list, and authority levels for decision-making.

The project scope statement contains elements, such as the following, that are relevant to risk management planning:

- **Assumptions and constraints.** Assumptions should be evaluated for their uncertainty and thereby the possible risks. Constraints represent fixed parameters, such as available funds and deadlines that can also pose risks to the project.
- **Project objectives and requirements.** You must address the risks that might prevent the team from meeting the project objectives and requirements.
- **Product description.** There might be risks involved in performing the work for meeting the product description.
- **Initial risk identification.** The project scope statement might contain some of the risks you initially identified. Now you have more information to build on that work.

The project management plan might have some information on which risk-related processes to use for this project. With these input items in place, the main technique used for risk management planning is meeting.

Tools and Techniques for Risk Management Planning

You develop the risk management plan by holding planning meetings, which might include the following attendees:

- Project manager
- Selected members from the project team
- Selected stakeholders
- Any member from the performing organization who has the responsibility for risk planning and executing

In these meetings, the input items are used to develop the risk management plan, the only output of the risk management planning process.

Output of Risk Management Planning

The only output of risk management planning is the risk management plan, which includes the following elements.

Methodology. This specifies the system of approaches, tools, and data sources that will be used to perform risk management on the project at hand. These tools and approaches might vary over the projects, so you have to make the best selection for the given project.

Identifying and assigning resources. This identifies and assigns the resources for risk management, such as human resources, cost, and time.

♦ **Roles and responsibilities.** This specifies the roles and responsibilities for each role involved in risk management. These roles are assigned to the members of the risk management team. The risk management team might include members from outside the project team.

♦ **Budgeting.** The cost for risk management activities needs to be estimated and included in the budget and the project cost baseline.

♦ **Timing and scheduling.** The plan specifies how often the risk management processes will be performed and which risk management activities will be included in the project schedule, which is planned and developed by using processes discussed in Chapter 5, "Planning the Project Schedule."

> **TIP**
>
> It's a good idea for the risk management team to include members from outside the project team to ensure unbiased risk evaluations.

Risk categories. This element specifies how the risks will be categorized. The risk categories typically correspond to the sources of risks. Depending upon the size and complexity of the project, you might need to develop a risk breakdown structure (RBS), which is a hierarchical structure that breaks the identified risk categories into subcategories. In developing this structure, you will end up identifying various areas and causes of potential risks. The performing organization might already have prepared a categorization of typical risks. However, you need to examine this categorization for each project and tailor it according to the needs of the project at hand. The risk categorization helps you identify the risks to the extent that you will be identifying various areas and causes of potential risks for your project.

> **TIP**
>
> Some project management literature and some PMP exam questions might use the terms "risk sources" and "risk categories" synonymously.

Risk probability and impact. Defining different levels of risk probabilities and impacts is necessary to ensure the quality and credibility of the qualitative risk analysis that we will discuss later in this chapter. The basic issues are defining the scale of likelihood that the risk will happen and defining the scale of the strength of its impact if the risk occurs. These definitions, even if they already exist in the organization, must be examined and tailored to the needs of the specific project.

You can define the risk probability scale from very unlikely to almost certainly, called the *relative scale*. As an alternative, you can define a numerical scale in which the probability is represented by numbers, in which a value close to 0.0 means very unlikely and a value close to 1.0 means almost certainly. The impact scale represents the size of the risk impact on the given project objective should the risk occur. Just like the probability scale, you can define the impact scale relatively or numerically. The relative scale can range from very low impact to very high impact, with points in the middle such as low, moderate, and high. As an alternative, you can define the impact numerically; it might be linear, such as the first point at 0.1, the second point at 0.2, and the tenth point at 1.0, or it might be nonlinear, such as the first point at 0.001, the second point at 0.01, and the third point at 0.1. Figure 4.5 shows an example of linear and nonlinear impact scales, in which the impact scale for objective 1 is nonlinear and the impact scale for objective 2 is linear. You can think of the X axis as a variable on which the risk impact depends.

Risks are prioritized according to the size of their impact on the project objectives, which can be recorded in what is called an *impact matrix* or *lookup table*. Even if your organization already has a typical impact matrix, you should examine it and tailor it to the needs of the specific project at hand. I will discuss the probability and impact matrix in more detail later in this chapter.

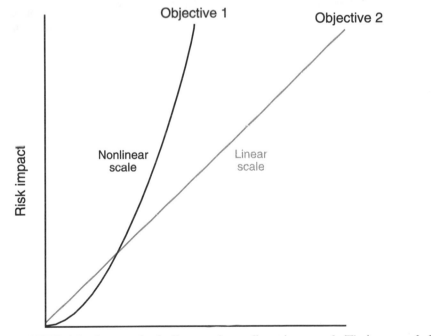

FIGURE 4.5 *An example of a linear and a nonlinear impact scale. The impact scale for objective 1 is nonlinear, whereas the scale for objective 2 is linear.*

As an example, Table 4.1 shows the risk impact definitions for four project objectives: cost, quality, scope, and time. Note that this example only shows the negative impact. The first row of the table presents the impact scale, and each cell in the following rows from column 2 to column 6 specifies the impact on a specific objective corresponding to a point on the overall impact scale. For example, the cell corresponding to the first row and fifth column reads that high impact (0.65) means a 50 to 80% increase in cost.

Table 4.1 Risk Impact Definitions for Four Project Objectives

Project Objectives	Risk Impact				
	Very Low (0.05)	Low (0.10)	Moderate (0.35)	High (0.65)	Very High (0.90)
Cost	Less than 1% cost increase	1–20% cost increase	20–50% cost increase	50–80% cost increase	80–100% cost increase
Time	Insignificant time increase	1–10% time increase	10–30% time increase	30–60% time increase	60–100% time increase
Scope	Scope decrease unnoticeable	Scope of only a few minor areas affected	Sponsor approval necessary for scope reduction	Scope reduction unacceptable to the sponsor	Project and item are effectively useless
Quality	Unnoticeable quality reduction	Only a few applications will be affected	Quality requires sponsor approval	Quality reduction unacceptable	Project and item are effectively useless

Risk reporting and tracking. This element describes the format of the risk reports, such as the risk register, a document that contains the results of risk analysis and risk response planning. Furthermore, it describes how different aspects of risk activities will be recorded so that the risks can be monitored for the current project. Also, should the performing organization decide to audit the risk management process, one should be able to track these activities. Another reason for recording these activities could be to save the information for the benefit of future projects in the form of lessons learned.

During the process of planning risk management for a specific project, you revisit the tolerance levels of the stakeholders for certain risks, and these levels may be revised. Risk management planning is the process that generates the risk management plan document, which contains the information that will be used in risk identification, risk analysis, and risk response planning.

Identifying Risks

Risks are identified by using the risk identification process. An unidentified risk is a danger lurking out of your sight and waiting to attack the project. The significance of the risk identification process cannot be overemphasized. You use the risk identification process to accomplish the following tasks:

◆ Identify which risks might affect the project at hand

◆ Document the characteristics of the identified risks in a document called the *risk register*

Figure 4.6 shows the input, tools and techniques, and the output for the risk identification process.

Note that the risk identification process has the risk management plan as an input item, in addition to all the input items that the quality planning and risk management planning processes have.

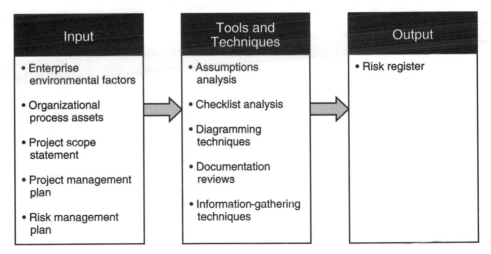

Input	Tools and Techniques	Output
• Enterprise environmental factors • Organizational process assets • Project scope statement • Project management plan • Risk management plan	• Assumptions analysis • Checklist analysis • Diagramming techniques • Documentation reviews • Information-gathering techniques	• Risk register

FIGURE 4.6 *The risk identification process: input, tools and techniques, and output*

Input to Risk Identification

The risk management plan, the project management plan, and the project scope statement are the key input items to the risk identification process. As in many other processes, the enterprise environment factors and organizational process assets relevant to the project at hand must also be considered.

◆ **Enterprise environment factors.** The environmental factors internal or external to the performing organization that can influence the project must be considered in the risk identification process. This might include academic and industry studies, benchmarking, and commercial databases.

◆ **Organizational process assets.** This might include information from previous projects (the knowledge base), including lessons learned.

◆ **Project scope statement.** Assumptions in the project scope statement are potential sources of uncertainty, hence the risk. Constraints pose a risk by presenting predetermined factors, such as hard deadlines and fixed cost, thereby posing questions such as, what is the probability that we can meet this constraint with the available resources?

◆ **Project management plan.** Identification of risks requires information from other processes, which can be found in the project management plan. For example, you might need to know the information about cost, quality, and scope before you can identify a risk.

◆ **Risk management plan.** The key items from the risk management plan useful for risk identification are risk categories, roles and responsibilities, and the budget and timing available for the risk management activities.

With this handful of input for your use, you are ready to use a number of tools and techniques available for risk identification.

Tools and Techniques for Risk Identification

Risk identification is crucial to risk management: If you fail to identify a risk, you will not be able to manage it. There are a multitude of tools and techniques available to aid you in identifying risks.

Assumptions analysis. Assumptions in the project scope statement represent uncertainty. You analyze these assumptions to identify the risks. Assumptions analysis is the technique used to examine the validity of the assumptions and thereby to identify the risks resulting from the inaccuracies, inconsistencies, or incompleteness of each assumption. For example, assume that there is only one person in the organization who has a rare skill needed for the project. An obvious assumption would be that the person will not quit the organization before completing the assignment. The inaccuracy of this assumption amounts to the risk.

Checklist analysis. The carefully prepared checklists in any process are great no-brainer time-savers. The projects in the same organization will more often than not have similarities. As a result, you can develop a risk identification checklist based on the information gathered from a similar set of projects previously performed. Also, if you developed the risk breakdown structure (RBS) in risk planning, the lowest level of RBS can be used as a checklist.

NOTE

Risk identification checklists are rarely exhaustive. Always explore what is left out of the checklist you are using. Also, improve the checklist when you close the project to enhance its value for future projects.

Diagramming techniques. These techniques use diagrams to identify risks by exposing and exploring the risks' causes. Here are a few examples:

♦ **Cause-and-effect diagram.** A cause-and-effect diagram illustrates how various factors (causes) can be linked to potential problems (effects).

♦ **Flowchart diagram.** A flowchart depicts how the elements of a system are related to each other and shows the logical flow of a process. By examining the flowchart of a process, the risk management team can identify the points of potential problems in the flowchart diagram.

♦ **Influence diagram.** An influence diagram is a graphical representation of situations that shows relationships among various variables and outcomes, such as causal influences and time-ordering of events. By examining these diagrams, the risk management team can recognize the potential problem areas and thereby identify risks.

Documentation reviews. A structured review of the relevant parts of input documents, such as the project scope statement and the project management plan, will certainly help in identifying risks. Furthermore, the knowledge base related to risk management from the previous projects can also be reviewed.

Information-gathering techniques. To identify risks, you need to gather risk-related information. Following are some of the information-gathering techniques used in risk identification:

♦ **Brainstorming.** The goal here is to get a comprehensive list of potential risks so that no risk goes unidentified. The project team, along with the relevant experts from different disciplines, can participate in the brainstorming session. Brainstorming is better performed under the guidance of a facilitator. You can use the categories of risks or the RBS as a framework to keep the session focused on the issue.

♦ **Delphi technique.** The goal here is for the experts to reach a consensus without biases toward each other. I'm sure you will have no problem recalling a time when a decision was made because somebody (usually higher in the management hierarchy) said so. Contrary to this, the Delphi technique is used to ensure that it is the quality of the information and the argument that are important, not who is saying them. A facilitator circulates a questionnaire among the experts to solicit ideas about the risks of the given project. The experts respond anonymously. The responses are compiled and circulated among the participating experts for further evaluation without attaching a name to a response. It might take a few iterations before a general consensus is reached.

♦ **Interviewing.** This is one of the common methods used for information-gathering for risk identification. You interview the appropriate stakeholders and subject matter experts to gather information that will help identify risks for the project at hand.

♦ **Root cause identification.** A powerful way to identify risk is to look for anything in the project that might generate a risk. In other words, if you can spot a potential cause for risks, it's simple to identify the risks resulting from that cause. Furthermore, if you know the cause of a risk, it helps to plan an effective response. You can also look for risks at the opposite side of causes—that is, impacts.

◆ **SWOT analysis.** While root cause identification techniques look into the causes of the risks to identify the risks, a SWOT analysis looks at the potential impacts of the risks to identify the risks. If you examine the strengths, weaknesses, opportunities, and threats (SWOT) of a given project, you will be exposing the risks involved. Remember that a strength is an opportunity, a weakness is a threat, and opportunities and threats are posed by risks. This helps broaden the spectrum of risks considered. For example, a strength of your project might be that most of its parts are well understood from previously executed similar projects. Therefore, the risks involved in those parts will be easy to identify. A weakness of your project might be that one of the parts involves new technology that is not well-tested. So, this is a source of unknown risks. An opportunity might be that your organization will be the first one to take this product to the market. An example of a threat might be that the government is considering a bill that, if it becomes a law, will have profound implications for your project.

You will generally be using more than one of these tools and techniques to identify the risks. During risk identification, you might discover the causes of the risks, and you might even think of some potential risk responses. All this is part of the output of the risk identification process.

The Risk Register: The Output of Risk Identification

The risk register is a document that contains the output of the risk identification process. You will see later in this chapter that the risk register, which is initiated in the risk identification process, will also contain the information from other risk management processes. To begin, you store the following information from the risk identification process in the risk register:

◆ **List of identified risks.** These are the risks that you identified in the risk identification process.

◆ **List of the root causes of the risks.** This is a list of events or conditions that might give rise to the identified risks.

◆ **Updated risk categories.** Risks categories were originally identified in the risk management planning process. However, in the process of identifying risks you might discover new categories or modify the existing categories. The updated risk categories must be included in the risk register.

◆ **List of potential responses.** Risk response planning is a separate process that is performed after risk analysis. However, during risk identification, you might identify potential risk responses that you must document in the risk register. These responses can be further examined and planned in the risk response planning process.

The risk register becomes part of the project management plan.

The results of the risk identification process usually lead to the qualitative risk analysis. However, depending upon the project and the experience of the risk management team, risk identification might lead directly to the quantitative risk analysis and even to risk response planning.

Analyzing Risks

Once the risks have been identified, you need to answer two main questions for each identified risk: What are the odds that the risk will occur and, if it does, what will its impact be on the project objectives? You get the answers by performing risk analysis, which comes in two forms: qualitative and quantitative.

◆ **Qualitative risk analysis.** This is used to prioritize risks by estimating the probability of their occurrence and their impact on the project.

◆ **Quantitative risk analysis.** This is used to perform the numerical analysis to estimate the effect of each identified risk on the overall project objectives and deliverables.

Usually, you prioritize the risks by performing qualitative analysis on them before you perform quantitative analysis.

Qualitative Analysis

Because the qualitative analysis is an estimate, it is less precise than the quantitative analysis, which is based on numbers and hence is more precise. However, qualitative analysis is quicker and cheaper. It gives you some feel about the risks, and then you can determine which risks needs to be analyzed further by using the quantitative analysis.

Figure 4.7 shows the input, tools and techniques, and output for the qualitative analysis, which are discussed in the following section.

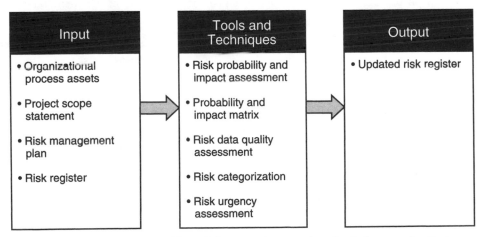

FIGURE 4.7 *The qualitative risk analysis process: input, tools and techniques, and output*

Input to Qualitative Risk Analysis

In addition to the risk register, the qualitative risk analysis can also use the risk management plan, the project scope statement, and the organizational process assets as input items.

Organizational process assets. While analyzing risks, you will make use of the risk-related components of the knowledge base from the previous projects, such as data about risks and lessons learned.

Project scope statement. When you are performing qualitative risk analysis, you want to know what kinds of risks you are dealing with. For example, are you already familiar with these risks? If your project is similar to previous projects, it might have well-understood risks. If it is a new and complex project, it might involve risks that are not well-understood in your organization. So, how do you know what kind of project are you dealing with? Simple—you take a look at the project scope statement.

Risk management plan. To generate the output of the qualitative risk analysis, you will need the following elements of the risk management plan:

◆ Budgeting
◆ Definitions of probabilities and impacts
◆ The probability and impact matrices
◆ Risk categories
◆ Risk timing and scheduling

If any of these input items was not developed during the risk management planning, it can be developed during the qualitative analysis.

Risk register. The risk register contains the list of identified risks that will be the key input to the qualitative risk analysis. Updated risk categories and causes of risks can also be useful elements of the risk register, which can be used in the qualitative risk analysis.

Tools and Techniques for Qualitative Risk Analysis

Prioritizing risks based on their probabilities of occurrence and their impact if they do occur is the central goal of the qualitative risk analysis. Accordingly, most of the tools and techniques used involve estimating probability and impact.

Risk probability and impact assessment. Risk probability refers to the likelihood that a risk will occur, and impact refers to the effect the risk will have on a project objective if it occurs. The probability for each risk and the impact of each risk on project objectives, such as cost, quality, scope, and time, must be assessed. Note that probability and impacts are assessed for each identified risk.

Methods used in making the probability and impact assessment include holding meetings, interviewing, considering expert judgment, and using an information base from previous projects. A risk with a high probability might have a very low impact, and a risk with a low probability might have a very high impact. To prioritize the risks, you need to look at both probability and impact.

Probability and impact matrix. Risks need to be prioritized for the quantitative analysis, response planning, or both. The prioritization can be performed by using the probability and impact matrix—a lookup table that can be used to rate a risk based on where it falls both on the probability scale and on the impact scale. Table 4.2 presents an example of a probability and impact matrix by showing both the probability scale and the impact scale. Here is an example of how to read this matrix: risk R45 has a probability of 0.70 (that is, seven out of 10 chances) for occurrence and an impact of 0.45 on the project objective for which this matrix is prepared. How to calculate the numerical scales for the probability and impact matrix and what they mean depends upon the project and the organization. However, remember the relative meaning: Higher value of a risk on the probability scale means greater likelihood of risk occurrence, and higher value on the impact scale means greater effect on the project objectives. The higher the value for a risk, the higher its priority is. For example, risk R38 has higher priority than risk R27.

Table 4.2 A Risk Probability and Impact Matrix for an Objective*

Probability		Impact							
0.00	0.05	0.15	0.25	0.35	0.45	0.55	0.65	0.75	0.90
0.10	R11	R12	R13	R14	R15	R16	R17	R18	R19
0.30	R21	R22	R23	R24	R25	R26	R27	R28	R29
0.50	R31	R32	R33	R34	R35	R36	R37	R38	R39
0.70	R41	R42	R43	R44	R45	R46	R47	R48	R49
0.90	R51	R52	R53	R54	R55	R56	R57	R58	R59

*R_{ij}, where i and j are integers, represent risks in the two-dimensional (probability and impact) space.

Each risk is rated (prioritized) according to the probability and the impact value assigned to it separately for each objective. Generally, you can divide the matrix in Table 4.2 into three areas—high-priority risks represented by higher numbers, such as R59; medium-priority risks represented by moderate numbers, such as R23; and low-priority risks represented by lower numbers, such as R12. However, each organization has to design its own risk score and risk threshold to guide the risk response plan.

Note that impact can be a threat (a negative effect) or an opportunity (a positive effect). You will have separate matrices for threats and opportunities. Threats in the high-priority area might require priority actions and aggressive responses. Also, you will want to capitalize on those opportunities in the high-priority area, which you can do with relatively little effort. Risks posing threats in the low-priority area might not need any response, but they must be kept on the watch list.

Assessment of the risk data quality. Qualitative risk analysis is performed to analyze the risk data to prioritize risks. However, before you do it, you must examine the risk data for its quality, which is crucial because the credibility of the results of qualitative risk analysis depends upon the quality of the risk data. If the quality of the risk data is found to be unacceptable, you might decide to gather better-quality data. The technique to assess the risk data quality involves examining the accuracy, reliability, and integrity of the data, and also examining how good that data is relevant to the specific risk and project for which it is being used.

Risk categorization. You defined the risk categories during risk management planning and the risk identification processes. Now you can assign the identified risks to those categories. You can also revisit the categorization scheme, such as RBS, that you developed for your project, because now you have more information about risks for the project. Categorizing risks by their causes often helps you develop effective risk responses.

Risk urgency assessment. This is a risk prioritization technique based on time urgency. For example, a risk that is going to occur now is more urgent to address than a risk that might occur a month from now.

You need to update the risk register with the output of the qualitative risk analysis.

Output of the Qualitative Risk Analysis: Updated Risk Register

The risk register was initiated during the risk identification process and is updated with the results from the qualitative risk analysis. The updates include the following:

- ◆ **Risk categorizations.** This means arranging risks in different categories. This helps you identify the causes of the risks and the areas of the project that might require special attention. Furthermore, categorizing risks can bring order to a chaotic situation and makes the management of these risks easier and more effective.

- ◆ **Prioritized list of risks.** The risk register has lists of risks prioritized according to the probability and impact matrix discussed earlier in this chapter. A separate list can be created for each project objective, such as cost, quality, scope, and time. These lists help you prioritize efforts for preparing and executing risk responses.

- ◆ **List of risks with time urgency.** This list includes urgent risks that require attention now or in the near future.

- ◆ **Watch list of low-priority lists.** This list contains the risks that are deemed unimportant by the qualitative risk analysis, but that need to be monitored continually.

- ◆ **List of risks for additional analysis and response.** This list includes risks that need further analysis, such as quantitative analysis or a response action.

- ◆ **Trends in the analysis results.** By examining the results from the qualitative risk analysis, you might recognize a trend for specific risks. That trend might suggest further analysis or a specific risk response.

The main output of qualitative risk analysis is the prioritization of risks based on a probability and impact matrix for each objective. So each objective can have its own prioritized list of risks.

Qualitative risk analysis is a relatively quick and cost-effective way to prioritize risks for risk planning. It also does the groundwork for the quantitative risk analysis if one is required for some risks.

Quantitative Analysis

Qualitative risk analysis is generally performed on the risks that have been prioritized by using the qualitative risk analysis. However, depending upon the experience of the team and their familiarity with the risk, it is possible to skip the qualitative risk analysis and move directly after the risk identification to the quantitative risk analysis. The quantitative risk analysis has three major goals:

◆ Assess the probabilities of achieving specific project objectives

◆ Quantify the effect of the risks on the overall project objectives

◆ Prioritize risks by their contributions to the overall project risk

Figure 4.8 shows the quantitative risk analysis process in terms of input, tools and techniques, and output.

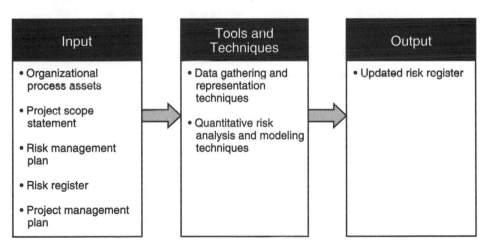

FIGURE 4.8 *The quantitative risk analysis process: input, tools and techniques, and output*

Input to Quantitative Analysis

All the items that are input for the qualitative risk analysis are also input for the quantitative risk analysis. Because the quantitative risk analysis generally requires more information, it also includes project management plans in its list of input items, which are discussed in the following list.

- ◆ **Organization process assets.** The following organizational process assets might be useful in the quantitative analysis:
  - ◆ Information on previously performed similar projects
  - ◆ Studies performed by risk specialists on similar projects
  - ◆ Proprietary risk databases or risk databases available from the industry

- ◆ **Project scope statement.** The project scope statement is especially important if the risk comes to the quantitative analysis directly after the identification. When you are performing risk analysis, you want to know what kind of risks you are dealing with. For example, are you already familiar with these risks? If your project is similar to the previous projects, it might have well-understood risks. If it is a new and complex project, it might involve risks that are not well-understood in your organization. So how do you know what kind of project are you dealing with? You take a look at the project scope statement.

- ◆ **Risk management plan.** To generate the output of the quantitative risk analysis, you need the following elements of the risk management plan:
  - ◆ Budgeting
  - ◆ Definitions of probabilities and impacts
  - ◆ Probability and impact matrix
  - ◆ Risk categories
  - ◆ Risk timing and scheduling

- ◆ **Risk register.** The key input items from the risk register are the following:
  - ◆ List of identified risks
  - ◆ Priority list of risks if the qualitative risk analysis was performed
  - ◆ Risks with categories assigned to them

- ◆ **Project management plan.** To analyze the effect of risks on the project objectives, you need to know the project schedule and the project cost. These can be found in the project management plan.

Obviously, the quantitative risk analysis will use techniques that are of a more numerical nature.

Tools and Techniques for Quantitative Analysis

The quantitative risk analysis can be looked upon as a two-step process—gathering and representing the data, and analyzing and modeling the data. Accordingly, all the techniques fall into two categories: data gathering and representation techniques, such as interviewing, probability distributions, and expert judgment; and analysis and modeling techniques, such as sensitivity analysis, EMV analysis, decision tree analysis, and modeling and simulation.

Interviewing. This technique is used to collect the data for assessing the probabilities of achieving specific project objectives. You are looking for results such as: We have a 70% probability of finishing the project within the schedule desired by the customer. Or perhaps: We have a 60% probability of finishing the project within the budget of $100,000. The goal is to determine the scale of probabilities for a given objective; for example, there is a 20% probability that the project will cost $50,000, a 60% probability that it will cost $100,000, and a 20% probability that it will cost $150,000.

The data is collected by interviewing relevant stakeholders and subject matter experts. Most commonly, you will be exploring the optimistic (best case), pessimistic (worst case), and most likely scenarios for a given objective. For example, for the project cost, the optimistic estimate might be $10 million, the pessimistic estimate might be $50 million, and the most likely estimate might be $25 million.

Probability distributions. After you have collected the data on meeting the project objectives, you can present it in a probability distribution for each objective under study. Note that a distribution represents uncertainty, and uncertainty represents risk. For example, if you know for sure the project will cost $25 million, there will be no distribution because it is only one data point. Distribution comes into the picture when you have several possible values with a probability assigned to each value. There are distributions of different shapes in which the data can be presented. Figure 4.9 shows some of them, such as for the cost objective. The X axis represents the cost, and the Y axis represents the corresponding probability that the project will be completed within that cost.

The beta distribution and the triangular distribution are the most frequently used distributions. The other commonly used distributions that could be suitable under given circumstances are normal distribution and uniform distribution. The uniform distribution is used when all the values of an objective have the same chance of being true.

Sensitivity analysis. This is a technique used to determine which risk has the greatest impact on the project. You study the impact of one uncertain element on a project objective by keeping all other uncertain elements fixed at their baseline values. You can repeat this analysis for several objectives, one at a time. You can also repeat this study for several uncertain elements (creating risks), one element at a time. This way, you can see the impact of each element (or risk) on the overall project separate from other elements (or risks).

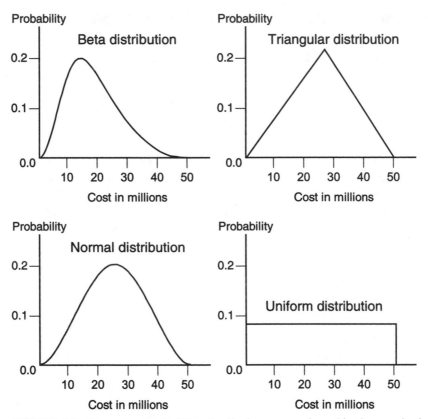

FIGURE 4.9 *Examples of probability distributions commonly used in the quantitative risk analysis*

Expected monetary value analysis. The expected monetary value (EMV) analysis is used to calculate the expected value of an outcome when different possible scenarios exist for different values of the outcome with some probabilities assigned to them. The goal here is to calculate the expected final result of a probabilistic situation. EMV is calculated by multiplying the value of each possible outcome by the probability of its occurrence and adding the results. For example, if there is 60% probability that an opportunity will earn you $1,000 and a 40% probability that it will only earn you $500, the EMV is calculated as follows:

$$EMV = 0.60 * 1000 + 0.40 * 500 = 600 + 200 = 800$$

So the EMV in this case is $800. When you are using opportunities and threats in the same calculation, you should express EMV for an opportunity as positive value, and that for a threat as negative value. For example if there is a 60% chance that you will benefit from a risk by $1,000, and a 40% probability that you will lose $400 as a result of this risk, the EMV is calculated as follows:

$$EMV = 0.60 * 1000 - 0.40 * 500 = 600 - 200 = 400$$

Therefore, the EMV in this case is $400.

The concept of EMV can be presented in a decision-making technique, such as a decision tree analysis.

Decision tree analysis. This technique uses the decision tree diagram to choose from different available options; each option is represented by a branch of the tree. This technique is used when there are multiple possible outcomes with different threats or opportunities with certain probabilities assigned to them. EMV analysis is done along each branch, which helps to make a decision about which option to choose.

Figure 4.10 presents a very simple decision tree diagram that depicts two options: updating an existing product or building a new product from scratch. The initial cost for the update option is $50,000, whereas the initial cost for the build-from-scratch option is $70,000. However, the probability for failure is 40% for the update option, compared to 10% for the build-from-scratch option, and the impact from failure in both cases is a loss of $200,000. As Table 4.3 shows, even though the initial cost for the update option is less than the initial cost for the build-from-scratch option, the decision will be made in favor of the build-from-scratch option because when you combine the initial cost with the EMV resulting from the probability of failure, the build-from-scratch option turns out to be a better deal.

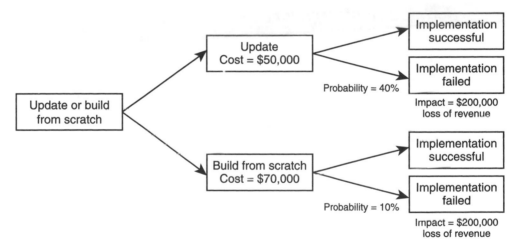

FIGURE 4.10 *Example of a decision tree diagram*

Table 4.3 Calculations for the Decision Tree Shown in Figure 4.10*

Option	Initial Cost	Risk Cost	Probability	EMV for Risk Cost	Total cost
Update	$50,000	$200,000	40%	0.40*$200,000= $80,000	$50,000+$80,000= $130,000
Build from scratch	$70,000	$200,000	10%	0.10*$200,000= $20,000	$70,000+$20,000= $90,000

*The total cost is the sum of the initial cost and the EMV for the risk cost.

Modeling and simulation. A *model* is a set of rules to describe how something works; it takes input and makes predictions as output. The rules might include formulas and functions based on facts, assumptions, or both. A *simulation* is any analytical method used to imitate a real-life system. Simulations in risk analysis are created using the Monte Carlo technique, which is named after Monte Carlo, France—known for its casinos that present games of chance based on random behavior. Monte Carlo simulation models take random input iteratively to generate output for certain quantities as predictions. This technique is used in several disciplines, such as physics and biology, in addition to project management. In risk analysis, the input is taken randomly from a probability distribution, and the output for impact on the project objectives is predicted. The name "Monte Carlo" refers to the random behavior of the input. (In that spirit, it could easily be called Las Vegas.)

Expert judgment. In the quantitative risk analysis, expert judgment can be used to validate the collected risk data and the analysis used for the project at hand.

The risk register is updated with the results of the quantitative risk analysis.

Output of the Quantitative Risk Analysis: Updated Risk Register

The risk register that was used as an input item to the quantitative risk analysis is updated with the results of this analysis. The updates include the following:

◆ **Probabilistic analysis of the project.** This includes the estimates of the project schedule and cost with a confidence level attached to each estimate. Confidence level is expressed in percentage form, such as 95%, and it represents how certain you are about the estimate. You can compare these estimates to the stakeholders' risk tolerances to see whether the project is within the acceptable limits.

◆ **Probability of achieving the project objectives.** Factoring in the project risks, you can estimate the probabilities of meeting project objectives, such as cost and schedule set forth by the current project plan. For example, the likelihood of completing the project within the current budget plan of $2 million is 70%.

◆ **Prioritized list of risks.** The risks are prioritized according to the threats they pose or the opportunities they offer. The risks with greater threats (or opportunities) are higher on the list. The goal is to prioritize the response plan efforts to eliminate (or minimize) the impact of the threats and capitalize on the opportunities. The priorities are determined based on the total effect of each risk to the overall project objectives.

◆ **Trends in the results.** By repeating the analysis several times and by examining the results, you might recognize a trend for specific risks. That trend might suggest further analysis or a specific risk response.

The emphasis in quantitative analysis is on two tasks: Assess the probabilities of meeting each project objective and prioritize the risks based on the total effect of each risk on the overall project objectives. Subsequently, the resultant prioritized list of risks can be used to prepare the risk response plan.

Planning the Risk Response

Depending on the project, the nature of risks, and the experience of the team, risk response planning can start after risk identification, qualitative risk analysis, or quantitative risk analysis. Recall that risks can include threats (negative risks) and opportunities (positive risks). Accordingly, the central task in risk response planning is to develop actions and options to meet the following two goals:

◆ Minimize threats to meeting project objectives

◆ Maximize opportunities

As shown in Figure 4.11, the risk management plan and risk register are the input items to risk response planning.

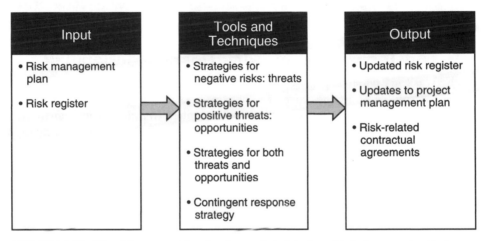

Input	Tools and Techniques	Output
• Risk management plan • Risk register	• Strategies for negative risks: threats • Strategies for positive threats: opportunities • Strategies for both threats and opportunities • Contingent response strategy	• Updated risk register • Updates to project management plan • Risk-related contractual agreements

FIGURE 4.11 *The risk response planning process: input, tools and techniques, and output*

Input to Risk Response Planning

The only two input items for risk response planning are the risk register and the risk management plan.

Risk register. The risk register contains the results from the risk identification, qualitative risk analysis, and quantitative risk analysis. The following elements of the risk register are especially useful for risk response planning:

◆ List of identified risks

◆ Root causes of risks

◆ Prioritized list of responses

◆ List of risks that need immediate attention

◆ Trends in analysis results

Risk management plan. The elements of the risk management plan that can be useful for risk response planning include the following:

- ◆ Organizations' and stakeholders' thresholds for low, moderate, and high risks to sort out those risks for which the response is needed.
- ◆ Roles and responsibilities that specify the positions and functions for each position involved in risk management. These roles are assigned to the members of the risk management team, which might include members from inside or outside the project team.
- ◆ Timing and a schedule that specify how often the risk management processes will be performed and which risk management activities will be included in the project schedule.

Because there is a wide spectrum of risks that can occur, there are a multitude of tools and techniques available to plan responses for these risks.

Tools and Techniques for Risk Response Planning

Risk, as you have already learned, can come in two categories: negative risks, which pose threats to meeting the project objectives, and positive risks, which offer opportunities. The goal is to minimize the threats and maximize the opportunities. In project management, there are three kinds of possible responses to risks—take an action, take no action, or take a conditional action. When you want to take an action, different response strategies for negative and positive risks need to be planned. Accordingly, there are three kinds of strategies available to handle three kinds of scenarios:

- ◆ Strategies to respond to negative risks (threats) when action is required
- ◆ Strategies to respond to positive risks (opportunities) when action is required
- ◆ Strategies that can be used to respond to both negative and positive risks when no action or a conditional action is taken

Response Strategies for Threats

There are only three commonsense ways to take an action against a potential problem: Get out of harm's way, pass it to someone else, or confront it to minimize the damage. In project management, these three strategies are called avoid, transfer, and mitigate—the ATM approach.

Avoid. You avoid the risk by changing your project management plan in such a way that the risk is eliminated. Depending upon the situation, this can be accomplished in various ways, including the following:

- ◆ Obtaining information and clarifying requirements for risks based on misunderstanding or miscommunication. This answers two questions: Do we really have this risk and, if yes, how can we avoid it?
- ◆ Acquiring expertise for risks that exist due to a lack of expertise.

◆ Isolating the project objectives from the risk whenever possible.

◆ Relaxing the objective that is under threat, such as extending the project schedule.

Transfer. Risk transfer means you shift the responsibility for responding to the risk (the ownership of the risk), the negative impact of the risk, or both to another party. Note that transferring the risk transfers the responsibility for risk management and does not necessarily eliminate the risk. Risk transfer almost always involves making payment of a risk premium to the party to which the risk has been transferred. Some examples include buying an insurance policy and contracting out the tasks involving risk.

Mitigate. Mitigation in general means taking action to reduce or prevent the impact of a disaster that is expected to occur. Risk mitigation means reducing the probability of risk occurrence, reducing the impact of the risk if it does occur, or both. A good mitigation strategy is to take action early on to first reduce the probability of the risk happening, and then to plan for reducing its impact if it does occur, rather than letting it occur and then trying to reduce the impact or repair the damage. Following are some examples of mitigation:

◆ Adopting less complex processes

◆ Conducting more tests on the product or service of the project

◆ Choosing a more stable supplier for the project supplies

◆ Designing redundancy into a system so that if one part fails, the redundant part takes over and the system keeps working

Each of these three strategies has a counter-strategy to deal with the opportunities.

Response Strategies for Opportunities

Just like in the case of threats, you have three strategies to deal with opportunities. Not surprisingly, each response strategy to deal with an opportunity is a counterpart of a response strategy to deal with a threat—a one-to-one correspondence:

◆ Share corresponds to transfer

◆ Exploit corresponds to avoid

◆ Enhance corresponds to mitigate

You use the SEE (share, exploit, enhance) approach to dealing with the opportunities presented by the positive risks.

Share. Sharing a positive risk that presents an opportunity means transferring the ownership of the risk to another party that is better equipped to capitalize on the opportunity. Some examples of sharing are:

◆ Forming risk-sharing partnerships

◆ Starting a joint venture with the purpose of capitalizing on an opportunity

◆ Forming teams or special-purpose companies to exploit opportunities presented by positive risks

Exploit. Exploiting an opportunity means ensuring that the opportunity is realized—that is, the positive risk that presents the opportunity does occur. This is accomplished by eliminating or minimizing the uncertainty associated with the risk occurrence. An example of exploiting is assigning more talented resources to the project to reduce the completion time and therefore to be the first to market. Another example could be to provide better quality than planned to beat a competitor. Whereas exploiting refers to ensuring that the positive risk occurs, enhancing refers to increasing the impact of the risk once it occurs.

Enhance. This strategy means increasing the size of the opportunity by increasing the probability, impact, or both. You can increase the probability by maximizing the key drivers of the positive risks or by strengthening the causes of the risks. Similarly, you can increase the impact by increasing the project's susceptibility to the positive risk.

You have just learned the different strategies that you need to plan for negative and positive risks if you intend to take action. If, on the other hand, you intend to take no action or a conditional action, then the response planning strategies for both negative and positive risks are the same.

Response Strategies for Both Threats and Opportunities

There are two response strategies that you need to plan for the risks for which you need to take either a conditional action or no action.

Acceptance. Acceptance of a risk means to let it be. Generally, it is not possible to take action against all the risks. Depending upon their probabilities and impacts, some risks will simply be accepted. There are two kinds of acceptance:

◆ Passive acceptance that requires no action

◆ Active acceptance that requires a conditional action, called a *contingent response*

Contingency. Generally speaking, contingency means a future event or condition that is possible but cannot be predicted with certainty. So, your action will be contingent upon the condition; that is, it will be executed only if the condition happens. In risk management, a contingent response is a response that is executed only if certain predefined conditions (or events) happen. These events trigger the contingency response. Some examples of such triggers are missing a milestone or escalating the priority of a feature by the customer. The events that can trigger contingency response must be clearly defined and tracked.

You use these strategies to generate the output of the risk response planning process.

Output of Risk Response Planning

The output of risk response planning might include risk register updates, risk-related contractual agreements, and project management plan updates.

Risk register updates. The appropriate risk responses planned and agreed upon by the risk management team are included in the risk register. The responses to high and moderate risks are entered in detail, while the low-priority risks can be put on a watch list for monitoring. After the risk register is updated, it includes the following main elements:

- A list of identified risks, descriptions of the risks, root causes of the risks, WBS elements affected by the risks, and the impacts of the risks on the project objectives.
- Roles and responsibilities in managing the risks—that is, risk owners and the responsibilities assigned to them.
- Results from qualitative and quantitative risk analyses, including a prioritized list of risks, a probabilistic analysis of the project objectives, and a list of risks with time urgency.
- Planned and agreed-upon risk response strategies and specific actions to implement each strategy.
- Symptoms and warning signs of risk occurrences, contingency plans, and triggers for contingency risks.
- Budget and schedule requirements to implement the planned responses, including the contingency reserve, which is the amount of funds, time, or both needed in addition to the estimates in order to meet the organization's and stakeholders' risk tolerances and thresholds.
- Fallback plans in case the planned responses prove to be inadequate.
- A list of risks to remain, which include the following:
    - Passive, accepted risks
    - Residual risks that will remain after planned responses have been performed
- A list of secondary risks that will arise as a result of implementing the responses. You must plan for these risks like any other risk.

Risk-related contractual agreements. The risk-related contractual agreements might result, for example, from transferring the risks.

Project management plan updates. The project management plan is updated to include the risk response activities that might affect other project management areas, such as cost and schedule.

NOTE

A residual risk is the remains of a risk on which a response has been performed, whereas a secondary risk is a risk that is expected to arise as a result of implementing a risk response; therefore, a response for a secondary risk must be planned.

Risk response planning deals with both kinds of risks—those that pose threats to meeting project objectives and those that present opportunities. Three kinds of responses can be planned—take action, take no action, or take a conditional action.

I have discussed quite a few processes used in quality management and risk management. It is time to put them together to show how they are related to each other in the big picture.

The Big Picture of Quality and Risk Management

In this chapter, I have introduced the processes used in managing the quality and risk of a project. As shown in Figure 4.12, quality management and risk management can begin after the project scope planning has been performed to the level of creating the WBS.

Note that Figure 4.12 presents a general and high-level view of the relationships between different processes used to manage quality and risk, and not all the interactions and data flow are shown. For example, depending on the nature of the risk and the experience of the risk management team, a risk might move directly from the identification process to the quantitative risk analysis or even to the risk response planning process.

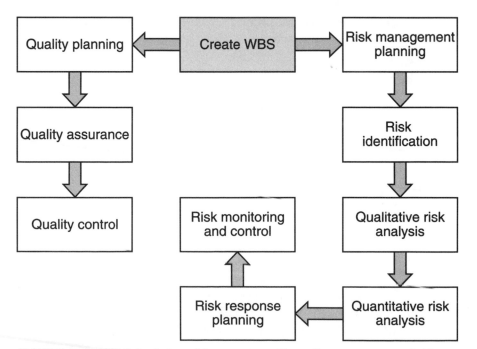

FIGURE 4.12 *A high-level view of the processes used in quality management and risk management*

You might be overwhelmed by the input items that go into various processes. Table 4.4 presents a unified picture of the main input items for various quality and risk-related processes. Following are the main points emerging from this picture:

◆ The quality planning and risk management planning processes have identical sets of input items.

◆ The qualitative risk analysis and quantitative risk analysis processes also have identical sets of input items with one exception: The quantitative risk analysis uses the project management plan as an input item, whereas the qualitative risk analysis does not.

◆ The risk register is initiated by the risk identification process and is an input item to, and is updated by, the following risk management processes: qualitative risk analysis, quantitative risk analysis, and risk response planning.

Table 4.4 Some Input Items for Various Processes Used to Manage Quality and Risk*

| | Processes | | | | | |
Input Items	Quality Planning	Risk Management Planning	Risk Identification	Qualitative Risk Analysis	Quantitative Risk Analysis	Risk Response Planning
Enterprise environment factors	Yes	Yes	Yes	No	No	No
Organizational process assets	Yes	Yes	Yes	Yes	Yes	No
Project scope statement	Yes	Yes	Yes	Yes	Yes	No
Project management plan	Yes	Yes	Yes	No	Yes	No
Risk management plan	No	No	Yes	Yes	Yes	Yes
Risk register	No	No	No	Yes	Yes	Yes

*"Yes" means the item is included in the input list of the corresponding process.

The three most important takeaways from this chapter are as follows:

◆ The goal for quality planning is twofold: Identify which quality standards are relevant to the project at hand and determine how to satisfy these standards.

◆ The risk identification process initiates the risk register by listing the identified risks in it. The qualitative risk analysis prioritizes these risks based on the probability and impact matrix for each objective, whereas the emphasis in quantitative risk analysis is on assessing the probabilities of meeting each project objective and prioritizing the risks based on the total effect of each risk on the overall project objectives.

◆ The goal for risk response planning is to minimize the threats (the negative effects of risks) and maximize the opportunities (the positive effects of risks).

Summary

Quality and risk are two interrelated aspects of any project and need to be managed. While quality refers to the degree to which a set of characteristics of project deliverables and objectives fulfill the requirements, risk refers to an uncertain event or condition that, if it occurs, has a positive or negative effect on meeting the project objectives. Quality management includes quality planning, quality assurance, and quality control. The quality management plan, quality baseline, and quality metrics are the major output items of the quality planning process. Quality planning and risk management planning processes have an identical set of input items—enterprise environmental factors, organizational process assets, project scope statements, and project management plans. The only output of risk management planning is the risk management plan, which includes elements such as a list of tools and approaches to be used for risk management, identification and assignment of resources for risk management, risk categories, risk probabilities and impacts, and the format of risk reporting and tracking. This information is used in the remaining processes of risk management—risk identification, risk analysis (qualitative and quantitative), risk response planning, and risk monitoring and control.

The risk management plan is an input item to the risk identification process. Its only output is the risk register, which includes a list of identified risks, a list of the root causes of the risks, and an initial list of potential responses. The risk register, initially prepared during the risk identification process, is updated during the following processes: qualitative risk analysis, quantitative risk analysis, risk response planning, and risk monitoring. The main output of qualitative risk analysis is the prioritization of risks based on a probability and impact matrix for each objective. Each objective might have its own prioritized list of risks. However, the emphasis in quantitative analysis is on two things—assessing the probabilities of meeting each project objective and prioritizing the risks based on the total effect of each risk on the overall project objectives. Subsequently, the resultant prioritized list of risks can be used to prepare the risk response plan.

Depending upon the priority of the risk, you can choose one of the three options—taking no action, taking an action if some event happens, or taking an action. When you decide to take an action, there are three ways to plan it: avoid, transfer, or mitigate in case of a negative risk; and share, exploit, or enhance in case of a positive risk.

After you have planned quality and risk management, you need to proceed toward scheduling the project before it can begin execution. The planning processes that lead to scheduling the project are discussed in the following chapter.

Exam's Eye View

Comprehend

◆ Risk categorization is a part of the risk management plan and it helps in the risk identification process.

◆ Defining the risk probability and risk impact are parts of the risk management plan and are used in the qualitative risk analysis and in prioritizing risks.

◆ Risk identification is performed before the risk analysis, and the qualitative risk analysis, if performed, is performed before quantitative risk analysis because it takes less effort and time and its results can be used for quantitative analysis.

◆ An important update added to the risk register by the qualitative risk analysis is the prioritized list of risks. Each objective can have its own prioritized list of risks.

◆ Two important updates added to the risk register by the quantitative risk analysis are:

    ◆ The probabilistic analysis of the project objectives—that is, the probability of meeting the project objectives.

    ◆ The prioritized list of risks based on the total effect of each risk on the overall project objectives.

Look Out

◆ Risk stems from elements of uncertainty and can have a negative or positive effect on meeting the project objectives.

◆ Quality planning and risk management planning processes have identical sets of input items.

◆ The only difference between the inputs to the qualitative risk analysis and those to the quantitative risk analysis is that the quantitative risk analysis has the project management plan as an input item, whereas the qualitative risk analysis does not.

◆ Depending upon the experience of the team and the nature of the risk, a risk can be moved directly after identification to the quantitative risk analysis or even to risk response planning.

Memorize
◆ The quality management plan, quality baseline, and quality metrics are the major output items of the quality planning process.   ◆ The risk register is initially prepared during the risk identification process and is updated during the following processes: qualitative risk analysis, quantitative risk analysis, risk response planning, and risk monitoring.   ◆ The risk register becomes part of the project management plan.   ◆ The input to the risk identification process contains all the items that are input to the risk management planning process, plus it contains the risk management plan as an input item, too.   ◆ The only output of risk management planning is the risk management plan.

Key Terms

◆ **assumptions analysis.** A technique used to examine the validity of an assumption and thereby identify the risk resulting from the inaccuracy, inconsistency, or incompleteness of each assumption.

◆ **benchmarking.** Benchmarking is comparing practices, products, or services of a project with those of some reference projects for the purposes of learning, improvement, and creating the basis for measuring performance.

◆ **confidence level.** A statistical term that refers to the certainty attached to an estimate and is often represented in percentage form, such as a 95% confidence level.

◆ **contingency.** A future event or condition that is possible but cannot be predicted with certainty. In this case, an action will be contingent upon the condition—that is, the action will be executed only if the condition happens.

◆ **contingency reserve.** The amount of funds, time, or both needed in addition to the estimates in order to meet the organization's and stakeholders' risk tolerances and thresholds.

◆ **decision tree analysis.** A technique that uses a decision tree diagram to choose from different options available; each option is represented by a branch of the tree. EMV analysis is done along each branch, which helps to make a decision about which option to choose.

◆ **Delphi technique.** An information-gathering technique used for experts to reach a consensus while sharing their ideas and preferences anonymously.

◆ **Expected Monetary Value (EMV) analysis.** A statistical technique used to calculate the expected outcome when there are multiple possible outcome values with probabilities assigned to them.

◆ **experiment design.** A statistical method that can be used to identify the factors that can influence a set of specific variables of a product or a process under development or in production.

◆ **methodology.** A system of procedures and techniques practiced in a discipline to accomplish a task. For example, risk management methodology is used in the discipline of project management to determine how risk management processes will be performed.

◆ **mitigation.** The process of taking actions to reduce or prevent the impact of a disaster that is expected to occur.

◆ **model.** A set of rules to describe how something works, which takes input and makes predictions as output.

◆ **Monte Carlo simulation.** An analysis technique that randomly generates values for uncertain elements (that is, variables) and takes them as input into a model to generate output. In other words, it simulates a model by feeding randomly selected input values.

◆ **performance measurement baseline.** An approved integrated plan for the project specifying some parameters to be included in the performance measurements, such as scope, schedule, and cost. The performance of the project is measured against this baseline. Some technical and quality parameters can also become part of this baseline.

◆ **quality.** The degree to which a set of characteristics of project deliverables and objectives fulfill the project requirements.

◆ **quality baseline.** A criterion that specifies the quality objectives for the project and thereby makes the basis for measuring and reporting the quality performance.

◆ **quality management plan.** A management plan that describes how the project management team will implement the quality policy of the performing organization for the specific project.

◆ **quality metrics.** An operational criterion that defines in specific terms what something (such as a characteristic or a feature) is and how the quality control process measures it.

◆ **quality planning.** The process of identifying the quality standards relevant to the project at hand and determining how to satisfy these standards.

◆ **quality policy.** Overall intentions and high-level direction of an organization with respect to quality, established by the management at executive level.

◆ **qualitative risk analysis.** A process used to prioritize risks by estimating the probability of their occurrence and their impact on the project.

◆ **quantitative risk analysis.** A process used to perform the numerical analysis to estimate the effect of each identified risk on the overall project objectives and deliverables.

◆ **residual risk.** A risk that remains after the risk response has been performed.

◆ **risk.** An uncertain event or condition that, if it occurs, has a positive or negative effect on meeting the project objectives.

◆ **risk breakdown structure (RBS).** A hierarchical structure that breaks down the identified risk categories into subcategories. In developing this structure, you will end up identifying various areas and causes of potential risks.

◆ **risk identification.** A process used to identify the risks for a given project and record their characteristics in a document called the *risk register*.

◆ **risk management plan.** A document that describes how risk management will be structured and performed for the project at hand. It becomes part of the project management plan.

◆ **risk management planning.** A process used to determine how to approach, plan, and execute risk management activities for a given project. This process produces risk management plan.

◆ **risk register.** A document that contains the results of risk analysis and risk response planning.

◆ **secondary risk.** A risk that arises as a result of implementing a risk response.

◆ **simulation.** Any analytical method used to imitate a real-life system.

◆ **strengths, weaknesses, opportunities, and threats (SWOT) analysis.** A technique used to gather information for risk identification by examining a given project from the perspectives of its strengths, weaknesses, opportunities, and threats.

Review Questions

1. Which of the following is a false statement about project risks?

   A. A risk arises out of uncertainty.

   B. A risk can only have a negative effect on a project.

   C. Identified risks are usually listed in a document called the *risk register*.

   D. Risks can be categorized by developing a risk breakdown structure (RBS).

2. The risk register is not an input to which of the following processes?

   A. Risk identification

   B. Qualitative risk analysis

   C. Quantitative risk analysis

   D. Risk response planning

3. Which of the following is not an information-gathering technique used in the risk identification process?

   A. Brainstorming

   B. Delphi technique

   C. SWOT analysis

   D. Web browsing

4. Which of the following statements about risk analysis is false?

   A. Quantitative risk analysis can only be performed on the risks on which a qualitative risk analysis has already been performed.

   B. Qualitative risk analysis is usually performed before quantitative risk analysis.

   C. An updated risk register is the output of both qualitative risk analysis and quantitative risk analysis.

   D. The risk register is an input to both qualitative risk analysis and quantitative risk analysis.

5. You are managing a project to set up data servers to support a Web site for an enterprise customer. The location for the servers has been chosen close to the customer due to their requirements. However, this location is prone to natural disasters, such as hurricanes and flooding. You have decided to install some redundant servers in another city that will act as backup if a disaster happens. This is an example of which of the following?

   A. Risk avoidance

   B. Risk mitigation

   C. Risk acceptance

   D. Risk transfer

6. The risk management team of a software project has decided that due to the lack of adequate talent in your company, development of a specific part of the system is under high risk, so they have decided to outsource it. This is an example of which of the following?

   A. Risk avoidance

   B. Risk mitigation

   C. Risk acceptance

   D. Risk transfer

7. You are in the process of evaluating the probability and impact of a risk by assigning numbers, such as expected monetary value. This is an example of which of the following?

   A. Monte Carlo simulation

   B. Qualitative analysis

   C. Quantitative analysis

   D. Risk response planning

8. Consider the following figure. It shows a risk with a 50% probability of occurrence. If the risk does occur, it could have a positive or a negative impact equivalent to $200,000 or $50,000, respectively, with the probabilities shown in the figure. What is the EMV for the positive impact?

   A. $80,000
   B. $200,000
   C. $50,000
   D. $40,000

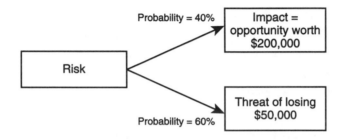

9. Consider the following figure. It shows a risk with a 50% probability of occurrence. If the risk does occur, it could have a positive or a negative impact equivalent to $200,000 or $50,000, respectively, with the probabilities shown in the figure. What is the EMV for the risk?

   A. $25,000
   B. $55,000
   C. $110,000
   D. $50,000

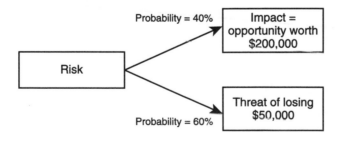

10. Which of the following is a correct statement about secondary risks?
    A. These are the residual risks.
    B. These are the risks that have medium or low priority.
    C. These are the risks that will be avoided.
    D. These are the risks that have been transferred.
    E. These are the risks that can result from responses to the identified risks.

11. Which of the following is not a valid risk response?
    A. Risk acceptance
    B. Risk sharing
    C. Risk mitigation
    D. Risk avoidance
    E. Risk rejection

12. Which of the following is a valid statement about SWOT?
    A. It is an analysis technique to identify risks.
    B. It refers to the analysis of scope, work, options, and timing.
    C. It is a technique used to plan a risk response.
    D. It is a technique used to perform quantitative risk analysis.

13. Which of the following is not an output of the qualitative risk analysis?
    A. A prioritized list of risks for a given project objective based on the probability and impact matrix of the objective
    B. A watch list of low-priority risks
    C. A list of risks prioritized based on the total effect of each risk on the overall project objectives
    D. A list of trends in the analysis results

14. Which of the following is not an output of the quantitative risk analysis?
    A. Probabilities of meeting the project objectives, such as cost and schedule
    B. Estimate of the project cost
    C. A list of risks prioritized based on the total effect of each risk on the overall project objectives
    D. A list of trends in the analysis results
    E. A risk-related contractual agreement

15. What is the name of a quality planning technique that involves comparing the results of similar activities?

    A. Brainstorming

    B. Benchmarking

    C. Cost/benefit analysis

    D. Quality metrics

    E. Quality checklists

Chapter 5

Planning the Project Schedule

PMP Exam Objectives

Objective	*What It Really Means*
2.2 Identify Project Team and Define Roles and Responsibilities 3.4 Manage Resource Allocation	Understand the activity resource estimating process and the human resource planning process.
2.3 Create the WBS	Understand the process of creating the WBS covered in Chapter 3. You must know how to define activities, sequence activities, estimate activity durations, and subsequently develop the schedule, starting with the WBS. These topics are covered in this chapter.
2.6 Obtain Plan Approval	You must know that the final project management plan must be approved before you start executing it. You must also know that you might end up developing multiple versions of the project schedule, but it is the approved version that will be considered as a schedule baseline against which the project progress will be measured.

Introduction

A project consists of two main components: the project work that needs to be performed and the schedule to perform that work. The overall project work is broken down into smaller manageable components. These components in the WBS are called *work packages*. However, a work package might not be suitable to assign to an individual to perform. So, work packages can be decomposed into smaller components called *activities*. A project schedule contains not only the activities to be performed, but also the order (sequence) in which the activities will be performed. The sequencing of activities is determined by dependencies among the activities.

A realistic project schedule can be created from the bottom up by identifying the activities, estimating the resources for the activities, and determining the time that each activity will take with the given resources available. The resources required to complete the activities include human resources. The core issue in this chapter is how to plan the project schedule. To enable you to put your arms around this issue, I will explore the following three avenues: generating the data about project activities, such as determining resource requirements and activity duration, building a project schedule from the data on the activities, and planning human resources that will perform the activities.

The Long and Winding Road to the Project Schedule

Planning the project schedule is all about time management. To complete a project, you need to perform some activities to produce the project deliverables. To make that happen, you need to assign resources to the activities and schedule them. But before all this can happen, you need to identify the activities. Although all this sounds like common sense, it makes sense to define the following terms so we are all on the same page.

◆ **Activity.** A component of project work.

◆ **Activity duration.** The time measured in calendar units between the start and finish of a schedule activity.

◆ **Schedule activity.** A scheduled task (component of work) performed during the life-cycle of a project.

◆ **Logical relationship.** A dependency between two project schedule activities or between a schedule activity and a schedule milestone.

◆ **Schedule milestone.** A milestone is a significant point (or event) in the life of a project, and a schedule milestone is a milestone on the project schedule. A milestone refers to the completion of an activity, marking possibly the completion of a set of activities, and therefore has zero duration. The completion of a major deliverable is an example of a milestone.

Project time management includes the processes required to complete the project in a timely manner. Figure 5.1 presents the flow diagram for the time management processes that lead to schedule development.

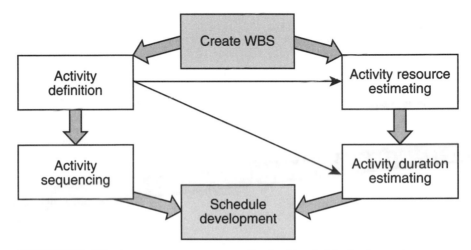

FIGURE 5.1 *The time management processes that lead to schedule development*

The usages of these processes are listed here:

◆ **Activity definition.** Identifies the specific schedule activities that must be performed to produce the project deliverables.

◆ **Activity sequencing.** Identifies the dependencies among the schedule activities and orders the activities accordingly.

◆ **Activity resource estimating.** Estimates the types and amounts of resources that will be required to perform each schedule activity.

◆ **Activity duration estimating.** Estimates the time in work periods individually for each schedule activity required for the activity's completion. A work period is a measurement of time when the work is in progress; it is measured in hours, days, or months, depending upon the size of the activity. This estimate is performed for given resources.

◆ **Schedule development.** Helps create the project schedule by analyzing schedule activity sequences, schedule activity durations, resource requirements, and schedule constraints.

> ### NOTE
>
> The underlying philosophy of project management for schedule development is to first develop the schedule based on the work required to complete the project tasks, and then see how you can make it conform to other constraints, calendar requirements, and strategic goals of the organization. You, the project manager, build the schedule through cold, hard mathematical analysis and you don't just accept whatever schedule goals come down the pipeline from elsewhere, such as from the customer or the project sponsor.

In a nutshell, the path to schedule development includes defining activities, arranging the activities in the correct order, and estimating the resources required to complete the activities. In other words, the work necessary for completing the project is expressed in terms of activities, and the resources are required to complete the activities. So, the first step toward schedule planning after creating the WBS is defining activities.

Defining Activities

Activities that need to be performed to produce the project deliverables are identified using the activity definition process shown in Figure 5.2. The starting point for defining the activities is the lowest level of the WBS that contains work packages. Each work package can be broken down into one or more activities.

So, the key input items to the activity definition process are the WBS and the WBS dictionary.

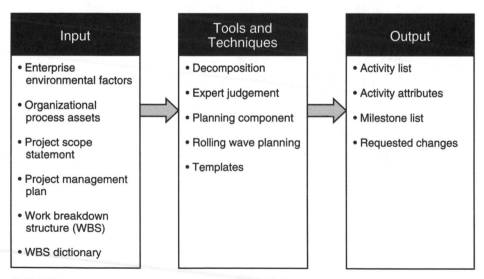

Input	Tools and Techniques	Output
• Enterprise environmental factors	• Decomposition	• Activity list
• Organizational process assets	• Expert judgement	• Activity attributes
• Project scope statemont	• Planning component	• Milestone list
• Project management plan	• Rolling wave planning	• Requested changes
• Work breakdown structure (WBS)	• Templates	
• WBS dictionary		

FIGURE 5.2 *The activity definition process: input, tools and techniques, and output*

Input to Activity Definition

Identifying project activities starts with the work packages in the WBS, which in turn are derived from the project scope statement. These two obvious input items, along with others, are discussed here:

◆ **WBS and WBS dictionary.** The work packages in the WBS are decomposed into project activities. To assign appropriate resources to these work packages, you need to know their details, which are provided in the WBS dictionary.

◆ **Project scope statement.** The WBS is built from the project scope statement. While dealing with the WBS, you might need to go back to the project scope statement. The following elements of the project scope statement are especially important to consider while identifying activities:

◆ Assumptions related to the activities or schedule planning, such as work hours per week

◆ Constraints that will limit the schedule options, such as predetermined deadlines on project milestones

◆ Project deliverables, to ensure everything is covered in WBS work packages

◆ **Project management plan.** The elements in the project management plan that can be useful for the activity definition process include the project scope management plan and the schedule management plan, which can provide guidance on identifying and scheduling activities.

◆ **Enterprise environmental factors.** The enterprise environmental factors relevant to identifying schedule activities include project management information systems and project scheduling software tools.

◆ **Organizational process assets.** Following are examples of organizational process assets that can be useful in the process of identifying activities:

◆ Organizational policies related to activity planning

◆ Organizational procedures and guidelines used in defining activities

◆ Knowledge base of lessons learned from previous projects regarding activity lists

So, the major input to the activity definition process is the WBS, whose work packages are decomposed into activities using some tools and techniques discussed in the following section.

Tools and Techniques for Activity Definition

The major task in the activity definition process is to decompose the work packages in the WBS into activities. This decomposition, along with other tools and techniques, is discussed here.

Decomposition. Recall that you used the decomposition technique to create the WBS by subdividing the project deliverables into smaller manageable tasks called *work packages*. Decomposition is also used in the activity definition process for subdividing the work packages into smaller, more manageable components called *schedule activities*.

> ### ◣ TIP
>
> You create the WBS and decompose the work packages to project activities with the help of the project team. Even though the schedule is not yet developed and the resources are not fully assigned, the project team in some initial form will be there. When decomposing a work package into activities, involve the individuals who either are familiar with the work packages or will be responsible for them.

Expert judgment. During the process of decomposing the work packages into schedule activities, you can use the help of team members and other experts who are experienced in developing WBS and project schedules.

Planning components for rolling wave planning. If there are areas of the project scope for which sufficient information is not available yet, there will definitely be corresponding components in the WBS that are not decomposed to the level of work packages. You can only develop a high-level schedule for these planning components. You accommodate this kind of high-level scheduling by using a technique called *rolling wave planning* to plan the project work at various levels of detail depending upon the availability of information. Work to be performed in the near future is planned to the low level of the WBS, whereas work to be performed far into the future can be planned at the relatively high level of the WBS. So, a WBS component at the bottom level of a branch of WBS hierarchy for which some planning can be performed is called a *planning component*. The planning components for which insufficient information is available to decompose them into work packages fall into the following two categories:

◆ **Control account.** From the management perspective, a control line is drawn in the WBS hierarchy levels. All planning components above this line belong to what is called the *control account*. All efforts performed for components in a control account are documented in the corresponding control account plan.

◆ **Planning packages.** The WBS components that are below the level of the control account and above the level of work packages are called *planning packages*. A planning package can have a budget, estimated start and finish dates, and a statement of work. The planning packages are ultimately converted into work packages.

> ### ◼ NOTE
>
> Rolling wave planning is an example of progressive elaboration, which was discussed in Chapter 1.

Templates. As a timesaver and a guide, you can use a standard activity list or an activity list from a previous project similar to the project at hand as a template. The template can also contain information about the activities in it, such as required hours of effort.

Using these techniques, you convert the work packages in the WBS into schedule activities, which, along with some other items, make the output of the activity definition process.

Output of Activity Definition

The key output item of the activity definition process is a comprehensive list of all the schedule activities that need to be performed to produce the project deliverables. This and other output items are discussed in this section.

Activity list. This is a list of all the activities that are necessary and sufficient to produce the project deliverables. In other words, these activities are derived from the WBS and hence are within the scope of the project. Also, the scope of each schedule activity should be described to sufficient detail in concrete terms, so that the team member responsible for it will understand what work needs to be performed. Examples of schedule activities include a book chapter with a summary of content, a computer program that will accomplish a well-defined task, and an application to be installed on a computer.

Activity attributes. These attributes are in addition to the scope description of the activity in the activity list. The list of attributes of an activity can include the following:

◆ Activity identifier and code
◆ Activity description
◆ Assumptions and constraints related to this activity, such as imposed date
◆ Predecessor and successor activities
◆ Resource requirements
◆ Team member responsible for performing the work and information about the work

These attributes are used to arrange the activities in the correct order (sequencing) and to schedule them.

Milestone list. A schedule milestone is a significant event in the project schedule, such as the completion of a major deliverable. A milestone can be mandatory, such as one required by a contract, or optional, such as one determined by the team to run the project more smoothly. The milestone list includes all the milestones and specifies whether a milestone is mandatory or optional. Milestones are used in building the schedule.

📦 NOTE

Once developed, the milestone list becomes part of the project management plan.

Requested changes. When you are converting the WBS elements to project activities, you might find problems with the WBS or with the project scope statement. For example, you might discover some holes in the scope or some gray areas, or you might realize that a deliverable cannot be produced within an imposed date. In such a case, you need to make change requests, which must be processed through the integrated change control process.

To summarize, the major output items of the activity definition process are a schedule activity list, a list of attributes for each activity, and a list of milestones. Before you can schedule them, the identified activities need to be arranged in the correct order, which is called *sequencing*.

Sequencing Schedule Activities

The activity sequencing process is used to arrange the schedule activities in the appropriate order, which takes into account the dependencies among the activities. For example, if activity B depends upon the product of activity A, then activity A must be performed before activity B. So the activity sequencing has a two-pronged goal—to identify the dependencies among the schedule activities and to order the activities accordingly. Figure 5.3 shows the activity sequencing process.

Comparing Figure 5.3 with Figure 5.2 reveals that all the output items of the activity definition process are the input into the activity sequencing process. Of course, only the approved change requests will make it into the plan. The project scope statement is an additional input item, and it can be used as a source to check the accuracy of the activity list and to ensure that the activity list covers the scope of the project.

You use the appropriate tools and techniques to determine the dependencies among the schedule activities and sequence them accordingly.

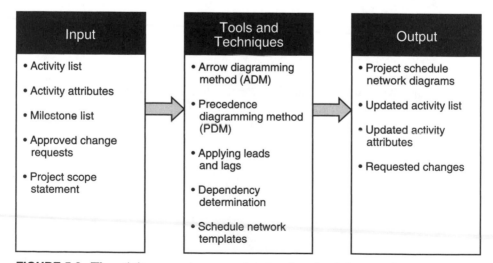

FIGURE 5.3 *The activity sequencing process: input, tools and techniques, and output*

Tools and Techniques for Activity Sequencing

Dependency determination is the prerequisite to determine sequencing. Therefore, most of the tools and techniques used for sequencing are focused on determining and displaying the dependencies.

Dependency determination. To properly sequence the schedule activities, you need to determine the dependencies among them. As illustrated in Figure 5.4, a dependency relationship between two activities is defined by two terms: predecessor and successor. In other words, when two activities are in a dependency relationship with each other, one of them is a predecessor of the other, and the other one is the successor. In Figure 5.4, activity A is a predecessor of activity B, and activity B is successor of activity A. That means A must start before B.

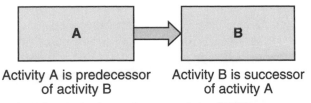

Activity A is predecessor
of activity B   Activity B is successor
of activity A

FIGURE 5.4 *Predecessor/successor relationship between two activities*

By definition, the successor activity must start after the predecessor activity has already started. But exactly when can the successor activity start after the predecessor activity has already been started? Well, both the predecessor and the successor have a start and a finish, and there are at maximum four possible combinations between the start and finish points of the predecessor and the successor activities. Accordingly, there are four kinds of dependencies, also called *precedence relationships*, listed here:

◆ **Finish to start.** The initiation of the successor activity depends upon the completion of the predecessor activity—that is, the successor activity cannot be started until the predecessor activity has already been completed.

◆ **Finish to finish.** The completion of the successor activity depends upon the completion of the predecessor activity—that is, the successor activity cannot be completed until the predecessor activity has already been completed.

◆ **Start to start.** The initiation of the successor activity depends upon the initiation of the predecessor activity—that is, the successor activity cannot be initiated until the predecessor activity has already been initiated.

◆ **Start to finish.** The completion of the successor activity depends upon the initiation of the predecessor activity—that is, the successor activity cannot be completed until the predecessor activity has already been initiated.

These types of dependencies describe the logical relationships between activities. Where do these relationships come from? To answer this question, the dependencies can be grouped into three categories:

◆ **Mandatory dependencies.** These are the dependencies inherent to the schedule activities. For example, a software program must be developed before it can be tested.

◆ **Discretionary dependencies.** These are the dependencies at the discretion of the project management team. For example, it was possible to perform activities A and B simultaneously or to perform A after B was finished, but the team decided, for whatever reason, to perform B after A was finished. Some of the guidelines for establishing discretionary dependencies can come from the knowledge of best practices within the given application area and from the previous experience of performing a similar project.

◆ **External dependencies.** An external dependency involves a relationship between a project activity and a non-project activity—that is, an activity outside the project. For example, in a movie production project, think of a project activity that involves shooting scenes with lots of tourists skiing. This scene is planned to be shot at a skiing resort during the skiing season. This is an example of an external dependency.

The dependency between two schedule activities is an example of the logical relationships defined earlier in this chapter. Logical relationships can be displayed in schematic diagrams, called *project schedule network diagrams*, or just *network diagrams* for brevity. There are two commonly used methods to construct these diagrams: the precedence diagramming method (PDM) and the arrow diagramming method (ADM).

Precedence diagramming method (PDM). The precedence diagramming method (PDM) is the method to construct a project schedule network diagram in which a box (for example, a rectangle) is used to represent an activity and an arrow is used to represent dependency between two activities. The boxes representing activities are called *nodes*. Figure 5.5 presents an example of a network diagram constructed by using PDM, in which activity A is a predecessor of activity B, activity C is a predecessor of activities D and G, and so on.

In this diagram, only C and I have more than one successor. In general, PDM supports all four kinds of precedence relationships discussed earlier, but the most commonly used dependency relationship in PDM is finish-to-start.

Although PDM is the most commonly used method, if you are only going to use the finish-to-start dependencies, the arrow diagramming method is another option to consider.

Arrow diagramming method (ADM). The arrow diagramming method (ADM) is the method to construct a project schedule network diagram in which a node (represented by a circle) acts as a junction between the predecessor activity and the successor activity, and the activity itself is represented by an arrow. The arrow representing an activity also points to the successor activity through a junction. However, there is a problem inherent to this definition. The problem arises from the fact that an activity might have multiple successors, multiple predecessors, or both. In such cases, you might need more arrows to show the dependencies than the number of activities. But an arrow does not just show the relationship; in ADM, it also represents an activity. So, you cannot have more than one arrow for one activity. How would you then represent, for example, that an activity has more than one successor? This problem is solved by introducing the concept of a dummy activity, represented by a broken arrow that is just used to show the relationship and does not represent any real activity.

Figure 5.6 displays a set of dependencies identical to that shown in Figure 5.5. The only difference between the two diagrams is that Figure 5.6 uses ADM instead of PDM, which was used in Figure 5.5. Note the use of dummy activities in Figure 5.6 to show the dependency between C and G, and between I and G.

Note that ADM is only used to represent finish-to-start types of dependencies.

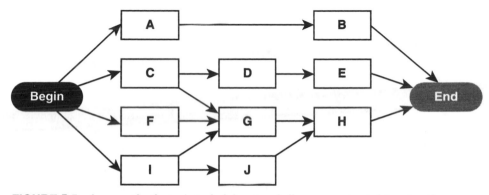

FIGURE 5.5 *An example of a project schedule network diagram constructed by using the Precedence Diagramming Method (PDM)*

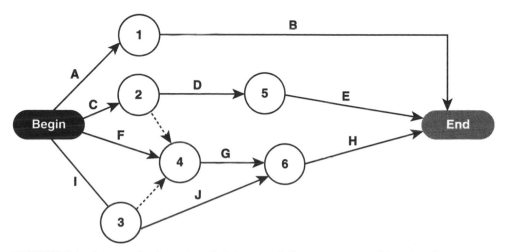

FIGURE 5.6 *An example of a project schedule network diagram constructed by using the arrow diagramming method (ADM)*

Applying leads and lags. The finish-to-start dependency means that the successor activity starts where the predecessor activity finishes. Applying a lead means you allow the successor activity to start before the predecessor activity finishes, and applying a lag means you start the successor activity a few days after the predecessor activity finishes. Sometimes you might need to make such adjustments in the schedule.

Schedule network templates. You can use the standardized network diagram templates to save time to expedite the process of activity sequencing. You can also use the network diagrams from previous projects and modify them for the project at hand.

Finish-to-start is the most commonly used precedence relationship in the PDM diagramming method, although this method can also be used to represent the other three precedence relationships: finish-to-finish, start-to-start, and start-to-finish. The ADM method can only be used to show the finish-to-start relationship.

You use these methods to construct project schedule network diagrams, which are the major output of the activity sequencing process.

Output of Activity Sequencing

The goal of the activity sequencing process is to determine the dependencies among the schedule activities and sequence the activities accordingly. The sequencing is presented in network diagrams. Following are the output items from the activity sequencing process:

◆ **Project schedule network diagrams.** These diagrams, discussed in the previous section, can be created manually or by using an appropriate project management software application. Depending upon a project's size, you might have multiple network diagrams for it.

◆ **Requested changes.** During the activity sequencing process, you might need to make changes to the activity list, the activity attributes, or both. For example, you might need to redefine an activity, decompose an activity into two, and so on. This situation will generate change requests, which must go through the integrated change control process for approval.

◆ **Updated activity list and attribute list.** Once approved, the requested changes regarding the activities must be added to the activity list. The attribute list must be updated accordingly as well.

You can make the activity list, and you can sequence the activities. These are important steps that must be executed. However, to perform the activities, you need resources.

Estimating Activity Resource Requirements

The resource requirements for an activity are estimated by using the activity resource estimating process. The main purpose of this process is to accomplish the following goals:

◆ Estimate the types of resources needed for a given activity

◆ Estimate the quantities of each type of resource needed for the activity

Figure 5.7 shows the activity resource estimating process with its input, tools and techniques, and output.

The activity list and attributes determined by the activity definition process are the major input items to the activity resource estimating process.

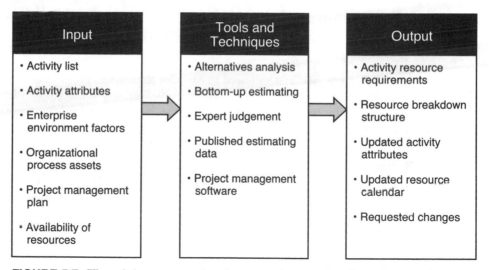

Input	Tools and Techniques	Output
• Activity list	• Alternatives analysis	• Activity resource requirements
• Activity attributes	• Bottom-up estimating	
• Enterprise environment factors	• Expert judgement	• Resource breakdown structure
• Organizational process assets	• Published estimating data	• Updated activity attributes
• Project management plan	• Project management software	• Updated resource calendar
• Availability of resources		• Requested changes

FIGURE 5.7 *The activity resource estimating process: input, tools and techniques, and output*

Input to Activity Resource Estimating

The activity list and attributes are the obvious and major input to the activity resource estimating process. These and other input items are discussed in the following list.

◆ **Activity list and activity attributes.** The activity list originally developed during the activity definition process identifies the schedule activities that need the resources. The activity attributes provide the details for the activities, which will be helpful in estimating the resources.

◆ **Enterprise environmental factors.** Information about the infrastructure of the performing organization, such as existing facilities, will be used in identifying the resources and their availability.

◆ **Organizational process assets.** The organizational process assets useful for activity resource estimating include organizational policies for staffing and purchase of supplies, historical information on what types of resources were used for similar activities in a previous project, and the like.

◆ **Project management plan.** Some components of the project management plan can be used in activity resource estimating. A schedule management plan, a component of the project management plan, is an obvious example that can be used in resource estimating.

◆ **Availability of resources.** Resource estimating will require information on the available quantity of resources of different types, such as human, equipment, and material.

Once you understand the activities, you can use some tools and techniques to determine the resources required to perform those activities.

Tools and Techniques for Activity Resource Estimating

Following are the tools and techniques used to determine the resources required to perform schedule activities.

◆ **Alternative analysis.** You will need to consider alternatives available for resources needed for some schedule activities. For example, you might need to decide whether you want to buy or develop a tool needed to perform an activity, what types of machines (for example, Windows or Linux) to use, which computers to use to do the development, or what level of skills is needed.

◆ **Bottom-up estimating.** You might discover that it is rather complex to estimate resources for a given schedule activity. If the problem is inherent to the activity, it might be helpful in certain cases to decompose the activity into smaller components for the purpose of resource estimating, then estimate the resource for each component, and then aggregate the resources to get an estimate for the whole activity. In aggregation, you must consider the possible relationships (overlaps and such) among different components of the activity so you don't double-count the resources.

◆ **Expert judgment.** Expert judgment can be used to assess the input and output of the resource estimating process.

◆ **Published estimating data.** Information published by various vendors, such as costs for resources, can be useful in estimating the resources.

◆ **Project management software.** Depending upon the sophistication of the resource requirements, project management software might be useful in estimating and managing the resources.

You can use a combination of these tools and techniques to generate the output of the resource estimating process.

Output of Activity Resource Estimating

The resource requirements are the major output of the resource estimating process. These and other output items are discussed in the following list.

Activity resource requirements. The main purpose of the activity resource estimating process is to determine the resource requirements for each schedule activity, and therefore this is the major output item from this process. You identify the types of resources required to perform each activity and estimate the required quantity of each identified resource. If a work package in the WBS has multiple activities, the resource estimates for those activities can be aggregated to estimate the resource requirements for the work package, if needed.

Resource breakdown structure. The resource breakdown structure (RBS) is a hierarchical structure of resource types required to complete the schedule activities of a project. The RBS can be used to identify and analyze the project human resource assignments.

Updated activity attributes. The identified types of required resources for an activity and the estimated quantity for each identified resource become activity attributes and must be added to the attribute list for the activity.

Resource calendar. The resource calendar contains the following useful information about the resources:

◆ Days and times of day when a resource is available

◆ The passive time for the resource—for example, holidays for human resources

◆ The quantity of each type of available resource

◆ The capability of each resource

Requested changes. The activity resource estimating process might generate change requests in the activity list—for example, to add or delete an activity. These change requests must be processed through the integrated change control process.

Once the activities have been identified and resources required to perform each activity have been estimated, you have enough information to begin estimating the time needed to complete each activity, which is called the *activity duration*.

Estimating Activity Duration

Activity duration is the time in calendar units between start and finish of a schedule activity. Activity duration is estimated in work periods by using the activity duration estimating process. A work period is a measurement of time when the work is in progress; it is measured in hours, days, or months, depending upon the size of the activity. This estimate can be converted to calendar units of time by factoring in the resource's passive time, such as holidays. For example, suppose you have estimated that it will take one programmer four days (with eight work hours in a day) to write a program. You also know that the work will start on a Friday and there will be no work on Saturday and Sunday. Therefore, the activity duration estimate is four days (or 32 hours) measured in work periods and six days measured in calendar units.

Figure 5.8 shows the input, tools and techniques, and output for the activity duration estimating process.

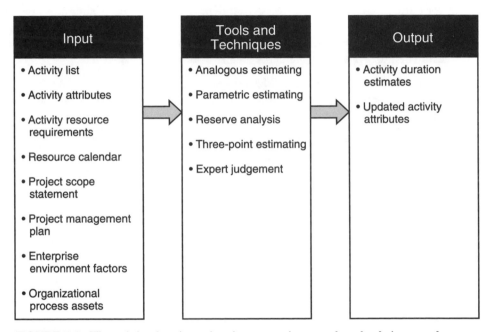

Input	Tools and Techniques	Output
• Activity list • Activity attributes • Activity resource requirements • Resource calendar • Project scope statement • Project management plan • Enterprise environment factors • Organizational process assets	• Analogous estimating • Parametric estimating • Reserve analysis • Three-point estimating • Expert judgement	• Activity duration estimates • Updated activity attributes

FIGURE 5.8 *The activity duration estimating process: input, tools and techniques, and output*

Input to Activity Duration Estimating

To estimate the activity duration, you will need information about the activity, the resource requirements for the activity, and the resources available for the activity. This underlines the major input items to the activity duration estimating process. These and other input items are discussed here.

Activity list and activity attributes. Because you want to estimate the duration of the activities, the activity list along with the activity attributes, originally developed in the activity definition process, are the obvious input items to the activity duration estimating process.

Activity resource requirements. The work periods required to complete an activity depend on the resources assigned to the activity. For example, suppose it will take four work days to complete an activity that involves having two programmers write two programs. If only one programmer is available, it will take roughly eight work days to finish this activity. However, while assigning additional resources to an activity, always consider the following:

◆ Sometimes assigning additional resources might reduce the overall efficiency and productivity. For example, think of two engineers with different skill levels assigned to work on the interrelated components of an activity.

◆ Most of the activities have a threshold beyond which assigning additional resources does not help. For example, installing an operating system on a machine will take the same amount of time regardless of how many system administrators have been assigned to this activity.

Resource calendar. The resource calendar, developed during the activity resource estimating process, contains the type, quantity, availability, and capability of each resource, including the skills of a human resource, which must be considered during activity duration estimating. For example, an experienced programmer can finish the same program in less time than a beginner can. Capability and quantity of available resources, both human and material, can affect the activity duration estimate. For example, if an activity will take four work days for an engineer to finish, and the engineer can work only four hours a day on this activity, it will take eight work days to finish.

Project scope statement. Some assumptions and constraints in the project scope statement can affect activity duration estimates and therefore must be considered. For example, there might be an assumption that part of the work related to an activity has already been performed in a previous project and can be used in this project. If the assumption is true, the activity duration will be less than otherwise. An example of a constraint might be that a specific work package must be finished before a predetermined deadline. This will put a maximum limit on the duration for the activities corresponding to this work package.

Project management plan. The following components of the project management plan are useful for activity duration estimating:

◆ **Activity cost estimates.** Within the project budget, there will be cost estimates assigned to each activity. This estimate will have an effect on the quantity of the resources you can use for the activity.

◆ **Risk register.** The risk register, originally developed during the risk identification process, contains the list of project risks, which must be considered while estimating durations for activities because these risks can influence activity durations. The effect of highly probable risks with high impacts must especially be considered and taken into account in the duration estimates.

Enterprise environmental factors. Examples of enterprise environmental factors are some databases that contain the reference data relevant to the activity duration—for instance, how long it takes for a specific government agency to respond to a request.

Organizational assets. Organizational assets that will be useful in estimating activity duration include information from previous projects and a calendar of working days and non-working days.

In a nutshell, the activity list and activity resource requirements are the major inputs to the activity duration process. The activity duration estimate is a non-trivial task, and there are various tools and techniques available to perform this task effectively and reliably.

Tools and Techniques for Activity Duration Estimating

The project schedule depends upon the activity duration estimates. The duration estimates of activities on the critical path will determine the finish date of a project for a given start date. However, there might be many uncertainties involved in the estimate. For example, two programmers, due to the differences in their experience, will take different amounts of time to write the same program. The good news is that there are a number of tools and techniques that you can use in activity duration estimating.

Analogous estimating. Analogous estimating techniques estimate the duration of an activity based on the duration of a similar activity in a previous project. The accuracy of the estimate depends upon how similar the activities are and whether the team member who will perform the activity has the same level of expertise and experience as the team member from the previous project. This technique is useful when there is not enough detail information about the project or a project activity available—for example, in the early stages of a project.

Parametric estimating. This is a quantitative technique used to calculate the activity duration when the productivity rate of the resource performing the activity is available. You use a formula such as the following one to calculate the duration:

Activity duration = Units of work in the activity / Productivity rate of the resources

For example, if you know that a team assigned to the activity of burying 40 miles of cable can bury two miles of cable in one day, the duration calculation can be performed as follows:

Activity duration = 40 miles / (2 miles/day) = 20 days

Three-point estimating. This method addresses the issue of uncertainty in estimating the activity duration. The uncertainty in the duration estimate can be calculated by making a three-point estimate in which each point corresponds to one of the following estimate types:

- ◆ **Most likely scenario.** The activity duration is calculated in most practical terms by factoring in resources likely to be assigned, realistic expectations of the resources, dependencies, and interruptions.
- ◆ **Optimistic scenario.** This is the best case version of the situation described in the most likely scenario.
- ◆ **Pessimistic scenario.** This is the worst case version of the situation described in the most likely scenario.

The spread of these three estimates determines the uncertainty. The resultant duration is calculated by taking the average of the three estimates. For example, if the duration for an activity is estimated to be 20 days for the most likely scenario, 18 days for the optimistic scenario, and 22 days for the pessimistic scenario, then the average duration is 20 days and the uncertainty is ± 2 days, which can be expressed as:

Duration = 20 ± 2 days

It's equivalent to saying that the activity duration is 20 days, give or take two days.

Reserve analysis. Reserve analysis is used to incorporate a time cushion into your schedule; this cushion is called a *contingency reserve*, a *time reserve*, or a *time buffer*. The whole idea is to accommodate the possibility of schedule risks. One method of calculating the contingency reserve is to take a percentage of the original activity duration estimate as the contingency reserve. Later, when more information about the project becomes available, the contingency reserve can be reduced or eliminated.

Expert judgment. Expert judgment can be used to estimate the whole duration of an activity when not enough information is available. It can also be used to estimate some parameters to be used in other methods—for example, what percentage of the original activity duration estimate should be used as a contingency reserve—and in comparing an activity to a similar activity in a previous project during analogous estimating.

Note that, in general, a combination of techniques is used to estimate the duration of an activity. For example, you can use the analogous technique and expert judgment to estimate the productivity rate of resources, and then use that productivity rate in parametric analysis to calculate the activity duration.

Output of Activity Duration Estimating

Guess what the output of the activity duration estimating process is. Yes, you are right: It is the activity duration estimates! Regardless of which technique you use, these estimates are quantitative assessments of the required time units to finish activities, such as five days or 10 weeks. As shown earlier, you can also assign an uncertainty to the estimate, such as 20±2 days to say that the activity will take at least 18 days and at most 22 days.

The duration of an activity is an attribute of the activity. Therefore, you update the activity attributes, originally developed in the activity definition process, to include the activity durations.

In a nutshell, there are two output items of the activity duration estimating process:

◆ Activity duration estimates
◆ Updates to activity attributes

By using various processes discussed in this chapter, you have identified schedule activities, arranged them in proper sequence, determined resource requirements for them, and estimated their durations. All these tasks and accomplishments are a means to an end called *project schedule development*.

Developing the Project Schedule

The project work is composed of individual activities. So, the processes previously discussed in this chapter deal with the activities. By using these processes, you work out a few schedule-related pieces at the activity level, which come together as the project schedule when you crank them through the schedule development process. Until you have a realistic project schedule, you do not have a project. A project schedule has schedule activities sandwiched between the project start date and the project finish date. Figure 5.9 shows the schedule development process used to develop the project schedule.

The major output items of all the processes discussed in this chapter are the input to the schedule development process.

Input to Schedule Development

The following output items from the schedule-related processes discussed in this chapter directly support the schedule development process:

◆ Activity list and activity attributes
◆ Project schedule network diagrams showing the dependencies among activities
◆ Activity resource requirements and resource calendars
◆ Activity duration estimates

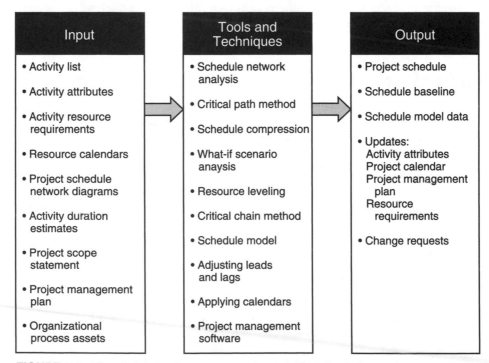

Input	Tools and Techniques	Output
• Activity list	• Schedule network analysis	• Project schedule
• Activity attributes	• Critical path method	• Schedule baseline
• Activity resource requirements	• Schedule compression	• Schedule model data
• Resource calendars	• What-if scenario anaysis	• Updates: Activity attributes Project calendar Project management plan Resource requirements
• Project schedule network diagrams	• Resource leveling	
• Activity duration estimates	• Critical chain method	• Change requests
• Project scope statement	• Schedule model	
• Project management plan	• Adjusting leads and lags	
	• Applying calendars	
• Organizational process assets	• Project management software	

FIGURE 5.9 *The schedule development process: input, tools and techniques, and output*

The project scope statement and project management plan are two other input items that can be useful in ways described in the following list.

Project scope statement. The assumptions and constraints in the project scope statement can affect the project schedule and therefore must be considered in developing the schedule. The following two types of time-related constraints should get special attention.

◆ **Hard deadlines on start and finish dates.** Some activities or work packages might have constraints on their start or finish dates. For example, there might be a situation in which an activity cannot be started before a certain date, or must be finished before a certain date, or both. Where do these date constraints come from? They can come from various sources, such as a date in the contract, a date determined by the market window, delivery of material from an external vendor, and the like.

◆ **Time constraints on deliverables.** These constraints can come from the customer, the sponsor, or any other stakeholder in terms of deadlines for certain major deliverables or milestones. Other projects inside or outside your organization might be depending on these constraints. So, once scheduled, these deadlines are constraints and can only be changed through the approval process.

Project management plan. The following components of the project management plan can be useful in developing the project schedule:

◆ Cost management plan

◆ Project risk management plan, especially the risk register

◆ Project scope management plan

◆ Schedule management plan

So, the output of various time management processes is used as input to the schedule development process, which uses a variety of tools and techniques to iron out the project schedule.

Tools and Techniques for Schedule Development

Once you have the network diagrams for the activities, as well as the activity duration estimates, you are well-equipped to start scheduling the project. The remaining main concerns include the following:

◆ The actual start date

◆ Uncertainty on the availability of resources

◆ Identification of and preparation for activities on the critical path

◆ Risks involved, or "what if" scenarios

◆ The hard start/finish dates for activities or for the project that came down the pipeline from very important stakeholders

Various tools and techniques discussed in this section can be used to address these concerns while you are hammering out the project schedule.

Schedule Network Analysis

A schedule network analysis is a technique used to generate a project schedule by identifying the early and late start and finish dates for the project. The analysis accomplishes this task by employing a schedule model and various analytical techniques, such as critical path method, critical chain method, "what if" analysis, and resource leveling. These techniques are discussed in this section.

Schedule model. You know by now that the resource requirements and activity durations are the estimates based on some assumptions, such as that a typical programmer will take five days to write a certain program. However, you use this data to build the project schedule. Changing the assumptions will change the data, hence the schedule. So, a set of assumptions on which this data is based is called a *schedule model*.

Critical path method. This is the schedule network analysis technique used to identify the schedule flexibility and the critical path of the project schedule network diagram. The critical path is the longest path (sequence of activities) in a project schedule network diagram. Because it is the longest path, it determines the duration of the project, and hence the finish date of the project given the start date. An example will explain this. Consider the network diagram presented in Figure 5.10. The boxes in the figure represent activities, such as activity A followed by activity B, and the number on top of a box represents the duration of the activity in time units, such as days.

Table 5.1 shows the calculations for the duration of each path of the network diagram by adding the durations of the individual activities on the path. You can see from Table 5.1 that the path Start-F-G-H-Finish is the critical path because it is the longest path in the diagram, at 21 days. This means if the project start date is January 2, the project finish date will be January 23 (2+21), given that the duration is shown in calendar time units.

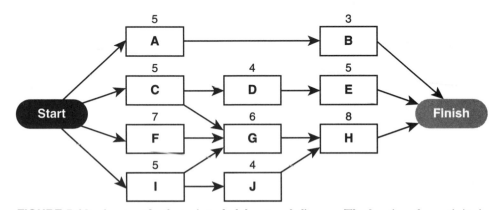

FIGURE 5.10 *An example of a project schedule network diagram. The duration of an activity is represented by the number shown on top of the box that represents the activity.*

Table 5.1 Path Durations Calculated from the Network Diagram Shown in Figure 5.10

Path	Durations of Activities	Path Duration
Start-A-B-Finish	5+3	8
Start-C-D-E-Finish	5+4+5	14
Start-C-G-H-Finish	5+6+8	19
Start-F-G-H-Finish	7+6+8	21
Start-I-G-H-Finish	5+6+8	19
Start-I-J-H-Finish	5+4+8	17

The second important feature of the critical path method is to identify the flexibility in the project schedule by calculating the early and late start and finish dates of each activity on each path. The schedule flexibility of an activity is measured by the positive difference between the late start date and the early start date for the activity, and is called *float time* or *total float*.

Table 5.2 shows calculations for the early and late start and finish dates and the float time for each activity in the network diagram being analyzed. The early start and finish dates of activities on a path are calculated by using the forward-pass method, which means you start your calculations from the start point (left-most) and make your way forward. As an example, consider the path Start-A-B-Finish in the network diagram shown in Figure 5.10. Because A is the first activity on the path, its early start is day 0. Because B depends on the completion of A, and A takes five days to finish, the early start date for B is the early start date of A plus the duration of A—that is, 0 + 5 = 5. The late start and finish dates are calculated using the backward-pass method, which means you start your calculations from the finish point. The project finish date determined by the critical path is day 21, given that the project start date is day 0. Because activity B has a duration of three days, it must be started no later than day 18 (21 − 3 = 18). Therefore, day 18 is the late start date of activity B. Activity A has duration of five days, so given that B must start on day 18, A must not start later than day 13 (18 − 5 = 13). Therefore the late start date for A is day 13. The float times are calculated as follows:

Float time for A = late start − early start = 13 − 0 = 13

Float time for B = late start − early start = 18 − 5 = 13

Note that each of the activities on the critical path (F, G, and H) has a float time of zero. This obviously is a source of schedule risk.

🔲 NOTE

Each activity on a critical path has zero float time, and therefore poses a schedule risk. Therefore, you must monitor the activities on all critical paths very closely during the execution of the project.

Table 5.2 Early and Late Start and Finish Dates for Activities in the Network Diagram Shown in Figure 5.10

Activity	Early Start	Early Finish	Late Start	Late Finish	Float Time
A	0	5	13	18	13
B	5	8	18	21	13
C	0	5	2 (not 7)	12	2
D	5	9	12	16	7
E	9	14	16	21	7
F	0	7	0	7	0
G	7	13	7	13	0
H	13	21	13	21	0
I	0	5	2 (not 4)	9	2
J	5	9	9	13	4

Critical chain method. This is an alternative schedule network analysis technique that takes into account the uncertainties of the activity durations due the uncertainty of the availability of resources. It uses the schedule network diagrams to identify the critical paths and the schedule flexibility, just like the critical path method. The only difference is that in this technique, you work from more than one network diagram. For example, the durations in the first network are based on the planned scenario regarding the availability of resources. You can draw another network diagram based on the pessimistic scenario regarding the availability of resources. The durations of some activities in the second diagram will be longer than the first diagram, and the second diagram might even have a different or an additional critical path. The extra durations in the second diagram are called *duration buffers*. So, the focus of the critical chain method is on managing the duration buffers and the uncertainties in the availability of resources applied to the planned schedule activities.

Resource leveling. Resource leveling is not an independent schedule network analysis method. It is applied to the schedule that has already been analyzed using other methods, such as the critical path method or the critical chain method. The resource leveling technique is applied to address the resource needs of activities that must be performed to meet specific delivery dates. Resource leveling involves taking a part of the resources from one activity and assigning it to another. This will change the activity durations and can also result in a change of critical paths.

"What if" scenario analysis. The purpose of the "what if" scenario analysis is to calculate the effects of a specific scenario on the schedule—for example, how the schedule will be affected if a vendor does not make the delivery of a major component on the promised date. Because a "what if" scenario by definition represents uncertainty, this analysis often leads to risk planning, which might include changing the schedule or changing the network diagram to get a few activities out of harm's way if possible.

As you have seen, the critical path method is used to develop a schedule for given resources, whereas the critical chain method factors in the uncertainty of the availability of the resources. The resource leveling technique is used to move the resources around to meet the resource needs of the activities that must be accomplished on a specific date. In other words, in an ideal world in which the required (or planned) resources are guaranteed, you do not need the critical chain method and resource leveling; just the critical path method will do.

Let's assume you have used the critical path method to determine the schedule for a project. You have also applied other techniques, such as the critical chain method and resource leveling. The final realistic schedule that you have come up with has an unacceptable project duration (the length of the critical path). What do you do? This is where the schedule compression technique comes to your rescue.

Schedule Compression

It is true that you, the project manager, build the schedule through cold, hard mathematical analysis and you don't just accept whatever schedule goals come down the pipeline from elsewhere, such as from the customer or the project sponsor. However, once you have the schedule built through analysis, you can attempt to accommodate some critical stakeholder expectations or hard deadlines, such as a predetermined project finish date. I have already discussed one such method, called resource leveling, to accommodate hard deadlines for activities. In this section, I will discuss two more methods for schedule compression: crashing and fast tracking.

Crashing. This is a project schedule compression technique used to decrease the project duration with minimal additional cost. A number of alternatives are analyzed, including the assignment of additional resources.

Fast tracking. This is a project schedule compression technique used to decrease the project duration by performing project phases or some schedule activities within a phase in parallel that would normally be performed in sequence. For example, testing of a product can start when some of its components are finished, rather than waiting for the whole product to be completed.

◀ **TIP**

Crashing usually involves assigning more resources and hence increasing the cost. However, guard yourself against the misconception that additional resources will linearly improve the performance. For example, if one programmer can develop a program in eight days, it does not necessarily mean that two programmers will develop the same program in four days, because there will be overheads, such as the initial less-productive stage of the newly assigned resource, the time taken to reallocate the work, the interaction among the resources, and so on.

Other Tools and Techniques

In addition to the main techniques to develop the project schedule, which I already discussed, there are some other tools and techniques for developing the project schedule that I will discuss in this list.

Applying calendars. Project calendars and resource calendars must be consulted during the schedule development process because they specify when the work can be performed. Project calendars can affect all project activities because they, for example, can identify when no work can be performed on a site during a certain period of the year. Resource calendars can affect project activities that require certain resources or a category of resources because they can identify when a resource or a category of resources is not available. The calendar might take into account holidays, restrictions on contract workers, overtime issues, other commitments within the organization, and the like.

Adjusting leads and lags. If you applied leads and lags during the activity sequencing process, it is time to consider whether you need to adjust those. This adjustment might be necessary to create a realistic schedule.

Project management software. After you have the data for the schedule development created by the processes discussed in this chapter, it is a common practice to use project management software to build the actual schedule.

In a nutshell, the main techniques to develop a project schedule include network diagram analysis (critical path method and critical chain method), schedule compression (fast tracking and crashing), and resource leveling. You use these techniques to generate the output of the schedule development process.

Output of the Schedule Development Process

The planned project schedule is an obvious output of the schedule development process. This and other output items are discussed in this section.

Project schedule. The project schedule includes a planned start date and a planned finish date for each schedule activity. The schedule will be considered preliminary until the resources have been assigned to perform the activities according to the schedule. Although a schedule for a simple project might be presented in a tabular form, typically a project schedule is presented in one of the following graphical formats:

- ◆ **Project schedule network diagram.** These diagrams present the schedule activities on a timescale with a start and finish date for each activity and hence show the dependencies of activities on each other.
- ◆ **Bar chart.** In these charts the activities are represented by bars, with each bar showing the start date, the finish date, and the duration of the activity.
- ◆ **Milestone chart.** These are typically the bar charts representing only the milestones, not all the schedule activities.

Schedule model data. This is the supporting data for the project schedule and consists of the following:

- Schedule activities, schedule milestones, activity attributes, and documentation of all identified assumptions and constraints
- Resource requirements by time periods
- Alternative schedules—for example, schedules based on best-case and worst-case scenarios
- Schedule contingency reserves

This data is used to create the version of the schedule that is approved by the project management team and becomes the schedule baseline.

Schedule baseline. This is a specific version of the project schedule that is approved by the project management team as a baseline against which the progress of the project will be measured. This version of the schedule is developed from the schedule network analysis of the schedule model data.

Changes and updates. The process of schedule development can generate requests for changes, which must be processed through the integrated change control process. Furthermore, some updates may be added to the following items:

- **Resource requirements.** The schedule development process might change the initial estimate for the types and quantities of the required resources.
- **Activity attributes.** Resource requirements or any other activity attributes that have changed must be updated.
- **Project calendar.** Any update to the project calendar must be documented.
- **Project management plan.** This plan should include any updates to reflect any changes that were realized during the schedule development regarding how the project schedule will be managed. Only the approved changes should be included.

NOTE

Project schedule development is an iterative process. For example, it might be necessary to review and revise the duration and resource estimates for some activities to create a project schedule that will be approved. The approved project schedule will act as a baseline against which project progress will be tracked.

The approved project schedule is used as a baseline to track the project progress. To some extent, the schedule development (or modification) continues throughout the project execution due to the approved changes and the risk occurrences.

While developing the project schedule, the availability of resources required to perform the schedule activities is an obvious assumption. An important category of resources is human resources—for example, a computer programmer who will write a computer program.

Planning Human Resources

Project roles, responsibilities of the roles, and reporting relationships need to be defined in order to perform a project. A role is a defined function to be performed by a team member, such as programmer or tester. The other issue that needs to be addressed before the project can be performed is how and when the project team members (who will perform the project work) will be acquired. The human resource planning process addresses these issues.

Therefore, two main goals of the human resource planning process are the following:

◆ Identify and document project roles, responsibilities for each role, and reporting relationships among the roles.

◆ Create the staff management plan.

Figure 5.11 shows the human resource planning process.

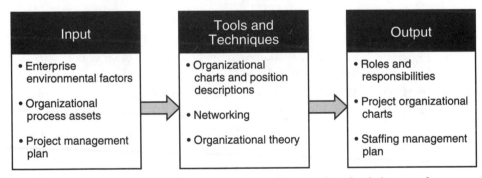

Input	Tools and Techniques	Output
• Enterprise environmental factors	• Organizational charts and position descriptions	• Roles and responsibilities
• Organizational process assets	• Networking	• Project organizational charts
• Project management plan	• Organizational theory	• Staffing management plan

FIGURE 5.11 *The human resource planning process: input, tools and techniques, and output*

Input to Human Resource Planning

Before you can assign the resources to a project, you need to know the resource requirements of the project, which are the main input item to the resource planning process. The other two input items are the familiar ones: enterprise environmental factors and organizational process assets.

Enterprise environmental factors. How do the different departments and the people within the performing organization interact with each other? This will have a profound effect on defining the roles and responsibilities. Overall, while planning human resources, you must consider the following enterprise environmental factors:

- **Interpersonal.** The interpersonal environmental factor should be explored while considering the candidates for the project team members. You should seek answers to interpersonal questions, such as the following:
  - What are the job descriptions of the candidates? This will tell you what kind of project activities they might be able to perform.
  - What types of formal and informal reporting relationships exist among the candidates?
  - What cultural or language differences will possibly affect the working relationships among the candidates?
- **Logistical.** The logistical factor deals with the issue of how the project team is spread out geographically. For example, a relevant question to ask is, are the team members spread out in different buildings, time zones, or countries?
- **Organizational.** The organizational factor relevant to human resource planning can be identified by the answers to the following questions:
  - Which departments of the performing organization will participate in the project?
  - What are the current relationships between these departments? In other words, how do these departments interact?
- **Political.** To explore the effect of the political factor on human resource planning, you should ask questions such as:
  - What are the individual goals and agendas of the project stakeholders?
  - Which individuals or groups are influential in areas important to the project?
  - What are the formal or informal alliances that exist between individuals or departments relevant to the project?
- **Technical.** Almost all projects these days include the use of some kind of technology. To explore the effects of technical factors on human resource planning, you should explore answers to questions such as:
  - What are the technical specialties, such as software, programming languages, and technical equipment, needed to perform the project?
  - Which of these specialties need to be coordinated?
  - Are there any technical challenges this project might face?

Organizational process assets. The organizational process assets that can be useful in human resource planning include checklists and templates. Some examples of checklists are common project roles in your organization, typical competencies, training programs to consider, team ground rules, and safety considerations. Examples of templates include project organizational charts and standard conflict management approach.

Project management plan. Following are the components of the project management plan relevant to resource planning:

◆ Activity resource requirements to determine the human resource needs of the project

◆ Descriptions of project management activities, such as quality assurance and risk management, which will help ensure that all the project roles and responsibilities are identified

The activity resource requirements are the raw material to determine the roles that will perform the activities. Various tools and techniques are available to convert some requirements into roles.

Tools and Techniques for Human Resource Planning

You need resources to complete the activities, and some of these resources will be human resources. For example, consider an activity in a project—writing a program. The program will be written by a programmer, which is a human resource. However, before you even know the name of the programmer, you can work with this programmer as a role and assign a real individual to fill this role later. The tools and techniques used to determine the roles for a project are discussed in this section.

Organizational charts. These charts identify and document the roles of the project team members, the responsibilities assigned to the roles, and the reporting relationships among the roles. Most of the chart formats fall into three categories—hierarchical, matrix, and text-oriented.

◆ **Hierarchical.** Hierarchical charts are the traditional way to represent the reporting relationships in an organization, in a top-down format. Such a chart is also called an *organizational breakdown structure (OBS)*, and is arranged according to the organization's existing departments, units, or teams. The OBS will help you to identify team members for the project.

◆ **Matrix.** A matrix is used to specify the relationships between schedule activities, roles, and team members. Such a matrix is generally called a *responsibility assignment matrix (RAM)*. Different matrices can show these relationships at different levels. For example, you can use the RAM to document resource requirements for each activity, as shown in Table 5.3. You can also use a RAM to document the specific responsibilities assigned to specific team members for the schedule activities, as shown in Table 5.4.

◆ **Text-oriented.** When the team-member responsibilities need to be described in detail, text-based documents might be more useful. These documents can be known by various names in different organizations, such as *responsibilities forms*, *position descriptions*, and *role-responsibility-authority forms*. Once established, these documents can act as templates for other projects.

Table 5.3 Example of a Responsibility Assignment Matrix (RAM) Depicting the Resources Required to Perform Schedule Activities

Activity	Designer	Developer	Tester	Marketer	Workstation	Server
A	1					
B		5			5	1
C			2		2	2
D				1		
E	1	1	1		1	

Table 5.4 Example of a Responsibility Assignment Matrix (RAM) Depicting the Roles Assigned to the Team Members for Various Activities

Activity	Deborah	Cathleen	Anil	Maya	Kiruba
Design	R	A	I	I	C
Develop	I	I	R	I	C
Test	C	R	A	I	C
Deploy	I	I	A	I	R

Depending upon the project needs, you can use both RAM and text-oriented charts to document roles and responsibilities. Also, remember that the RAM can be used for various purposes. For example, the RAM in Table 5.3 documents the resource requirements for the schedule activities, while the RAM in Table 5.4 depicts the roles of team members for schedule activities.

The RAM in Table 5.4 is also called the *RACI chart* because it assigns four roles to team members for various activities: responsible (R), accountable (A), consult (C), and inform (I). For example, Deborah has the responsibility of designing the product, Cathleen will be held accountable for the design, Kiruba will play the role of a consultant for designing the product, while Anil and Maya will play the role of keeping everybody informed of the status and progress.

Networking. Burn it in your head: Networking is one of the golden secrets you have for succeeding as a project manager, especially in an organization in which functional managers hold all the power (hiring, firing, bonuses), and the project managers are running around with nothing in their hands other than the project schedules and status reports. To network effectively, you should understand the influence of political and interpersonal factors in your organization that might impact various staffing management options. Some of the essential networking happens at the beginning of each project, and you must make full use of it. However, networking is a regular practice, and you should be using all the human resource network activities, such as proactive correspondence, informal conversations, luncheon meetings, and trade conferences.

Organizational theories. Various organizational theories provide information and insight on how people behave in a team or an organization, what motivates team members, and the like. If you have knowledge of these theories, it will help you plan human resources quickly and use them more effectively.

To summarize, organizational charts, networking, and organizational theories are the main tools and techniques used to determine roles and develop the staff management plan, which are the major output items of the human resource planning process.

Output of Human Resource Planning

The output of the human resource planning process includes roles and responsibilities, as well as the staff management plan. These and other output items are discussed in this list.

Roles and responsibilities. The schedule project activities will be completed by individuals working in certain roles and performing responsibilities that come with the roles. So, roles and responsibilities are an important output of human resource planning. While determining roles and responsibilities, you must be clear about the following concepts:

◆ **Role.** In real life, most activities are performed by people playing certain roles, such as a parent, a teacher, or a student. Similarly, in project management, a role is essentially a set of responsibilities, such as the responsibilities of a developer, a tester, or a manager. A role is assigned to a team member who will perform the responsibilities included in the role to complete one or more project activities.

◆ **Responsibility.** A responsibility is a piece of work (task) that must be performed as part of completing a project activity. Responsibilities can be grouped together as a role.

◆ **Competency.** Competency is the ability of a team member to play a certain role—that is, to perform the responsibilities assigned to the role. While assigning a role to a team member, you should know whether the team member possesses the skills required to perform the responsibilities of the role. You might need to respond to a mismatch with training, hiring, schedule changes, or scope changes.

◆ **Authority.** Authority is a right assigned to a role that enables the person playing the role to apply project resources, make certain decisions, or sign approvals.

TIP

Roles must be clarified by specifying the responsibilities and the authorities assigned to each role. A good match between the levels of responsibility and authority for each team member generally produces the best results. This gives the team members a sense of ownership.

Project organizational charts. A project organizational chart displays the project team members and the reporting relationships among them. The level of formality and detail of these charts depends upon the size and needs of the project at hand.

Staffing management plan. After you have determined the roles to perform the activities, you need to identify individuals to fill those roles. The staff management plan describes when and how human resource requirements for a project will be met. When preparing the staff management plan for your project, you must consider the following items:

◆ **Staff acquisition.** While planning staff acquisition, you might need to struggle with some of the following questions:

  ◆ What are the levels of expertise needed for the project, and what are the assigned costs?

  ◆ Will the human resources come from within the organization, outside the organization, or both?

  ◆ Will the team members be required to work in a central location, or can they work from distant locations?

  ◆ Will you need the assistance of the human resources department of your organization to acquire the staff?

◆ **Timetable and release criteria.** You need to have a timetable for the human resource requirements, describing when and for how long a staff member is needed. The project schedule will help you determine that. You should also determine the release criteria and time to release each team member from the project. Planning of release criteria is very important for a smooth transition of team members from one project to another, and for the optimal use of the resources.

◆ **Training needs.** If some team members lack the adequate level of skills needed for the project, a training plan can be developed as part of the project.

◆ **Compliance and safety.** The staff management plan can also include strategies for complying with relevant government regulations, union contracts, and human resource policies. Your organization might have some policies and procedures that protect the team members from safety hazards. These policies and procedures must be included in the staff management plan.

◆ **Recognition and rewards.** Recognition and rewards are good tools to promote and reinforce desired behavior. However, to use this tool effectively, you must have clear criteria for rewards based on activities and performance of team members. The potential candidate for a reward must have an appropriate level of control over the activity for which the reward will be offered. For example, if a team member is to be rewarded for completing the project within the budget, the team member must have an adequate level of control over the decision-making that affected the spending.

The human resource planning accomplishes two things: It determines roles to perform the schedule activities, and it develops a staff management plan to fill those roles with team members.

The three most important takeaways from this chapter are as follows:

◆ Various time management processes are used to produce schedule model data—a list of schedule activities and attributes for each activity, such as required resources and the duration of the activity.

◆ The schedule model data is used to develop the project schedule, which is an iterative process due to the uncertainties in the schedule data and due to the changes during the project execution. However, the approved version of the planned schedule is used as a baseline to track the project progress.

◆ The human resource planning process is used to determine roles to perform the schedule activities and to develop a staff management plan to fill these roles with team members.

Summary

Project schedule development is a journey that begins with decomposing the work packages in the WBS to project activities and ends with determining resources, including team members who will perform those activities at certain times. The schedule planning addresses some basic questions: What are the activities that need to be performed to complete the project, who is going to perform these activities, and when?

The activity definition process is used to decompose the work packages in the WBS into schedule activities. The resulting activity list is used by the activity sequencing process to generate network diagrams, which display the dependencies among the activities. Two methods are commonly used to construct network diagrams: the precedence diagramming method (PDM), which can be used to display any of the four kinds of dependencies, and the arrow diagramming method (ADM), which can be used only to show finish-to-start dependencies. The activity list and attributes are also used to determine the resource requirements for the project. Given the available resource, you can estimate the activity duration—that is, the time it will take to perform the activity.

By using various time-management processes discussed in this chapter, you identify schedule activities, arrange them in proper sequence, determine resource requirements for them, and estimate their durations. All these tasks and accomplishments are a means to an end called *project schedule development*. You typically use the critical path method to develop the project schedule from a network diagram. After you have a schedule, you can use schedule compression methods, such as fast tracking and crashing, to accommodate hard deadlines. Schedule development is an iterative process that can continue well into the project execution due to approved changes and risk occurrences. However, the approved planned project schedule is used as a baseline to track the project progress.

The human resource planning process is used to determine roles to perform the activities in the project schedule and to develop a staff management plan to fill these roles with team members. When the project starts executing, it needs to be monitored, which is the topic of the next chapter.

Exam's Eye View

Comprehend

◆ The major task of the activity definition process is to generate the activity list (output) by decomposing the work packages of the WBS (input) into activities.

◆ The major task of the activity sequencing process is to determine the dependencies among the activities in the activity list (input) and display those dependencies in the network diagrams (output).

◆ After the activity resource requirements have been determined, the duration for an activity can be estimated for a given resource.

◆ The approved project schedule acts as a baseline against which the project progress is tracked.

◆ The human resource planning process is used to determine roles to perform the schedule activities and to develop the staff management plan to fill the roles with team members.

Look Out

◆ Activity duration is estimated for a given resource. Changing the quantity of the resource will change the duration estimate.

◆ Activity duration measured in work periods does not include holidays, whereas the duration measured in calendar units does. For example, the activity duration from Friday to the following Tuesday is three days when measured in work units and five days when measured in calendar units, given that no work is done on Saturday and Sunday.

◆ Each activity on a critical path has zero float time and thus poses a schedule risk. Therefore, you must monitor the activities on all critical paths very closely during the execution of the project.

Memorize

◆ The activity list, generated as an output of the activity definition process, becomes a component of the project management plan.

◆ In PDM, finish-to-start is the most commonly used dependency relationship, whereas ADM only uses finish-to-start dependency.

◆ Fast tracking compresses the schedule by performing activities simultaneously that would otherwise be performed in sequence, whereas crashing compresses the schedule by assigning more resources.

Key Terms

◆ **activity.** A component of project work.

◆ **activity definition.** The process of identifying the specific schedule activities that need to be performed to produce the project deliverables.

◆ **activity duration.** The time measured in calendar units between the start and finish of a schedule activity.

◆ **activity duration estimating.** The process of estimating the time in work periods individually for each schedule activity required for its completion. A work period is a measurement of time when the work is in progress; it is measured in hours, days, or months depending upon the size of the activity.

◆ **activity resource estimating.** The process of estimating the types and amounts of resources that will be required to perform each schedule activity.

◆ **activity sequencing.** The process of identifying and documenting the dependencies among schedule activities.

◆ **analogous estimating.** A technique that is used to estimate the duration of an activity based on the duration of a similar activity in a previous project.

◆ **arrow diagramming method (ADM).** A technique used to draw a project schedule network diagram in which an arrow represents an activity and also points to the successor activity through a junction represented by a node (box).

◆ **control account.** A level in the WBS at which the WBS components can be planned to a limited detail.

◆ **crashing.** A project schedule compression technique used to decrease the project duration with minimum additional cost. A number of alternatives are analyzed, including the assignment of additional resources.

◆ **critical path.** The longest path (sequence of activities) in a project schedule network diagram. Because it is the longest path, it determines the duration of the project.

◆ **critical path method (CPM).** A schedule network analysis technique used to identify the schedule flexibility and the critical path of the project schedule network diagram.

◆ **fast tracking.** A project schedule compression technique used to decrease the project duration by performing project phases or some schedule activities within a phase simultaneously, when they would normally be performed in sequence.

◆ **float time.** The positive difference between the late start date and the early start date of a schedule activity.

◆ **lag.** A technique to modify a dependency relationship by delaying the successor activity. For example, a lag of five days in a finish-to-start relationship means the successor activity cannot start until five days after the predecessor activity has ended.

◆ **lead.** A technique to modify a dependency relationship by accelerating the successor activity. For example, a lead of five days in a finish-to-start relationship means the successor activity can start up until five days before the finish date of the predecessor activity.

◆ **logical relationship.** A dependency between two project schedule activities or between a schedule activity and a schedule milestone.

◆ **milestone.** A significant point (or event) in the life of a project.

◆ **parametric estimating.** A quantitative technique used to calculate the activity duration when the productivity rate of the resource performing the activity is available.

◆ **planning component**. A WBS component at the bottom level of a branch of WBS hierarchy for which some planning can be performed.

◆ **planning package.** A WBS component that is below the level of a control account and above the level of a work package.

◆ **precedence diagramming method (PDM).** A technique used to construct a project schedule network diagram in which a node (a box) represents an activity and an arrow represents the dependency relationship.

◆ **project calendar.** A calendar of working days or shifts used to establish when a schedule activity can be performed. A calendar typically specifies holidays and weekends when a schedule activity cannot be performed.

◆ **project schedule.** A schedule that consists of planned dates for performing schedule activities and meeting schedule milestones.

◆ **project schedule network diagram.** A schematic display of logical relationships among the project schedule activities. The time flow in these diagrams is from left to right.

◆ **resource breakdown structure.** The resource breakdown structure (RBS) is a hierarchical structure of resource types required to complete the schedule activities of a project.

◆ **role.** A defined function that contains a set of responsibilities to be performed by a team member, such as a programmer or a tester.

◆ **rolling wave planning.** A technique used to plan the project work at various levels of detail, depending upon the availability of information. Work to be performed in the near future is planned at the low level of the WBS, whereas work to be performed far into the future is planned at a relatively high level of the WBS.

◆ **schedule activity.** A scheduled task (component of work) performed during the life-cycle of a project.

◆ **schedule baseline.** A specific version of the project schedule that is approved by the project management team as a baseline against which the progress of the project will be measured. This version of the schedule is developed from the schedule network analysis of the schedule model data.

◆ **schedule development.** The process of creating the project schedule by analyzing schedule activity sequences, schedule activity durations, resource requirements, and schedule constraints.

◆ **schedule milestone.** A significant event in the project schedule, such as the completion of a major deliverable.

◆ **Schedule network analysis.** A technique used to generate a project schedule by identifying the early and late start and finish dates for the project.

Review Questions

1. Which of the following is the most widely used network diagramming method?
   A. Critical path method (CPM)
   B. Critical chain method (CCM)
   C. Precedence diagramming method (PDM)
   D. Arrow diagramming method (ADM)

2. What is the crashing technique used for?
   A. Network diagramming
   B. Duration compression
   C. Cost reduction
   D. Activity sequencing

3. Which of the following is a true statement about the critical path?
   A. Each activity on the critical path has zero float time.
   B. It controls the project finish date.
   C. It controls the project start date.
   D. It is the shortest sequence in the network diagram.
   E. Both A and B are true.

4. In your research project on tourism, you must collect data before the tourist season ends because the project involves interviewing the tourists. The data-collection activity has which of the following kind of dependency?
   A. Mandatory
   B. External
   C. Internal
   D. Discretionary
   E. Finish-to-start

5. You know from a network diagram that activity B cannot start until activity A is finished. Which of the following are true?

   A. Activities A and B have a start-to-finish dependency.

   B. Activities A and B have a finish-to-start dependency.

   C. Activity B has a mandatory dependency on activity A.

   D. Activities A and B are on a critical path.

   E. Activity B is a successor to activity A.

6. Why should you monitor the activities on the critical path more closely?

   A. Because each activity on the critical path has a zero float time and thereby poses a schedule risk.

   B. Because the activities on the critical path need to be performed before the activities on other paths.

   C. Because the activities on the critical path are critical to the organization's strategy.

   D. Because the activities on non-critical paths depend upon the activities on the critical path.

7. You estimate the duration of an activity as five days because an expert told you that it took five days to complete a similar activity in a previous project. Which of the following methods have you used for your activity duration estimate?

   A. Parametric estimating

   B. Expert judgment

   C. Analogous estimating

   D. Delphi technique

8. You have developed the schedule for your project and you've called the kickoff meeting. A team member who is responsible for an activity comes to you and tells you that the activity cannot be performed within the allocated time because some pieces were left out during activity definition. The revised estimate will add two more days to the activity duration, but the activity is not on the critical path. Which of the following actions will you take?

   A. Go to the team member's functional manager and find out whether the team member's estimate is correct.

   B. Accept the new estimate but do not change the schedule.

   C. Accept the new estimate and update the schedule accordingly.

   D. Put the new estimate through the integrated change control process.

   E. Ask for the replacement of the team member who is adding two more days to the already scheduled activity.

   F. Accept the change after consulting with the project sponsor.

9. The amount of time by which an activity can be delayed without changing the project finish date is called:

   A. Float time

   B. Lag time

   C. Grace time

   D. Activity gradient

10. You are the project manager of a project that is running behind schedule. The project sponsor is very unhappy at the new finish date that you proposed, but he has accepted it. However, you also requested extra funds to support the extended time of work, and the sponsor has refused to supply more funds and is threatening to cancel the project if you cannot finish the project within the planned budget. What are your options?

    A. Crashing

    B. Fast tracking

    C. Asking the executive management for a new sponsor

    D. Speaking with the customer directly without involving the sponsor to see whether the customer can increase the budget

    E. Offering to complete some project activities yourself in your spare time

11. Consider the following network diagram. Which of the following is the critical path?

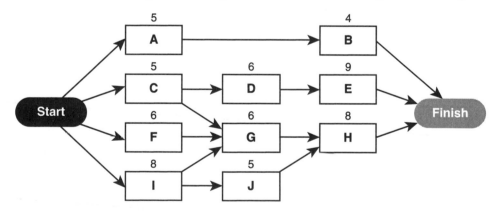

    A. Start-C-D-E-Finish

    B. Start-I-G-E-Finish

    C. Start-I-G-H-Finish

    D. Start-I-J-H-Finish

    E. Start-I-G-H-E-Finish

12. What is the float for activity G in the network diagram in question 11?

   A. 3

   B. 2

   C. 1

   D. 0

13. What is the length of the critical path in the network diagram shown in question 11?

   A. 20

   B. 21

   C. 22

   D. 31

   E. 9

14. You use a three-point estimate for activity duration estimating. An activity has a duration of nine days for an optimistic scenario, 18 days for a pessimistic scenario, and 12 days for the most likely scenario. Which of the following will you take as the duration estimate for this activity?

   A. 13 days

   B. 13.5 days

   C. 12 days

   D. 18 days

   E. 9 days

15. Which of the following is not an input item to the activity definition process?

   A. The WBS

   B. The activity duration

   C. The project scope statement

   D. The WBS dictionary

16. The management has asked you to produce a chart that depicts the resource needs for all the activities in the project. Which of the following charts is the management referring to?

   A. The project organizational chart

   B. The WBS

   C. The roles and responsibilities chart

   D. The responsibility assignment matrix

17. Which of the following is not an output of the human resource planning process?

    A. A project organizational chart

    B. Roles and responsibilities

    C. A project schedule

    D. A staff management plan

18. Which of the following is a true statement about the staff management plan?

    A. It is created by the human resources department.

    B. It is a tool for team development.

    C. It is created by the project management team as an output of the human resource planning process.

    D. It is provided by the project sponsor.

Chapter 6

Executing the Project

PMP Exam Objectives

Objective	*What It Really Means*
2.7 Conduct Kick-Off Meeting	You need to know how to conduct an effective kickoff meeting for a project. Understand that the main purpose of the kickoff meeting is to bring every team member onto the same page regarding the big picture of the project. You also must understand the project charter, project plan, and the organizational structure to run a successful kickoff meeting.
3.1 Execute Tasks Defined in the Project Plan	You must understand the direct and manage project execution process.
3.2 Ensure Common Understanding and Set Expectations 3.8 Improve Team Performance	You must understand that during the process of directing and managing the project execution, you need to manage the stakeholders' expectations and keep them on the same page. You must also understand how to improve team performance by using the develop project team process.
3.3 Implement the Procurement of Project Resources	You need to know how to implement the procurement plan by performing the request seller responses process and the select sellers process. Also understand the different types of contracts.

PMP Exam Objectives

Objective	*What It Really Means*
3.5 Implement a Quality Management Plan	You must understand how to implement the quality management plan to ensure that the project work is being performed in conformance with the planned quality standards. That involves understanding the perform quality assurance process.
3.6 Implement Approved Changes 3.7 Implement Approved Actions and Workarounds	You must understand that implementing approved changes and approved actions and recommendations is part of the project execution and must be managed by using the direct and manage project execution process. Also know that these changes and recommendations can originate from various sources, one of them being the processes in the monitoring and controlling process group, discussed in Chapter 7.

Introduction

After a project has been planned using the processes in the planning process group, it needs to be executed using the processes in the executing process group. The project team determines which of the processes in the executing process group is relevant to the project at hand. The goal of the execution stage is to complete the project work specified in the project management plan to meet the project requirements. To accomplish that, you will need to acquire, develop, and manage the project team. Your organization might not have the resources to finish certain parts of this work. You will need to use procurement for those parts of the work. You also need to ensure that all the planned quality activities are performed. This is accomplished by using the quality assurance process.

So the core question in this chapter is how to execute a project as planned. In search of an answer, you will explore three avenues—performing the project work by acquiring, developing, and managing the project team; implementing procurement; and performing quality assurance.

Executing a Project

The project work defined in the project management plan is executed by using the processes in the executing process group, shown in Figure 6.1. It is up to the project team to determine which of these processes is relevant for the project at hand. The processes in this group are used to accomplish the following:

- ◆ Coordinate people and resources
- ◆ Integrate and perform project activities
- ◆ Implement the project scope
- ◆ Implement the approved changes

The following list defines the processes shown in Figure 6.1:

- ◆ **Direct and manage project execution.** Process to manage various interfaces in the project to execute the project work smoothly.
- ◆ **Acquire the project team.** Process to obtain the project team members needed to perform the project work.
- ◆ **Develop the project team.** Process to improve the interaction among team members to enhance the project performance.

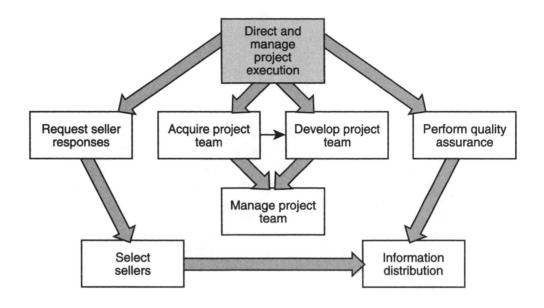

FIGURE 6.1 *The processes used in executing a project. All of these processes (except the manage project team process) belong to the executing process group.*

◆ **Manage the project team.** Process to manage the project team, which includes tracking the performance of team members, providing feedback, resolving issues, and coordinating changes to improve project performance.

◆ **Perform quality assurance.** Process to implement the planned quality activities so that the project meets all the requirements.

◆ **Distribute information.** Process to keep the project stakeholders informed about the project progress in a timely manner.

◆ **Request seller responses.** Process to obtain responses in terms of quotations, bids, offers, and proposals from sellers outside the project team for their products or services needed for the project.

◆ **Select seller responses.** Process to select sellers based on their responses and to negotiate written contracts with the selected sellers.

Once the project execution starts, it needs to be managed, which is accomplished using the direct and manage execution process.

Directing and Managing Project Execution

The project work defined in the project management plan is performed using the direct and manage process. While executing this process, you will be interacting with other processes and departments in your organization. In general, a project team includes people from different departments. Usually the reporting relationships within the same department are very well-defined and structured. However, the relationships between different departments (especially between individuals from different departments at the same level of authority) are not well-defined. So, managing such project interfaces is a crucial function of a project manager during project execution. Generally speaking, project interfaces are the formal and informal boundaries and relationships among team members, departments, organizations, or functions—for example, how the development department and the QA department interact with each other while working on the same project. Directing and managing project execution is the process used to manage various technical and organizational interfaces in the project to facilitate smooth execution of the project work.

The main purposes of directing and managing project execution are

◆ Producing the project deliverables by executing the project management plan
◆ Implementing the approved changes, defect repairs, and other actions
◆ Implementing the planned methods, processes, and standards
◆ Producing and distributing the status information

The key words during execution are *implement*, *manage*, and *inform* (status). Figure 6.2 shows the direct and manage project execution process with its input, tools and techniques, and output.

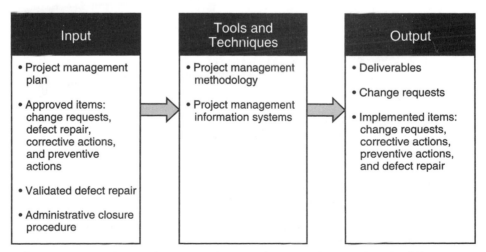

Input	Tools and Techniques	Output
• Project management plan • Approved items: change requests, defect repair, corrective actions, and preventive actions • Validated defect repair • Administrative closure procedure	• Project management methodology • Project management information systems	• Deliverables • Change requests • Implemented items: change requests, corrective actions, preventive actions, and defect repair

FIGURE 6.2 *The direct and manage project execution process: input, tools and techniques, and output*

Input to Directing and Managing Project Execution

The input to directing and managing project execution mainly consists of the items that need to be implemented. The information on the project work that needs to be performed to produce project deliverables is the major input to this process. The specific input items are discussed in the following list:

Project management plan. The project management plan contains all the major subsidiary plans, such as the project scope management plan, the schedule baseline, the cost baseline, and the quality baseline. It describes how the work will be executed to meet the project objectives and produce deliverables.

Approved items. The following approved items are input to the project execution because they must be implemented.

- ◆ **Change requests.** The approved requests for changes to the project schedule, scope, cost, policies, procedures, and project management plan need to be implemented, and therefore are the input to the execution process. These change requests are scheduled for execution by the project management team.

- ◆ **Defect repairs.** This is the list of the defects found during the quality assurance (QA) process that have been approved for repairs.

- ◆ **Corrective actions.** The QA process can recommend corrective actions to improve quality, which are directions for executing the project work to bring expected project performance into conformance with the project management plan. The approved corrective actions must be scheduled for implementation.

- ◆ **Preventive actions.** These are the directions to perform an activity that will reduce the probability of negative consequences associated with project risks. These preventive actions are recommended by the QA process during process analysis.

Validated defect repairs. This is a list with information on whether a previously performed defect repair has been accepted or rejected. This will tell you whether you need to implement the defect repair again.

Administrative closure procedure. This procedure describes how to properly close a cancelled or completed project. You might need to perform some work during the project execution (such as creating some documents to archive information) that is required for the closure procedure. Therefore, you must consult this procedure during the project execution.

There are mainly three kinds of items that need to be implemented and therefore are input to the direct and manage project execution process: the original deliverables, the approved changes, and defects. You direct and manage the execution by using some tools, which will be discussed in the next section.

Tools and Techniques for Directing and Managing Project Execution

Project execution includes the execution of the project management plan. Each organization might have a different method to execute the project management plan, called a *project management methodology*. Also, to manage the execution you might use a set of tools and techniques called the *project management information system*. So, project management methodology and the project management information system are the two main tools and techniques for the direct and manage project execution process.

Project management methodology. The project management plan contains the output of the project planning processes. This plan defines how the project is executed, monitored/controlled, and closed. But how do we implement (that is, execute) the project management plan? Every organization will have its own method to implement the project management plan for its projects, called a *project management methodology*. This is a high-level method on top of the project management processes. In other words, project management methodology defines a process that helps the project team in executing the project management plan.

Project management information system. This is a collection of tools and techniques—manual and automated—used to gather, integrate, and disseminate the output of project management processes. This system is used to facilitate processes from the initiation stage all the way to the closing stage. Microsoft Project, a product that lets you create a project schedule, is an example of such a tool.

The project is executed to produce some results, which will be the output of directing and managing the execution.

Output of Directing and Managing Project Execution

When the project is being executed, at each point in time there are some deliverables completed and there is a status for the project that can be reported to the stakeholders. These two important output items, along with others, are discussed in this section.

Deliverables. A deliverable is a unique and identifiable product, service, or result identified in the project management plan that must be executed to complete the project. The main purpose of executing the project management plan is to produce deliverables.

Change requests. During the execution of the project work, requests for changes in the following areas might arise:

◆ Project scope
◆ Project cost
◆ Project schedule
◆ Policies or procedures

These change requests might come from inside or outside the performing organization and can be optional or mandated legally or contractually. These change requests must be approved before they can be processed and implemented.

Implemented items. When you are directing and managing the project execution, obviously the items are being implemented. In addition to the work that produces original deliverables, the following items are implemented during project execution:

◆ Approved change requests

◆ Approved corrective actions recommended by the QA process

◆ Approved preventive actions recommended by the QA process

◆ Approved defect repairs recommended by the QA process

Work performance information. Monitoring the project status is one of the crucial functions of a project manager during project execution. Work performance information is basically the project status information that is regularly collected and distributed among the stakeholders. It includes the following items:

◆ The schedule progress information:

   ◆ Schedule activities that have been finished and those that have started

   ◆ Estimate to complete the schedule activities that have started and hence are in progress

   ◆ The portion of each in-progress activity completed in a percentage—for example, activity A is 30% complete

   ◆ Deliverables that have been completed and those that have not yet been completed

◆ Incurred costs compared to authorized costs

◆ Resource utilization details

◆ How well the quality standards are being met

◆ Lessons learned and added to the knowledge base

The main output of the direct and manage project execution process are the project deliverables specified in the project management plan. Between planning the project and producing the deliverables, many things need to happen, and you need processes for them too. Therefore, the direct and manage project execution process is a high-level process, and to execute it you need to perform some other processes too, which are discussed in this chapter. To start with, you need to put together a project team.

Acquiring a Project Team

The project work will be executed by the project team, and therefore the role of the team in the success of the project is crucial. Therefore, it is critical to acquire the right project team for your project. You accomplish this through the acquire project team process, shown in Figure 6.3. Roles and responsibilities for the roles required to complete the project are defined during

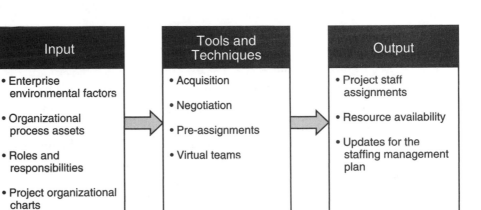

FIGURE 6.3 *The acquire project team process: input, tools and techniques, and output*

the human resource planning process, discussed in the previous chapter. Before the work can start, the roles need to be assigned to real individuals who will become the members of the project team. These individuals might comes from different departments, and the project management team might have no direct control over them. So, these team members need to be acquired through a process like the one shown in Figure 6.3.

The major input to the acquire team process comes from the human resource planning discussed in the previous chapter.

Input to Acquiring the Project Team

The human resource planning process generates the output that contains the staffing management plan, the project organizational chart, and the roles and responsibilities. These items are major inputs into the process of acquiring a project team. These and other input items are discussed in this section.

Enterprise environmental factors. The enterprise environmental factors are important in obtaining the project team members because the team members can come from various sources inside and outside the performing organization. For example, the team might include current employees of the performing organization and contractors hired for the project. Depending on your enterprise environment, you, the project manager (or the project management team), may or may not be able to direct or influence the hiring and staff assignments. In either case, you must try to obtain the best team you can. To determine who will be the best team, you need to do your homework, which includes finding out the availability and abilities of the candidate team members.

When you do have an influence on making the staff assignments, you should consider the following characteristics:

- ◆ **Availability.** It is important to know whether and when the candidate is available before you attempt to obtain that member.
- ◆ **Competency.** Does the candidate have the skills needed to complete the schedule activities?
- ◆ **Experience.** Has the candidate performed similar work well in the past?
- ◆ **Interests.** What is the candidate's interest level in this project and in the work that will be assigned to him or her?
- ◆ **Cost.** What is the cost attached to each candidate in terms of pay? This is even more important if the member is a contractor.

Based on this information, build your dream team on paper and attempt to obtain that team. If the team is spread out over different departments and hence the team members are under the control of different functional managers, plan who you will ask for from each functional manager. To make a request, meet with the manager and ask for your most wanted team member first, even though it is very unlikely that you will get everyone you ask for. Before meeting the functional managers, you need to prioritize your staffing needs. The most complex activities and the activities on the critical paths should get special attention, and you should make sure these activities have the best members because they have the highest risk potential. Having assigned staff to these activities first, you have more flexibility to agree to a different resource assigned to activities that are less complex and have a non-zero float time. Even though you want to negotiate for the best team, keep a backup plan—that is, if you don't get the best member, try to get the second best member, and so on.

> **NOTE**
>
> In a traditional organizational structure, you will not have direct control over the project team members, and you will need to acquire them by negotiating with the functional managers. But you still need to do the homework that you would do if you were to interview the candidates because you still want to get the best members available for the job.

Organizational process assets. In the process of acquiring the project team, you should consider the following organizational process assets:

- ◆ Guidelines, policies, or procedures governing staff assignments that your organization may have
- ◆ Help from the human resources department in recruitment of and orientation for the team members

Roles and responsibilities. Roles with specific responsibilities are defined in the human resource planning process based on the project work that needs to be performed. These roles will be the guide to finding suitable candidates for the project team, because the team members will play these roles.

Project organizational chart. This chart gives you a quick overview of the number of team members needed and their relationships to each other.

Staffing management plan. A staffing management plan is an important input item to acquiring the project team because it provides detailed information about the roles that need to be filled, such as the start and finish dates for a role. This information is necessary to match the candidates with the roles.

> **TIP**
>
> In the worst case scenario, you will not be able to negotiate for staff and you will have no influence on the staff assignments. Unless a team member is not qualified to do the job, you will have to live with the staff assignment decision and make the best of it. If you choose to challenge one of these assignments, make sure you are doing this based on hard facts, such as the lack of skills required to perform the assigned activity.

To put together the best team, you need to understand the tools and techniques available for acquiring the team.

Tools and Techniques for Acquiring the Project Team

You will either negotiate with the functional manager for a team member to fill a role, or you will acquire the team member from outside your organization, such as a contractor. Negotiation and acquisition are discussed in this section, along with other tools and techniques.

Acquisition. If the performing organization does not have the human resources to fill one or more roles needed to finish the project, the required team member can be obtained from outside the organization as a contractor, or the corresponding work can be given to the source outside the performing organization. We will talk more about this area of procurement management later in this chapter.

Negotiation. You will most likely need to negotiate with functional managers for the staff assignments for your project. In these negotiations, you have a two-prong goal—to obtain the best available person for an activity and to obtain the person for the required timeframe. As described in the previous section, you must do your homework in order to get the best results from the negotiations.

> ### ◢ TIP
>
> While negotiating with a functional manager, sometimes it's important to understand the functional manager's perspective in light of the politics of the organization. For example, a functional manager will weigh the benefits (for example, visibility of your project compared to that of competing projects) in determining where to assign the best performers. In this case, it is to your advantage to explain the importance of your project and the activity for which you are asking for the best performer.

Pre-assignment. In some cases, there will be some staff members already assigned to the project. This can happen, for example, due to the following situations:

◆ A staff member was promised as part of a specific proposal to compete with another proposal. Acceptance of this proposal automatically affirms that staff-member assignment.

◆ There is only one person in the organization who has the expertise to perform a specific activity.

◆ A staff assignment was specified in the project charter.

Virtual teams. Welcome to the information age triggered by the Internet. The process of working for an organization from outside its physical location is called *telecommuting*. The Internet (along with other technological advances, such as teleconferencing, cellular phones, and pagers) makes it possible to telecommute from your home in the same city where the organization is or from a location on the other side of the globe with almost the same ease. Teams composed of telecommuters are called *virtual teams* because the team works together on the same project without holding face-to-face meetings. It is not difficult to find people who have worked on virtual teams and have never seen the other team members face to face. I have worked on several such teams, and I'm sure you either have or you will in the near future. The virtual team format expands the team definition to offer the following benefits:

◆ People working for the same organization but living in different locations can join the same team.

◆ A needed expert can join a team even if the expert does not live in the same location as the rest of the team.

◆ The organization has the option to accommodate employees who can only work from their home offices for a certain period of time.

◆ Due to the availability of asynchronous communication means, such as e-mail and online bulletin boards, it is possible to form a team of members who have different work hours or shifts.

◆ Virtual teams eliminate or reduce the need to travel by using means of communication that are abundantly available, such as e-mail, video conferencing, and the World Wide Web. This enables organizations to perform projects that were previously impossible due to the anticipated travel expenses.

Note that because the virtual team members are not at the same location and do not have regular face-to-face meetings, the effective communication is that much more important for the success of the project being performed by the virtual team. Therefore, communication management is crucial to the success of virtual teams.

The team you are going to acquire could be a team at one location or a virtual team, and a team member might be from your organization or from outside your organization. Whatever the case may be, the team itself is the major output of the acquire team process—no surprise there.

Output of Acquiring the Project Team

The major output of the acquire project team process are the staff assignments to fill the roles defined during human resource planning and the list of time periods for which the staff members will be available. These and other output items are discussed in the following list.

◆ **Project staff assignments.** This document contains the list of individuals assigned to the project. It can also include the memos sent to the team members, the project organization chart, and the schedule with the names inserted.

◆ **Resource availability.** This document includes the time periods for which each assigned member can work on the project. Possible schedule conflicts, commitments to other projects, and times when a team member is not available can also be recorded.

◆ **Updates to the staffing management plan.** The project team is acquired by matching the staffing requirements specified in the staffing management plan to the candidates. Hardly ever is there a perfect match between the two. During the process of acquiring the project team, you might realize that the staffing management plan needs to be updated. The other updates to the staffing management plan might come from the following sources:

  ◆ Promotions
  ◆ Retirements
  ◆ Illnesses
  ◆ Performance issues
  ◆ Changing workloads

After the staff assignments have been made, you have the raw material out of which you need to develop the special team for your project.

Developing the Project Team

Your project team can consist of members from different departments and disciplines, regular employees and contractors, and experts from different disciplines. Some of these individuals might not have much appreciation for others' disciplines. You have a challenge to develop this diverse group into a cohesive and efficient team that will perform the project on time, within budget, and with quality. There are two major goals for team development:

◆ Improve the competencies of team members

◆ Improve the interaction among team members

This will help you develop a cohesive and competent team to meet the project objectives effectively.

As Figure 6.4 shows, the output of the acquire project team process is the input to the develop project team process. The team development starts with a list of team members and the staff assignments made during the acquire project team process. The resource availability list provides information about when the team members are available for the team development activities. The following items of the staff management plan can be useful for team development:

◆ Training strategies

◆ Plans for developing the project team

◆ Recognition and rewards systems

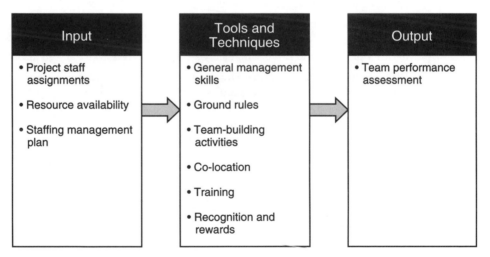

FIGURE 6.4 *The develop project team process: input, tools and techniques, and output*

As discussed in the following list, there are some standard tools and techniques that you can use to develop a winning team.

General management skills. You and the project management team can minimize problems and maximize cooperation by understanding the sentiments of each team member, anticipating their actions, acknowledging their concerns, and following up on their issues. To accomplish this, the following interpersonal management skills are necessary:

◆ **Effective communication.** This is needed to facilitate the smooth flow of necessary information among the team members.

◆ **Ability to influence the organization.** This is needed to get things done.

◆ **Leadership.** This is needed for developing a vision and strategy and for motivating people to achieve that vision. During the time of possible uncertainty, such as changes in upper management, you should clarify the situation and help the team stay focused on the project.

◆ **Motivation.** This is needed for energizing team members to achieve high levels of performance and to overcome barriers to change. During the times when the team is in a low-morale mode, you should be able to lift the team morale and thereby contribute to team development.

◆ **Negotiation and conflict management.** This is needed to work with the team members to resolve their conflicts and facilitate negotiations when necessary in resolving conflicts or in task assignments. Depending on the nature of the conflict, you can take it as a team development opportunity. An effective resolution of a conflict contributes to team building.

◆ **Problem solving.** This ability is needed to define, analyze, and solve problems.

Team management is further discussed later in this chapter.

Ground rules. A very important management technique is to establish clear expectations at the very beginning of a project. The expectations can be established by establishing a set of ground rules. Early commitment to these guidelines will increase cooperation and productivity by decreasing misunderstandings.

Team-building activities. Team-building activities can range from indirect team-building activities, such as participating in constructing the WBS, to direct team-building activities, such as social gatherings where the team members can get to know each other and start feeling comfortable with each other. While planning such activities, you should keep in mind that the team members might have different interests and different levels of tolerance for games and different icebreakers.

The project kickoff meeting is another indirect method to start team development. This can be used as a formal way to introduce team members and other stakeholders and spell out the project goals for everyone at the same time. An ideal kickoff meeting is a combination of serious business and fun. The goal is to align the team with the project goals and to help the team members feel comfortable with each other.

In planning the kickoff meeting, you can assume that team members have the following questions in their heads that need to be answered before the end of the meeting:

◆ Why am I here?

◆ Who are you and what are your expectations of me?

◆ What is this team going to do?

◆ How is the team going to do its work?

◆ How do I fit into all this?

Consider the following steps to make your kickoff meeting successful:

◆ **Agenda.** Putting the meeting agenda in the hands of the team members always helps to run the meeting more smoothly and effectively and keep it on track.

◆ **Welcome.** Take immediate charge of the meeting by introducing yourself and welcoming the participants. Quickly walk through the agenda and set the stage for the rest of the meeting.

◆ **Project overview.** Define the project, its goals, and its deliverables. Introduce the project team members and briefly describe their roles. The goal is to provide a big picture and to help individual team members figure out how they fit into the big picture.

◆ **Expectations.** Many of the project team members might not already know you and your management style. You should take this opportunity to set expectations about how the team will function. For example, state that you expect all team members to attend the weekly status meetings. Remind the team to focus on the project goal, to do their part, and to look out for one another in a team spirit.

◆ **Guest speakers.** Depending upon the size and the visibility of the project, you might also invite relevant guest speakers, such as the project sponsor, the customer, or an executive stakeholder. Before the meeting, spend some time communicating with the guest speaker about the message to deliver.

◆ **Closure.** Ask for feedback and hold the question-and-answer session before closing the meeting.

Remember that the main purpose of the kickoff meeting is to bring every team member onto the same page regarding the big picture of the project. Don't get bogged down discussing every item in detail.

You should know that team development is not an instant process. Generally speaking, when you form a team it goes through five stages of development (according to the Tuckman model), as shown in Figure 6.5 and explained in the following list.

◆ **Forming.** This is the orientation stage, with high dependence on the leader (the project manager, in this case) for guidance and direction. Individual roles and responsibilities are unclear, and there is little agreement on the team goals other than those received from the leader. Processes are often ignored, and the team members test the tolerance of the system and the leader. It's time to establish the ground rules and clear expectations. The leader directs in this stage.

◆ **Storming.** This stage represents the struggle for control and power as team members work to establish themselves relative to other team members. The clarity of team goals increases, but some uncertainties persist. Compromises might be required to make progress. Coaching and training can play effective roles during this stage.

◆ **Norming.** This is the routine stage during which the consensus and agreement about team goals generally prevails among the team members. Roles and responsibilities are clear and accepted by the team members. Major decisions are made by group agreements, and smaller decisions can be delegated to the appropriate team members. During this stage, the leader facilitates.

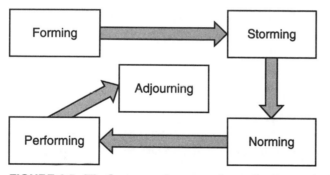

FIGURE 6.5 *The five progressive stages of team development in the Tuckman model*

◆ **Performing.** This is the productivity stage in which the team knows what it's doing and why. The team is functioning in a cohesive mode and working toward the common goal in a more autonomous fashion. Disagreements might arise, but they are resolved within the team in a constructive way. During this stage, the leader delegates and oversees.

◆ **Adjourning.** This is the closure stage. When the mission for which the team was formed is accomplished (or cancelled), the team is adjourned to free the team members to move on to other things.

Being aware of these stages of team development will help you to better understand the behaviors of the team members and thereby develop your team more effectively.

Training. The goal of training is to improve the competencies of the project team members, which in turn helps in meeting the project objectives. It might be aimed at the individual members or at the team as a whole, depending upon the needs. The training might be scheduled in the staff management plan or it might result from the observations, conversations, and project performance appraisals as the project progresses. Following are examples of some training methods:

◆ Coaching
◆ Mentoring
◆ On-the-job training of a team member by another team member
◆ Online training
◆ Instructor-led classroom training

Co-location. This technique keeps all (or most) of the project team members in the same physical location to improve communication and to create a sense of community among the team members. In this age of virtual teams, this is not an increasingly popular technique, but when most of the team members are in the same location, this technique is a default choice. It can include a war room, which is a meeting room used for regular face-to-face meetings.

Recognition and rewards. The recognition and rewards strategy set up during the human resource planning process can be used to develop the project team. Remember the following rules in setting up a fair reward system:

- ◆ Only desirable behavior should be rewarded.
- ◆ Any member should be able to win the reward.
- ◆ Win-lose rewards, such as team member of the month, can hurt the team cohesiveness.
- ◆ The cultural diversity of the team should be considered and respected.

The effects of the team development efforts are measured by the team performance assessment, which includes the following indicators:

- ◆ Improvement in individual skills that enables a team member to perform project activities more efficiently
- ◆ Improvement in team skills that help the team to improve overall performance and work more effectively as a group
- ◆ Reduced staff turnover rate

The project team needs to be managed throughout the project. Managing the team is part of controlling the project, a topic discussed in the next chapter. However, I will discuss managing the team in this chapter for sake of flow.

Managing the Project Team

You manage the project team by using the manage project team process, which is aimed at improving the project performance by executing the following tasks:

- ◆ Resolving issues
- ◆ Coordinating changes
- ◆ Tracking the performance of each team member
- ◆ Providing feedback to the team members

Figure 6.6 depicts the manage project team process.

NOTE

The manage project team process belongs to the monitoring and controlling process group, whereas all other processes discussed in this chapter belong to the executing process group.

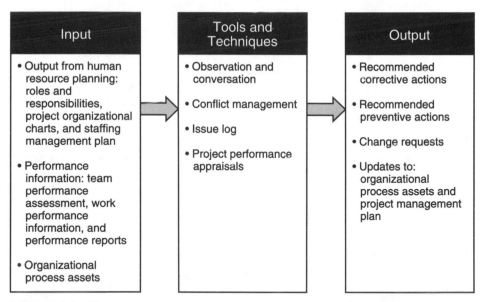

Input	Tools and Techniques	Output
• Output from human resource planning: roles and responsibilities, project organizational charts, and staffing management plan • Performance information: team performance assessment, work performance information, and performance reports • Organizational process assets	• Observation and conversation • Conflict management • Issue log • Project performance appraisals	• Recommended corrective actions • Recommended preventive actions • Change requests • Updates to: organizational process assets and project management plan

FIGURE 6.6 *The manage project team process: input, tools and techniques, and output*

Input to Managing the Project Team

The main input to managing the project team comes from the output of the human resource planning, acquire project team, and develop project team processes.

Output from human resource planning. The following output items from the human resource planning process are the input to the manage project team process:

◆ **Roles and responsibilities.** Used to monitor and evaluate performance.

◆ **Project organizational charts.** Used to find out the reporting relationships among project team members.

◆ **Staffing management plan.** Contains information such as training plans, compliance issues, and certification requirements, along with the time periods when the team members are expected to work.

Performance information. The following items regarding performance are the input to the manage project team process:

◆ **Team performance assessment.** This is the output of the develop project team process discussed earlier in this chapter.

◆ **Performance reports.** Performance reports contain the progress of the project against the baseline data, such as the schedule baseline, the cost baseline, and the quality baseline. They basically reflect how the project resources are being used to achieve the project objectives. The information from the performance reports helps determine future human resource requirements, updates to the staffing management plan, and recognitions and rewards.

◆ **Work performance information.** This is an output item from the direct and manage project execution process discussed earlier in this chapter. It involves observing the performance of each team member, which includes participating in meetings, following up on action items, effectively performing the assigned activities, and communicating clearly.

Organizational process assets. The project management team can use the following organization assets in managing the project team:

◆ The organization's policies, procedures, and system for rewarding the team members

◆ Other items that should be available to the project management team for use in managing the team, such as organizational recognition dinners, certificates of appreciation, bulletin boards, newsletters, and internal Web sites for information sharing

To manage the team effectively, you should be aware of the tools and techniques that can be used for that.

Tools and Techniques for Managing the Project Team

The tools and techniques used in managing the team include observation and conversation, conflict management, an issue log, and project performance appraisals.

Observation and conversation. Observations and conversations are both means to stay in touch with the work and attitudes of the project team members. The indicators to monitor these include the following:

◆ Progress toward completion of assigned activities and therefore project deliverables

◆ Distinguished accomplishments contributing to the project performance

◆ Interpersonal issues

Conflict management. The purpose of conflict management is to nourish the positive working relationships among the team members that result in increased productivity. The common sources for conflicts include the following:

◆ Scarce resources resulting in unsatisfied needs

◆ Scheduling priorities

◆ Personal work styles

◆ Perceptions, values, feelings, and emotions

◆ Power struggles

You can reduce the number of conflicts by setting ground rules, clearly defining roles and goals, and implementing solid project management practices.

> **▲ TIP**
>
> Differences of opinions should not be considered as sources of conflict. If managed properly, differences can be very healthy and can lead to better solutions and thereby increase productivity.

Initially, the project team members who are parties to a conflict should be given the opportunity to resolve it themselves. If the team members fail to resolve the conflict and it becomes a negative factor for the project, you, the project manager, should facilitate the conflict resolution, usually in private and using a direct and collaborative approach. If the conflict continues, you might have no option other than to use formal procedures, such as disciplinary actions.

The first step in conflict management is analyzing the nature and type of conflict, which might involve asking questions. You can meet with (interview) the parties involved in the conflict. The next step is to determine the management strategy. Different management strategies are summarized here:

◆ **Avoidance.** In this strategy, at least one party to the conflict ignores (or withdraws) from the conflict and decides not to deal with the problem. This strategy can be used by the project manager as a cooling-off period, to collect more information, or when the issue is not critical. However, if the issue is critical, this is the worst resolution strategy and can give rise to lose/lose situations if both parties withdraw or yield/lose situations if one party withdraws. This strategy is also called *withdrawal strategy*.

◆ **Competition.** In this approach, one party uses any available means to get its way, often at the expense of the other party. This is a win/lose situation. It can be justified under some situations, such as when the basic rights of a party in conflict are at stake or when you want to set a precedent. However, if used unfairly from a power position (such as if it is a management style), it can be destructive for team development. This strategy can cause the conflict to escalate, and the losing party might attempt to retaliate. When used by a party in power, competition is also called *forcing*.

◆ **Compromising.** In this strategy, both parties gain something and give up something. This is a lose-win/lose-win strategy. You can use this strategy to achieve temporary solutions and to avoid a damaging power struggle when there is a time pressure. The downside of this approach is that both parties can look at the solution as a lose/lose situation and can be distracted from the merits of the issues involved. In this way, this short-term solution can hurt the long-term objectives of the project.

◆ **Accommodation.** This strategy is opposite of the competition strategy. One party attempts to meet other party's needs at the expense of their own. This might be a justifiable strategy when the concerns of the accommodating party are less significant than the concerns of the other party in the context of the project. Sometimes it's used as a goodwill gesture. However, it is a lose/win approach (the accommodating party loses and the accommodated party wins), and the accommodating party runs the risk of losing credibility and influence in the future.

◆ **Collaboration.** This strategy is based on reaching consensus among the parties in the conflict. Both parties work together to explore several solutions and agree on the one that satisfies the needs and concerns of both parties. This is a win/win strategy and is generally considered the best of all the strategies because it helps build commitment and promotes goodwill between the parties involved.

TIP

You should always look for how the different processes overlap and interact with each other. For example, conflict management is a technique for managing the team. However, the purpose of conflict management is to nourish the positive working relationships among the team members that result in increased productivity, so resolving a conflict can also be looked upon as a team development activity.

Issue log. Issues generally involve obstacles that can stop the project team from achieving the project objectives. A written log should be maintained that contains the list of team members responsible for resolving the issues by target dates. The purpose of the issue log is to monitor the issues until they are closed.

Project performance appraisals. Conducting project performance appraisals includes evaluating the performance of the project team members and providing them with feedback based on the evaluation. The evaluation is based on information collected from several people interacting with the team member. This method of collecting information is called the *360-degree feedback principle* because the information comes from several sources.

The objectives for conducting performance appraisals include the following:

◆ Providing positive feedback to team members in a possibly hectic environment

◆ Clarifying roles and responsibilities

◆ Discovering new issues and reminding of unresolved issues

◆ Discovering the needs of individual training plans

◆ Setting specific goals for the future

While you are managing the team using these techniques, you might recommend some actions as an output of the manage project team process.

> ◢ **TIP**
>
> You might find that the project managers in your organization are not responsible for performance appraisals. The need for formal or informal performance appraisals depends on the organization's policy, the contract requirements, and the size and complexity of the project.

Output of Managing the Project Team

The output from managing the project team includes recommended corrective and preventive actions, change requests, and updates to organization process assets and the project management plan.

Recommended actions. The manage project team process might generate recommendations for corrective and preventive actions, as discussed here:

- ◆ **Recommended corrective actions.** A corrective action is a direction for executing the project work to bring the future performance in line with what is expected in the project management plan. The corrective actions recommended during project team management might include the following:
    - ◆ Staffing changes, such as changing assignments of the team members, replacing team members (for example, the ones who leave), and outsourcing some work
    - ◆ Training for the team or for individual team members
    - ◆ Recognition and rewards based on the reward system
    - ◆ Disciplinary actions
- ◆ **Recommended preventive actions.** A preventive action is a direction to perform an activity to stop or reduce the probability of an anticipated event occurrence generally associated with a project risk. Preventive action can also be taken to reduce the anticipated impact of an event in case it happens. The preventive actions recommended during project team management might include the following:
    - ◆ Cross-training so that in the absence of a team member, another team member can take over the assignment
    - ◆ Role clarifications to ensure that all the responsibilities associated with the role are performed
    - ◆ Planning for overtime in anticipation of extra work that might be needed to meet project deadlines

Change requests and updates. Managing the project team can generate the change requests and updates discussed here:

◆ **Change requests.** The team management activities can generate some change requests for the project management plan. For example, staffing changes can generate requests for extending the schedule, increasing the budget, or reducing the scope. The change requests should be processed through the integrated change control system.

◆ **Updates to organizational process assets.** Two kinds of organizational process assets can be updated as a result of project team management:

◆ **Performance appraisals.** The project staff member that interacts with a project team member in a significant way can offer input to the performance appraisal for that team member.

◆ **Lessons-learned database.** The lessons-learned database should be updated with the lessons learned during team management, which can come from different areas that include the following:

◆ Issues and solutions in the issue log

◆ Special skills and competencies discovered during the project work for the team members

◆ Successful and unsuccessful ground rules, conflict management techniques, and recognition events

◆ **Updates to the project management plan.** Approved change requests and corrective actions can result in updates to the staffing management plan, which is a part of the project management plan. New role assignments, training plans, and reward decisions are some examples of updates.

In addition to performing the project work to produce the project deliverables, a significant task to perform during project execution is quality assurance.

TIP

Managing the project team is a complex task when the team members are accountable to both the project managers and the functional managers—for example, in a matrix organization. Effectively managing this dual relationship is critical to the success of the project and is therefore generally the responsibility of the project manager.

Performing Quality Assurance

Quality planning, discussed in Chapter 4, is used to identify which quality standards are relevant to the project at hand and to determine how to meet these standards. Implementing quality management consists of the following two components:

◆ **Quality assurance (QA).** Quality assurance is the application of the planned systematic quality activities. The perform quality assurance process is used for applying the planned systematic quality activities to ensure that the project employs all the planned processes needed to meet all the project requirements. This process is used during the execution of the project, and I discuss it in this section.

◆ **Quality control.** This refers to monitoring the project results to ensure they meet the agreed-upon quality standards. This topic is covered in the next chapter.

Performing organizations typically have a department called quality assurance (QA) that oversees the quality assurance activities and fosters continuous process improvement, which is an iterative method for improving the quality of all processes.

Figure 6.7 depicts the perform quality assurance process.

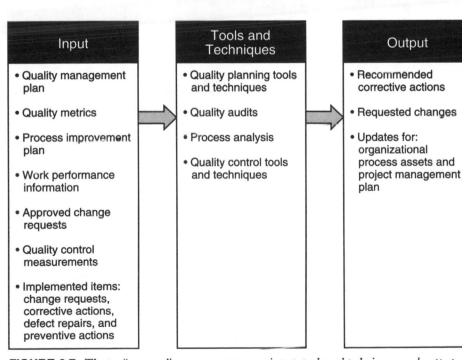

FIGURE 6.7 *The perform quality assurance process: input, tools and techniques, and output*

> **TIP**
>
> Continuous process improvement enhances the efficiency and effectiveness of the processes by minimizing waste (unnecessary activities) and duplication of efforts. It includes identifying and reviewing the business processes inside the organization, such as coding of modules within software programs and the process of project approval.

Input to Performing Quality Assurance

The input to the quality assurance process comes largely from three sources: quality planning, direct and manage project execution, and quality control. The quality-related output items of these three processes become the input to the quality assurance process. These input items are discussed here.

Output from quality planning. The following output items from the quality planning process become the input into the quality assurance process:

◆ **Quality management plan.** This plan is the output of the quality planning process discussed in Chapter 4, and it describes how QA will be performed for this project.

◆ **Quality metrics.** A quality metric is an operational criterion that defines in specific terms what something (such as a characteristic or a feature) is and how the quality control process measures it. The quality metrics developed during quality planning, such as defect density, failure rates, reliability, and test coverage, must be employed during QA.

◆ **Process improvement plan.** The process improvement plan, discussed in Chapter 4, helps improve the quality of the project and must be implemented during QA.

Output from directing and managing project execution. When you are directing and managing the project execution, information about the work performance and the implementation of a few items will help you determine how the quality is being implemented. Therefore, during QA, you must consider the work performance information and a specific set of implemented items discussed here:

◆ **Work performance information.** Monitoring the project status is one of the crucial functions of a project manager during project execution. Work performance information is basically the project status information that is regularly collected and distributed among the stakeholders. It includes the following items:

　◆ Schedule progress information:

　　◆ Schedule activities that have been finished and those that have started

　　◆ Estimates for the completion of the schedule activities that have started and hence are in progress

- ◆ Percentages to show the portion of each in-progress activity—for example, activity A is 30% complete
- ◆ Deliverables that have been completed and those that have not yet been completed
- ◆ Incurred cost as compared to authorized cost
- ◆ Resource utilization details
- ◆ How well the quality standards are being met
- ◆ Lessons learned added to the knowledge base
- ◆ **Implemented items.** When you are directing and managing the project execution, obviously the items are being implemented. The following quality-related implemented items must be considered during QA:
  - ◆ Implemented change requests
  - ◆ Implemented corrective actions
  - ◆ Implemented defect repair
  - ◆ Implemented preventive actions

Quality control measurements. Quality control involves monitoring specific project results to verify whether they meet quality standards. The quality control process sends its results back to QA as feedback.

Approved change requests. Approved change requests, such as modification of work methods, product requirements, quality requirements, scope, and schedule, must be analyzed for their effect on the quality management plan and quality metrics.

Some tools and techniques can be used to facilitate the QA process.

TIP

All approved changes should be formally documented. Unapproved and undocumented changes (for example, changes just verbally discussed) must neither be processed nor be implemented.

Tools and Techniques for Performing Quality Assurance

Quality audits and process analysis along with the tools and techniques used in quality planning and quality control processes can be used in the QA process.

Quality audits. A quality audit is a structured and independent review to determine whether project activities comply with the policies, processes, and procedures of the project and the performing organization. It verifies the implementation of approved change requests, corrective actions, defect repairs, and preventive actions. The audits can occur as scheduled or at random, and can be conducted by a third party or by the properly trained in-house auditors of the performing organization. These audits accomplish the following:

◆ Because one of the objectives of a quality audit is to identify inefficient and ineffective policies, processes, and procedures being used for the project, audits reduce the cost of quality on the subsequent projects.

◆ Audits increase customer satisfaction and acceptance of the product or service delivered by the project.

Process analysis. This is a technique used to identify the needed improvements in a process by following the steps outlined in the process improvement plan. It examines the problems, constraints, and unnecessary (non-value-added) activities identified during the implementation of the process. Process analysis typically includes the following steps:

1. Identify a technique to analyze the problem.
2. Identify the underlying causes that led to the problem.
3. Examine the root cause of the problem.
4. Create preventive actions for this and similar problems.

Other tools and techniques. The tools and techniques used in the following processes can also be used in the QA process:

◆ Quality planning, already discussed in Chapter 4
◆ Quality control, discussed in the next chapter

The quality assurance process recommends corrective actions as an output item.

Output of Performing Quality Assurance

The main output of performing quality assurance includes recommended corrective actions and change requests. These and other output items are discussed in this section.

Recommended corrective actions. This is an important output of the QA process. Implementation of recommended corrective actions will increase the effectiveness and efficiency of the policies, processes, and procedures of the performing organization, and will also improve the quality of the product or service delivered by the project. Following are examples of the types of recommended actions:

◆ Audits
◆ Process analysis that itself might produce a list of preventive actions
◆ Defect repair, such as bug fixes in a software program

Requested changes. The goal of quality assurance is improving quality, which involves taking actions to increase the effectiveness and efficiency of the policies, procedures, and processes of the performing organization. One way of accomplishing this is to implement the quality-related changes recommended and approved during the process of directing and managing the project execution, including:

◆ Modifications to policies and procedures

◆ Modifications to project scope, cost, and schedule

Updates. As a result of the QA process, you might need to add updates to the following:

◆ **Organizational process assets.** The quality standards, policies, procedures, and processes of the performing organization are the organization assets that can be updated during the QA process.

◆ **Project management plan.** The quality assurance process can result in updates to the project management plan in the following ways:

   ◆ Changes to the quality management plan, which is a part of the project management plan

   ◆ Changes to the quality assurance processes

In some projects you might not find the resources in your organization to complete certain parts of the project. This is where the concept called *procurement* comes into the picture.

Procurement of Project Resources

Procurement refers to obtaining (purchasing or renting) products, services, or results from outside the project team to complete the project. Procurement management is an execution of a set of processes used to obtain (procure) the products, services, or results from outside the project team to complete the project. There are two main roles involved in procurement management:

◆ **Buyer.** The party purchasing (procuring) the product or service.

◆ **Seller.** The party delivering the product or service to the buyer.

Procurement management includes the following processes:

◆ **Plan purchases and acquisitions.** This is the process used to determine what needs to be obtained and when and how it will be obtained.

◆ **Plan contracting.** This is the process used to determine and document the requirements for the products, services, or results to be obtained and to identify the potential sellers.

◆ **Request seller responses.** This is the process used to solicit information, quotations, bids, offers, or proposals from potential sellers.

◆ **Select sellers.** This is the process of selecting sellers by reviewing offers, choosing from the candidate sellers, and negotiating a written contract with the sellers.

◆ **Contract administration.** This is the process used to manage the contract and the relationship between the buyer and the seller by monitoring the seller's performance.

◆ **Contract closure.** This is the process used to complete a contract by resolving an open issue.

Planning for Procurement

The plan purchases and acquisitions and plan contracting processes are used to plan the procurement, whereas the request seller responses and select seller processes are used to implement the procurement. Although the procurement planning should be done early in the project, like any other planning, it might be necessary at any stage of the project as the need arises due to approved changes or other circumstances.

Make or Buy Decision

Obviously, procurement refers to buying something as compared to making it in-house. The decision to buy or make can be based on one or more of the reasons listed in Table 6.1. Buy can mean to purchase or rent. The decision to purchase or rent should be based on the effective cost in the long term. For example, if it is a piece of hardware that will be used only in this project, you do not anticipate its use in any future project, and renting is significantly cheaper than buying, you should probably rent it. You might decide to buy it if this hardware is of common use in the kind of work your organization does and therefore it will be used in other projects as well.

Table 6.1 Reasons to Make or Buy

Factor	Reasons to Make In-House	Reasons to Buy
Cost	Less cost.	Less cost.
Skills availability	Use in-house skills.	In-house skills don't exist or are not available.
Skills acquisition	Learn new skills that will be used even after this project.	These skills are not important to the organization.
Risks	Deal with the risk in-house.	Transfer the risk.
Work	Core project work.	Not core project work.
Human resource availability	Staff available.	Vendor available.

NOTE

An output of the procurement planning process is the statement of work (SOW), which is a document summarizing the work to be performed. The SOW can be written by the buyer or the seller to specify what products will be delivered or what services will be performed. It is also called the *contract statement of work*.

Before you can buy, you need to get information from the sellers. In other words, you need to request seller responses. Make or buy analysis is a technique used in the plan purchases and acquisitions process. Also in this process, you need to use a technique to determine the type of contract you will use for the procurement.

Determining Contract Types

A contract is a mutually binding agreement between a buyer and a seller that obligates the seller to provide the specified product, service, or result and obligates the buyer to make the payment for it. Contracts generally fall into the three categories discussed in this list.

Fixed-price (lump-sum) contracts. A fixed-price contract, also called a *lump-sum contract* or a *firm fixed-price contract*, is an agreement that specifies the fixed total price for the product, service, or result to be procured. An example of a fixed-price contract is a purchase order for the specified item to be delivered by a specified date for a specified price. This category of contracts is generally used for products and services that are well-defined and have good historical information. A fixed-price contract for a poorly defined product or a service with very little historical record is a source of high risk for both the seller and the buyer.

Cost-reimbursable contracts. A contract in this category includes two kinds of costs:

◆ **Actual cost.** This is the payment (reimbursement) to the seller for the actual cost of the item, which includes the direct cost and the indirect cost (overhead). An actual cost, such as the salary of the project staff working on the item, is incurred directly from the work on the item, whereas an indirect cost, such as the cost of utilities and equipment for the office of the staff member, is the cost of doing business. Indirect cost is generally calculated as a percentage of the actual cost. The actual cost is also called the *project cost*. The project here refers to the project of the seller to produce the items for the buyer.

◆ **Fee.** This typically represents the seller's profit.

As discussed in the following list, there are three types of cost-reimbursable contracts:

◆ **Cost plus fee (CPF) or cost plus percentage of cost (CPPC).** The payment to the seller includes the actual cost and the fee, which is a percentage of the actual cost. Note that the fee is not fixed; it varies with the actual cost.

◆ **Cost plus fixed fee (CPFF).** The payment to the seller includes the actual cost and a fixed fee, which can be calculated as a percentage of the estimated project cost. Note that the fee is fixed and does not vary with the actual project cost.

◆ **Cost plus incentive fee (CPIF).** The payment to the seller includes the actual cost and a predetermined incentive bonus based on achieving certain objectives.

> **NOTE**
>
> Both fixed-price contracts and cost-reimbursable contracts can optionally include incentives—for example, a bonus from the buyer to the seller if the seller meets certain target schedule dates or exceeds some other predetermined expectations.

Because cost overrun can occur in any type of cost-reimbursable contract, and the cost overrun will be paid by the buyer, this category of contract poses risk to the buyer.

Time and material (T&M) contracts. This category of contracts is a hybrid that contains some aspects from both the fixed-price category and the cost-reimbursable category. The contracts in this category resemble the contracts in the cost-reimbursable category because the total cost and the exact quantity of the items is not fixed at the time of the agreement. The contracts resemble fixed-price contracts because the unit rates can be fixed in the contract. These types of contracts are useful when you do not know the quantity of the procured items. For example, you do not know how much time a contract programmer will take to develop a software program, so you determine the hourly rate in the contract, but not the total cost for writing the program. In this category of contracts, the risk is high for the buyer because the buyer agreed to pay for all the time the seller takes to produce the deliverables.

Table 6.2 lists different types of contracts and the corresponding risk bearers.

Table 6.2 Risk Bearers in Different Categories of Contracts

Contract Type	Risk Bearer	Explanation
Fixed price	Buyer and seller	The cost overrun is borne by the seller, whereas the price fixed higher than the actual cost hurts the buyer.
Time and material	Buyer	The increased cost due to the increased quantity of resources, such as work hours by a contractor, is borne by the buyer.
Cost plus fixed fee	Buyer	Cost overrun is paid by the buyer.
Cost plus percentage of cost	Buyer	Cost overrun is paid by the buyer. Because the fee increases with the increase in cost, this type poses maximum risk to the buyer.
Cost plus incentive fee	Buyer	Cost overrun is paid by the buyer.

The major tasks of procurement planning are making buy or make decisions, preparing the procurement management plan, preparing the statement of work, determining the suitable type of contract, and preparing or acquiring the procurement documents. Once you have these elements in place, you are ready to implement the procurement plan.

Implementing the Procurement of Project Resources

The plan purchases and acquisitions and the plan contracting processes are used to plan the procurement, whereas the request seller responses and select seller processes are used to implement the procurement.

Requesting Seller Responses

Seller responses are requested by using the request seller responses process. The responses can be solicited in form of bids, quotations, proposals, or offers. The major input to the request seller process comes from the procurement management plan.

Input to the Request Seller Responses Process

The input items to the request seller responses plan include the procurement management plan, procurement documents, and procurement-related organizational process assets. These input items are discussed in the following list.

Procurement management plan. The major input to the request seller responses process is the procurement management plan, which in turn is an output of the plan purchase and acquisition process. The procurement management plan includes the following:

◆ Identifying any prequalified selected sellers

◆ Procurement metrics to be used to manage contracts and evaluate sellers

◆ Types of contracts to be used and the format for the contract statement of work

◆ Assumptions and constraints that could affect planned purchases and acquisitions

◆ Scheduled dates for the contract deliverables

◆ Directions to be provided to the seller on developing and maintaining a contract work breakdown structure

Procurement documents. Another input item is the set of procurement documents, which is an output of the plan contracting process. The buyer structures these documents with two goals in mind:

◆ To facilitate an accurate and complete response from each prospective seller

◆ To facilitate easy evaluation of the responses

These documents include the following:

◆ A description of the desired form of the response

◆ A relevant contract statement of work

◆ Any required contractual provisions, such as a copy of a model contract, and non-disclosure provisions

---

◢ TIP

In government contracting, some or all of the content and structure of a procurement document might already be defined by regulations.

Different terms are used for these documents for different purposes:

◆ A term such as *bid*, *tender*, or *quotation* is used when the seller selection decision will be based on the price, when buying commercial or standard items.

◆ A term such as *proposal* is used when multiple factors are considered, such as cost, technical skills, and technical approach.

◆ Common names for these different kinds of documents include *invitation for bid*, *request for quotation*, *tender notice*, *request for proposal*, and *contractor initial response*.

The procurement documents should be rigorous enough to ensure consistent responses from different sellers that can be fairly compared with one another and flexible enough to allow the sellers to offer suggestions on better ways to satisfy the requirements. How are the requests sent to the potential sellers? This is done according to the policies of the buyer's organization—for example, publication of the request in the public media, such as newspapers, magazines, and the Internet.

◼ NOTE

Bids and quotations are typically used to ask for prices, whereas proposals are used to ask for solutions. Invitations for bid, requests for quotation, and requests for proposal travel from buyer to seller, whereas bids, quotations, and proposals travel from seller to buyer.

Organizational process assets. The organizational process assets relevant to requesting seller responses include the following:

◆ A list of prospective sellers

◆ A list of previously used or qualified sellers

◆ Information about the past experiences with previously used sellers

With the availability of this input, requests can be facilitated using various techniques.

Tools and Techniques for the Request Seller Responses Process

The goal for the tools and techniques here is to find the sellers and provide them with the information about the requests for responses. Main techniques used in requesting seller responses are advertising and bidder conferences. These and other techniques are discussed in this section.

Developing a list of qualified sellers. The list of potential sellers can be developed from various sources, such as the World Wide Web, library directories, relevant local associations, trade catalogs, and the performing organization's internal information base.

Advertising. The request for seller responses can be advertised in the public media or in relevant professional journals. Whether to use advertising depends on the organization's policy. However, some government jurisdictions require public advertising of pending government contracts.

Bidder conferences. This refers to meetings with prospective sellers prior to preparation of a response to ensure that the sellers have a clear understanding of the procurement, such as the technical and contractual requirements. These meetings can generate amendments to the documents. All potential sellers should be given the same amount of information (or help) during this interaction so that each seller has an equal opportunity to produce the best response. These conferences are also called *contractor conferences*, *vendor conferences*, or *pre-bid conferences*.

By using these techniques, you can generate the output of the request seller responses process.

Output from the Request Seller Responses Process

The output of the request seller responses process includes the list of qualified sellers, the request material to be submitted to the sellers, and the responses submitted by the sellers. These output items are discussed in the following list.

◆ **List of qualified sellers.** This is the list of sellers who will be asked to submit a response for this procurement, such as a bid, quotation, or proposal.

◆ **Procurement document package.** This is a set of documents that comprises the formal request prepared by the buyer that will be sent to the qualified sellers.

◆ **Proposal.** A proposal is a response provided by a qualified seller to a request by the buyer. In other words, a proposal constitutes a formal and legal offer in response to a buyer's request.

NOTE

In some cases, after a proposal is submitted the buyer can request the seller to supplement its proposal with an oral presentation to provide some additional information, which can be used to evaluate the seller's proposal.

After proposals (responses) have been submitted, you need to evaluate those proposals and select the sellers.

Selecting Sellers

Proposals obtained during the request seller responses process are evaluated in the select sellers process—that is, the process used to select one or more sellers for procurement. The main tasks performed during the select sellers process are the following:

- ◆ Review seller responses to buyer requests
- ◆ Select one or more sellers based on their responses
- ◆ Negotiate written contracts with the selected sellers

Figure 6.8 shows the select sellers process.

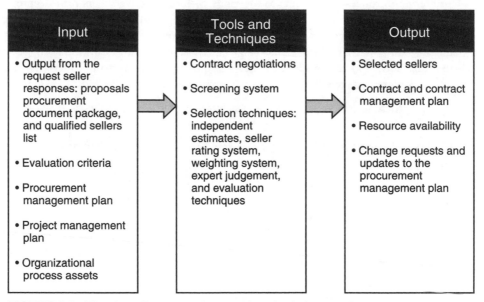

FIGURE 6.8 *The select sellers process: input, tools and techniques, and output*

Input to Selecting Sellers

The procurement management plan and the output from the request seller responses process are the major input items to the select sellers process. These and other input items are discussed in this section.

Output from the request seller responses process. The following output items from the request seller responses process, discussed earlier in this chapter, become the input items to the select sellers process:

◆ Proposals

◆ Procurement document package

◆ Qualified sellers list

Evaluation criteria. The buyer develops the evaluation criteria to rate the responses from the sellers. The evaluation criteria could be as simple as the price for off-the-shelf standard items, or it could be a combination of factors for a more complex proposal. Following is a list of some examples of evaluation criteria:

◆ **Cost.** To evaluate the overall cost, you should consider all cost-related factors, such as:

  ◆ Purchase price

  ◆ Delivery cost

  ◆ Operating cost

◆ **Business aspects.** This can include the following factors:

  ◆ **Business size and type.** Does the business size or type meet a condition set forth in the contract, such as being a small business or a disadvantaged small business?

  ◆ **Financial capacity.** Does the seller have the financial capacity to do the job, or is the seller in a position to obtain the necessary financial resources to do the job?

  ◆ **Production capacity and interest.** Does the seller have the capacity and the interest to meet future potential requirements?

  ◆ **References.** Can the seller provide reliable references (such as from previous customers) verifying the seller's work experience and history of compliance with contractual requirements?

◆ **Management approach.** If the procurement itself involves a project, does the seller have the ability to execute management processes and procedures to run a successful project?

◆ **Rights.** The following rights can be considered:

  ◆ **Intellectual property rights.** Will the seller own the intellectual property rights for the work processes or services that will be used to produce the deliverables?

  ◆ **Proprietary rights.** Will the seller have the proprietary rights for the work processes or services that will be used to produce the deliverables?

◆ **Technical aspects.** This includes the technical approach and capability:

  ◆ **Technical approach.** Will the technical methodologies, techniques, solutions, or services proposed by the seller meet the procurement requirements, or will they provide more than the expected results?

  ◆ **Technical capability.** Does the seller have or is the seller capable of acquiring the technical skills and knowledge required to produce the deliverables?

Procurement management plan. I discussed this plan earlier in this chapter.

Project management plan. As you know by now, the project management plan provides an overall plan for managing the project, and it consists of subsidiary plans and components. Out of these the following can be useful in the select seller process: the procurement management plan, the risk management plan, the risk register, and the risk-related contractual agreements.

Organizational process assets. The buyer organization might have formal policies that could affect the evaluation of responses from the sellers.

With this input in place, you use some tools and techniques to select the sellers.

Tools and Techniques for Selecting Sellers

The tools and techniques used to select the sellers include contract negotiations, a screening system, and selection techniques.

Evaluation techniques. These techniques are used to make the final selection of the sellers. These techniques are discussed in the following list:

◆ **Independent estimates.** The purpose of independent estimates is to have a check on the proposed pricing by the seller. The procuring organization prepares the independent estimate in-house or has it done by a third party. Significant differences between the proposed price and the independent estimate mean that either the market has changed or the seller has failed to offer reasonable pricing due to reasons such as failure to understand the contract statement of work. The independent estimates are also called *should-cost estimates*.

◆ **Seller rating system.** A seller's rating does not depend on a specific response that you are evaluating. Rather, the seller's rating comes from the seller's rating system, which is developed by multiple organizations based on multiple factors related to seller's past performance, such as delivery performance, contractual compliance, and quality rating.

◆ **Weighting system.** The purpose of putting a weighting system in place is to have an objective evaluation as opposed to a subjective evaluation influenced by personal prejudice. The weighting system uses a method to quantify the qualitative data and typically involves the following steps:

1. Assign a numerical weight to each of the evaluation criteria according to its importance, such as $w1$, $w2$, and $w3$ for three criteria, and make these weights the same for each seller.

2. Rate the seller on each criterion, such as $r1$, $r2$, and $r3$. These ratings depend upon the seller.

3. Multiply the weight by the rate for each criterion.

4. Add the results in the previous step to compute an overall score, such as $s1$ for seller 1: $s1 = r1 * w1 + r2 * w2 + r3 * w3$.

◆ **Expert judgment.** The expert judgment is made by an experts committee that consists of experts from each of the disciplines covered by the procurement documents and the proposed contract. The committee can include experts from functional disciplines, such as accounting, contracts, engineering, finance, legal, manufacturing, and research and development.

◆ **Proposal evaluation techniques.** Different techniques can be used to evaluate responses from sellers. All these techniques can use expert judgment and evaluation criteria. The factors that can be considered in the evaluation include the following:

 ◆ **Price.** This can play a primary role in the selection of off-the-shelf standard items. However, you should consider that the lower price does not mean lower cost if the seller does not deliver in time.

 ◆ **Multiple aspects.** Proposals are usually evaluated for different aspects, such as technical and commercial. Technical refers to the overall approach, whereas commercial refers to the cost.

 ◆ **Multiple sources.** For products critical to the project, multiple sources (sellers) might be required. This redundancy will help mitigate such risks as failure to meet the delivery schedule or quality requirements.

▲ TIP

Sellers in procurement are sometimes also called *sources*.

The evaluation criteria are discussed in detail as the input to the select sellers process.

Screening system. A screening system consists of minimum requirements as a threshold that must be met if the seller has to stay in the list of candidate sellers. It might, for example, consist of one or more evaluation criteria. The screening system can also use the weighting system and independent estimates.

Contract negotiations. The contract negotiations have the following goals:

◆ Clarify the structure and requirements of the contract

◆ Reach an agreement

The subjects covered during the negotiations might include the following:

◆ Applicable terms and laws

◆ Authorities, rights, and responsibilities

◆ Business management and technical approaches

◆ Contract financing

◆ Payments and price

◆ Proprietary rights

◆ Schedule

◆ Technical solutions

The conclusion of contract negotiations is a document, the contract, which can be signed by both the buyer and the seller. The final contract signed by both parties can be an offer by the seller or a counteroffer by the buyer. Sometimes for simple procurement items, the contract is non-negotiable.

TIP

A contract is a mutually binding legal relationship subject to remedy in the court. The project manager might not be the lead negotiator on the contract. However, the project manager might be required to be present during negotiations to provide any necessary clarification on the project requirements.

In the select sellers process, you basically evaluate, screen, and negotiate. In general, multiple tools and techniques are used to evaluate responses and make a selection.

Output of Selecting Sellers

Using the select sellers process, the sellers are selected, the contracts are signed, and the contract management plan is prepared. These and other output items of the select sellers process are discussed in this section.

Selected sellers. This is the list of sellers that you have selected as a result of response evaluations.

Contract management. The contract management includes the contract and its management plan.

◆ **Contract.** This is the contract awarded to a selected seller. It is a legal document that obligates the seller to provide the specified products, services, or results, and obligates the buyer to make the payment to the seller. The contract can be a simple purchase order or a complex document, depending on the nature of the procurement. A contract can include, but is not limited to, the following sections:

◆ Acceptance criteria

◆ Change-request handling

◆ Inflation adjustments

◆ Insurance

- Limitation of liability
- Penalties and incentives
- Pricing and payment
- Product support
- Roles and responsibilities
- Schedule
- Statement of work
- Termination and dispute-handling mechanism
- Warranty
- **Contract management plan.** Depending upon the size and complexity of the procurement, a contract can be administered through its lifecycle by a contract management plan, which becomes a subset of the project management plan.

Resource availability. This contains the information on the quantity and availability of the resources—for example, the dates on which a resource will be active or idle.

Changes and updates. The select sellers process can generate the following changes and updates:

- **Change requests.** The selection process can generate change requests for the project management plan and its subsidiary plans and components, such as the project schedule and the procurement management plan. These change requests must be processed through the integrated change control system before implementation.
- **Updates to the procurement management plan.** If a procurement-related change request is approved, the procurement management plan should be updated to reflect the change.

The three most important takeaways from this chapter are as follows:

- Direct and manage project execution is a high-level process to produce the project deliverables. To accomplish this, you need to do two things:
  1. Acquire the project team, develop it, and manage it to perform the project activities.
  2. Procure the items that cannot be produced by the project team.
- Procurement involves preparing the procurement management plan and implementing the plan by requesting seller responses, evaluating seller responses, selecting sellers based on the evaluation, and negotiating and signing contracts with the selected sellers.
- Use the perform quality assurance process to apply the planned systematic quality activities to ensure that the project employs all the planned processes needed to meet all the project requirements.

Summary

The project management plan is executed using the processes in the executing process group. The high-level process in this group is the direct and manage project execution process, whose main goal is to produce the project deliverables. To make that happen, you need to put together a project team, and then you and the team need to perform multiple actions, such as performing schedule activities, training and managing the project team members, and obtaining proposals from the seller for the project items that need to be procured. These actions are performed using processes discussed in this chapter. For example, you put together a project team using the acquire project team process. The main output of the acquire project team process are the project staff assignments, which become the input to the develop project team process. This process uses training, recognition and rewards, and other team-building techniques to develop a cohesive and efficient team with high performance. You manage the project team using the manage project team process to improve the team performance.

Due to a lack of resources in the performing organization, you might need to obtain some products, services, or results from outside the project team to complete the project. This is called *procurement*. The plan purchases and acquisitions as well as the plan contracting processes are used to plan the procurement, which includes preparing the procurement management plan and the procurement documents. The request seller responses and select sellers processes are used to implement the procurement plan, which involves obtaining seller responses, selecting sellers based on the responses, and reaching an agreement with the selected sellers, such as a contract to obtain (procure) the products, services, or results.

In addition to performing the project work to produce the project deliverables, a significant task to perform during the project execution is quality assurance. The goal of quality assurance is to improve quality, which involves taking actions to increase the effectiveness and efficiency of the policies, procedures, and processes of the performing organization.

The project execution, along with initiation, planning, and closing, needs to be monitored and controlled. This is the topic of the next chapter.

Exam's Eye View

Comprehend

◆ The goal of the acquire project team process is to fill the roles defined in the staffing management plan with real individuals who will perform those roles to execute the project.

◆ Regardless of how much control you have over staff assignments, always try to obtain the best person for the job by doing your homework, which includes finding out the availability and competencies of the candidate team members.

◆ The staff assignments made in the acquire project team process are the input to the develop project team process, which uses techniques such as training, recognition and rewards, and other team-building activities.

◆ The main output items from the human resource planning, acquire project team, and develop project team processes become the input to the manage project team process.

Look Out

◆ Invitations for bid, requests for quotation, and requests for proposal travel from buyer to seller, whereas bids, quotations, and proposals travel from seller to buyer.

◆ Of all the contract types discussed in this chapter, only the firm fixed-price contract can present risk to the seller.

◆ The contract type that presents the most risk to the buyer is the cost plus percentage of cost contract because the fee (which is a percentage cost) also increases if cost overrun occurs.

Memorize

◆ Team development goes through five progressive stages: forming, storming, norming, performing, and adjourning.

◆ The strategies used to resolve conflicts include avoidance, competition, compromise, accommodation, and collaboration. Collaboration is the best strategy because it offers a win/win resolution.

◆ The input of the quality assurance (QA) process comes from the output of three processes: quality planning, quality control, and direct and manage project execution.

◆ In procurement, a term such as *bid*, *tender*, or *quotation* is used when the seller selection decision will be based on the price when buying commercial or standard items, whereas a term such as *proposal* is used when multiple factors are considered, such as cost, technical skills, and technical approach.

Key Terms

◆ **asynchronous communication.** A communication in which the two communicating entities do not have to be present on both ends of the communication line at the same time. E-mail is an example of asynchronous communication because when the sender of the e-mail pushes the send button, the intended recipient of the e-mail message does not have to be logged on to the e-mail server.

◆ **contract.** A mutually binding agreement between a buyer and a seller that obligates the seller to provide the specified product, service, or result and obligates the buyer to make the payment for it.

◆ **corrective actions.** Directions for executing the project work to bring expected project performance in conformance with the project management plan. This is an output item of the QA process.

◆ **perform quality assurance.** A process used for applying the planned systematic quality activities to ensure that the project employs all the planned processes needed to meet all the project requirements.

◆ **preventive actions.** Directions to perform an activity that will reduce the probability of negative consequences associated with project risks. These preventive actions are recommended by the QA process during process analysis.

◆ **process analysis.** A technique used to identify the needed improvements in a process by following the steps outlined in the process improvement plan.

◆ **procurement.** Refers to obtaining (purchasing or renting) products, services, or results from outside the project team to complete the project.

◆ **procurement management.** An execution of a set of processes used to obtain the products, services, or results from outside the project team to complete the project.

◆ **project interfaces.** The formal and informal boundaries and relationships among team members, departments, organizations, or functions. An example might be how the development department and the QA department interact with each other while working on the same project.

◆ **project management methodology.** A method that an organization uses to execute the project management plan for a project. This methodology is built on top of the standard project management processes discussed in this book.

◆ **quality.** The degree to which the set of characteristics inherent to the product or services offered by the project meets the project requirements.

◆ **quality assurance.** The application of the planned systematic quality activities.

◆ **quality audit.** A structured and independent review to determine whether project activities comply with the policies, processes, and procedures of the project and the performing organization. It verifies the implementation of approved change requests, corrective actions, defect repairs, and preventive actions.

◆ **virtual team.** A team of members working on the same project with few or no face-to-face meetings. Various technologies, such as e-mail, video conferencing, and the World Wide Web, are used to facilitate communication among team members.

◆ **war room.** A conference room used for project team meetings.

Review Questions

1. Which of the following is not the output of directing and managing project execution?

   A. Deliverables

   B. Implemented defect repairs

   C. Work performance information

   D. Recommended corrective actions

2. Which of the following is not the input to the QA process?

   A. Quality metrics

   B. Implemented defect repairs

   C. Work performance information

   D. Recommended corrective actions

3. In procurement, which of the following contract types presents the highest risk for the buyer?

   A. Firm fixed-price

   B. Cost plus fixed fee

   C. Cost plus percentage of cost

   D. Cost plus incentive fee

   E. Time and material

4. In procurement, which of the following contract types presents the highest risk for the seller?

   A. Firm fixed-price

   B. Cost plus fixed fee

   C. Cost plus percentage of cost

   D. Cost plus incentive fee

   E. Time and material

5. The analysis to make a buy or make decision is performed during which of the following stages of procurement?

   A. Request for seller responses

   B. Select sellers

   C. Procurement planning

   D. Contract administration

6. You are managing a software project. The project is already in the execution stage when you discover that a whole software module is missing from the work breakdown structure. Your company does not have the programmers to write the module in a timely fashion, so you decide to procure this piece of work. The module will have a number of small programs working together, and it will take almost the same effort to write any of these programs. The software experts have given you an estimate for the effort. However, it is not clear at this stage how many programs will be needed. Which type of contract will you choose in this situation?

   A. Time and material

   B. Cost plus fixed fee

   C. Cost plus percentage of cost

   D. Firm fixed-price

7. Your company is outsourcing a part of your project, and therefore preparing the procurement documents. Which of the following is true about the procurement documents?

   A. The documents should have a rigidly fixed format so there are no variations in the responses from different sellers.

   B. The documents should be completely open-ended so each seller has the complete freedom to suggest the requirements and present their solutions.

   C. The documents should follow the standards required by the sellers.

   D. The documents should be flexible enough allow the sellers to be creative in offering solutions for meeting the requirements.

8. Your organization is playing the seller role in doing a part of the project for another company, the buyer. The buyer has incomplete specifications for the work involved and wants you to start the work immediately after signing the agreement. Which of the following contract types will be the most beneficial for your organization?

   A. Fixed-price

   B. Time and material

   C. Cost plus percentage of cost

   D. Cost plus time

9. Which of the following is generally the best conflict-resolution technique in most situations?

    A. Avoidance

    B. Compromise

    C. Accommodation

    D. Competition (forcing)

    E. Collaboration

10. You are the project manager for the ABC project. You are going to meet with your project team to discuss how to ensure that the project will be completed without any deviations from the project requirements. Which of the following processes are you performing?

    A. Quality control

    B. Quality planning

    C. Quality assurance

    D. Manage project team

11. Quality audits are part of which of the following quality management processes?

    A. Quality assurance

    B. Quality control

    C. Quality planning

    D. Quality inspection

12. Karl, one of your team members, is arguing with you over how to perform a specific task. At the end of a long discussion, you say, "Karl, please do me a favor and do it this way for my peace of mind." Which conflict resolution technique are you using?

    A. Avoidance

    B. Compromise

    C. Accommodation

    D. Forcing

    E. Collaboration

13. Which of the following is not a situation well-suited for team development efforts?

    A. The kickoff meeting

    B. A conflict between two groups within the team

    C. Low team morale

    D. Management changes within the organization

    E. Changes in the budget

Chapter 7

Monitoring and Controlling Projects

PMP Exam Objectives

Objective	What It Really Means
4.1 Measure Project Performance	You must understand how to measure project performance against cost, schedule, and scope baselines. You must also understand the terms involved in cost and schedule performance analysis, such as BAC, EV, AC, CV, SV, CPI, and SPI.
4.2 Verify and Manage Changes to the Project 2.4 Develop Change Management Plan	You should know how to manage changes to the project scope, project schedule, and project cost. That means you must understand the integrated change control process, quality control process, and schedule control process. You also must understand the impact of a change across the project—for example, the triple constraint.
4.3 Ensure Project Deliverables Conform to Quality Standards	You must understand how to perform the quality control process by using appropriate tools and techniques, such as control charts, flowcharting, Pareto diagrams, statistical sampling, and inspection.
4.4 Monitor All Risks	You need to know that you must actively monitor the identified risks and identify and respond to the new risks as they appear. You must understand the risk monitoring and controlling process. You should also be familiar with the risk response techniques, such as acceptance, transference, and mitigation, discussed in Chapter 4.

Introduction

You need to continually monitor and control your project. Executing a project means executing the project work according to the project management plan based on some baselines, such as a schedule baseline, a scope baseline, and a cost baseline. In general, monitoring means watching the course, and controlling means taking action to either stay the course or change the wrong course. You monitor the project by generating, collecting, and distributing information about project performance against the baselines. Deviations of the performance results from the plan might indicate that some changes to the original project plan are required. Other change requests might come from stakeholders, such as expanding the project scope by adding new requirements. You control all these changes by influencing the factors that generate them, processing them through a system called the *integrated change control system* that contains a process called the *integrated change control process*, evaluating their impact across the project, and ensuring the implementation of the approved change requests.

In addition to the schedule activities that need to be executed, the project management plan also contains a list of risks and the risk management plan. You monitor the risks by looking out for the risk triggers (the alerts that tell you a risk has occurred or is about to occur) for the already identified risks and by identifying new risks as the project progresses. You control the risks by executing the risk response plan and taking corrective and preventive actions.

Therefore, the core question in this chapter is, how do you monitor and control a project? In search of an answer, we will explore three avenues in the area of monitoring and controlling: performance, changes, and risks.

Monitoring and Controlling the Project Work

You monitor and control your project by monitoring and controlling the project performance, changes, and risks. Monitoring includes measuring the project performance, collecting and distributing information about the project performance, and evaluating the performance information to see the trends. Continuous monitoring helps the project management team identify the areas that need to be controlled closely by, for example, taking corrective or preventive actions.

Some of the major tasks involved in monitoring and controlling the project are the following:

◆ Monitoring project performance by measuring it against the project management plan in terms of parameters such as cost, schedule, and scope

◆ Monitoring the project by collecting information to support status reporting, progress measurement, and predictions, and then distributing this information among the stakeholders

◆ Evaluating performance to determine whether it needs to be controlled by taking corrective or preventive actions

◆ Monitoring risks by tracking and analyzing the already identified project risks and by identifying new risks

◆ Controlling risks by managing the execution of risk response plans when the risks occur

◆ Maintaining an accurate and timely information base regarding the project as it progresses

◆ Monitoring and controlling changes and monitoring the implementation of approved changes

---

▣ NOTE

Monitoring and controlling does not start only after the project starts execution. Rather, the project needs to be monitored and controlled all the way from initiation through closing.

A project is monitored and controlled using the monitor and control project work process, which is a high-level process that is performed by executing more specific processes, such as cost control, schedule control, and scope control, as shown in Figure 7.1. All these processes are in the monitoring and controlling process group.

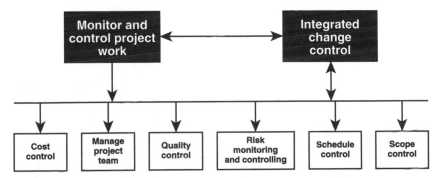

FIGURE 7.1 *Some processes in the monitoring and controlling process group*

The change requests arising from monitoring and controlling the project or originating from any other source, such as the stakeholders, must be processed through the integrated change control process.

Integrated Change Control Process

The integrated change control process is used to manage changes to the project from project initiation through project closure. A project rarely runs exactly according to the project management plan, and therefore changes will inevitably appear. The change requests can come from evaluating the project performance to bring the project in line with the project management plan, or they can come from other sources, such as the stakeholders. Regardless of where they originate from, all changes need to be managed (monitored and controlled), which includes getting the changes rejected or approved, seeing the approved changes implemented, and changing the affected plans accordingly. You, the project manager, must manage changes proactively, which includes the following activities:

- Identifying a change that has occurred and receiving a change request.
- Getting the requested changes approved or rejected. Depending on the project and the performing organization, the authority to determine whether a change is eventually rejected or approved might lie with the project manager, a customer, a sponsor, or a committee.
- Monitoring and controlling the flow of approved changes, which includes:
  - Making sure they are implemented.
  - Maintaining the integrity of the project baseline (cost, schedule, and scope) by updating it to incorporate the approved changes.
  - Coordinating changes and their impact across the project and updating the affected documentation. For example, an approved schedule change might impact cost, quality, risk, and staffing.
- Controlling project quality—for example, through defect repairs and recommended corrective and preventive actions.
- Making sure that only the approved changes are implemented.

▲ TIP

Especially in a startup organization, you will notice quite often the changes making their way through the back door—for example, a product manager talking to an engineer directly and introducing changes. Do not consider yourself an opponent of changes by default, but you do need to manage changes and make sure each change goes through the integrated change control process. So, when it comes to changes, the keyword is control, and not necessarily oppose.

Figure 7.2 shows the integrated change control process. The change requests that need to be approved are the obvious input to this process.

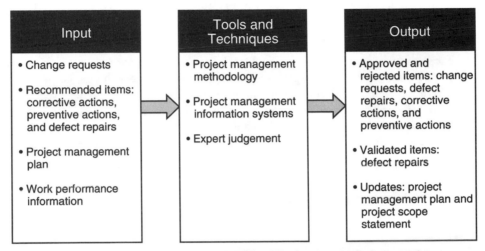

FIGURE 7.2 *The integrated change control process: input, tools and techniques, and output*

Input to Integrated Change Control

Each requested change and recommended action must be processed through the integrated change control process. The approved changes have their effects on the project management plan, and therefore the plan needs to be updated accordingly. Following are the input items to the integrated change control process:

◆ **Requested changes.** This is the obvious input. A requested change goes through the integrated change control process.

◆ **Recommended items.** The following recommended items should also go through the integrated change control process.

  ◆ Recommended corrective actions

  ◆ Recommended preventive actions

  ◆ Recommended defect repairs

  These recommendations might arise from performance evaluations, and they are the output of various processes discussed in this chapter.

◆ **Project management plan, including deliverables.** This is needed to help identify the changes and make updates after the changes have been approved.

◆ **Work performance information.** The performance information is the input because performance deviations from the plan will trigger change requests or recommended corrective or preventive actions to improve the situation.

So what tools and techniques are available to process these requests and recommendations? Read on....

Tools and Techniques for Integrated Change Control

You can use project management methodology and project management information systems to implement the integrated change control process. You can also use the expertise of the stakeholders to approve and reject change requests. Following are the tools and techniques available for the integrated change control process.

Project management methodology. Recall that the project management plan contains the output of the project planning processes. This plan defines how the project is executed, monitored/controlled, and closed. But how do you implement (that is, execute) the project management plan? Every organization will have its own method for implementing the project management plan for its projects; this is called its *project management methodology*. This is a high-level method on top of the standard project management processes discussed in this book.

The project management methodology of an organization will also define the high-level process for the project management team to implement the integrated change control for the project. For example, different organizations might have different answers to the following questions:

> **NOTE**
>
> It's important to distinguish between the project management body of knowledge (which is essentially a set of processes) canned by PMI and the project management methodology, which is a structured approach to developing and executing the project management plan. The methodology refers to the issues such as which of the PMI processes to implement and how to implement them. It facilitates the implementation through, for example, templates, best practices, and procedures.

◆ How will the change requests be submitted?
◆ Who will reject or approve the change requests?

Once you have the methodology in place, you need a system to implement the methodology.

Project management information system. This is a collection of tools and techniques (manual and automated) used to gather, integrate, and disseminate the output of project management processes. This system is used to facilitate processes from the initiation stage all the way to the closing stage. Microsoft Project, a product that lets you create a project schedule, is an example of such a tool. Another example of the components of the project management information system could be a document management system to create, review, change, and approve the documents to facilitate the change control procedure.

The project management information system might also have tools that can help the project management team implement the integrated change control process.

Expert judgment. The project management team can use the experts on the change control board to make approval or rejection decisions about change requests.

The rejection or approval of the change request is an obvious output of the integrated change control process.

Output from Integrated Change Control

The changes that are processed through the integrated change control process will either be rejected or approved. As a result of the approved changes, the project management plan might need to be updated. Accordingly, following are the output items of the integrated change control process:

Approved and rejected items. The items processed through the integrated change control process will either be approved or rejected. These items include change requests, suggested defect repairs, recommendations for corrective actions, and recommendations for preventive actions.

Validated items. Some change-related items that have been implemented, such as defect repairs, will be validated.

Updates. As a result of approved changes, items such as the project management plan and the project scope statement might need to be updated.

So, the requested changes are either rejected or approved in the integrated change control process.

Project performance, a factor that you monitor and control, is closely related to quality, which is the degree to which the project requirements are fulfilled. For example, a good-quality project is a project that is completed within its planned cost, scope, and schedule. Any variations from the planned cost, schedule, and scope performance indicate the degradation of project quality. So, controlling the performance correlates strongly to controlling the quality.

Controlling Quality

Controlling quality involves monitoring specific results to determine whether they comply with the planned quality standards, which include project processes and product goals, and controlling the results by taking actions to eliminate unsatisfactory performance. The perform quality control process is used to monitor and control quality by accomplishing the following goals:

◆ Monitor specific project results, such as cost performance and schedule performance, to determine whether they comply with the planned quality standards, which include project processes and product goals.

◆ Identify ways to eliminate the causes of unsatisfactory performance.

The results under scrutiny include both deliverables and performance measurements by the project management team. Quality control is performed throughout the project. While dealing with quality control, you must be able to distinguish the two terms in each of the following pairs from each other:

◆ Prevention and inspection

  ◆ Prevention is a direction to perform an activity that will keep an error from entering the product and the process.

  ◆ Inspection is a technique to examine whether an activity, component, product, result, or service complies with planned requirements. The goal of inspection is to ensure that errors do not reach the customer.

◆ Attribute sampling and variable sampling

  ◆ Attribute sampling is a technique to determine whether a result conforms to the specified standard.

  ◆ Variable sampling is a technique to rate a result on a continuous scale that measures the degree of conformity.

◆ Common cause and special cause

  ◆ Common cause is a source of variation that is inherent to the system and is predictable. Such variations are also called *normal variations*, and the common causes for them are also called *random causes*.

  ◆ Special cause is a source of variation that is not inherent to the system and is removable. It can be assigned to a defect in the system.

◆ Control limits and tolerances

  ◆ Control limits are the area occupied by three standard deviations on either side of the central line or the mean of a normal distribution of data plotted on a control chart that reflects the expected variation of the data. If the results fall within the control limits, they are within the quality control.

  ◆ Tolerance is the range within which a result is acceptable if it falls within the limits of the range.

Figure 7.3 shows the perform quality control process.

TIP

QC can be performed by the QA department or by the QC department if the performing organization has one. Nevertheless, the project management team should have a working knowledge of statistical aspects of quality control, such as sampling and probability. This will help evaluate the QC output.

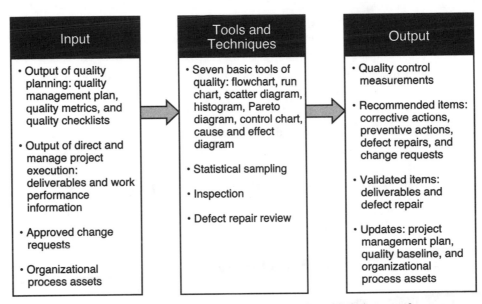

FIGURE 7.3 *The perform quality control process: input, tools and techniques, and output*

Input to Quality Control

The goal of quality control is to ensure that the performance from the project execution meets the planned quality standards. Therefore, the outputs from the project execution and from the quality planning are the obvious inputs to the perform quality control process. These and other input items are discussed here:

◆ **Quality planning output.** The following items from the output of the quality planning process, discussed in Chapter 4, are the input into the perform quality control process:

   ◆ The quality management plan lets you know how the quality standards are supposed to be implemented.

   ◆ Quality metrics specify which quality features to monitor and how to measure them.

   ◆ Quality checklists show which quality steps need to be performed.

◆ **Output from direct and manage project execution.** The following items from the output of the direct and manage project execution process, discussed in Chapter 6, are input into the perform quality control process:

   ◆ A list of deliverables from the project execution to ensure that all the required deliverables are produced before the project completion

   ◆ Work performance information to monitor performance

◆ **Approved change requests.** You need this list to ensure that all the approved changes are implemented in a timely fashion. The list of approved change requests also includes modifications, such as revised work methods and a revised schedule.

◆ **Organizational process assets.** These include quality policies and procedures, change control procedures, and quality-related historical data. These items will be used in the quality control process.

Quality control is a very involved process and has a plethora of tools and techniques, discussed next.

Tools and Techniques for Quality Control

The tools and techniques used for quality control include inspection, defect repair reviews, and the so-called seven basic tools of quality.

Seven Basic Tools of Quality

Table 7.1 shows the seven kinds of charts used in quality control, also known as the seven basic tools of quality. These tools are described in the following sections, too.

Table 7.1 Seven Basic Tools of Quality

Chart	Purpose
Flowchart	To anticipate what quality problems might be and where they might occur
Run chart	To perform trend analysis—that is, predict future results based on past performance
Scatter diagram	To find the relationship between two variables, such as cause and effect, or two causes
Histogram	To display the relative importance of different variables
Pareto diagram	To identify and rank errors based on the frequency of defects caused by them
Control chart	To monitor whether the variance of a specified variable is within the acceptable limits dictated by quality control
Cause and effect diagram	To explore all the potential causes of a problem, not just the obvious ones

Flowcharts

A flowchart is a diagram that depicts inputs, actions, and outputs of one or more processes in a system. Flowcharts, commonly used in many disciplines of knowledge, show the activities, decision points, and order of processing. They help to understand how a problem occurs. You can also use flowcharts to anticipate what quality problems might be, where they might occur, and how you might deal with them.

Run Charts

Run charts are used to perform trend analysis, which is the science of predicting future performance based on past results. In quality control, trend analysis can be used to predict such things as the number of defects and the cost to repair them. You can use the results of trend analysis to recommend preventive actions if needed.

Scatter Diagrams

A scatter diagram is used to show the pattern of the relationship between two variables—an independent variable and another variable that depends on the independent variable. The dependent variable is plotted corresponding to the independent variable. For example, a variable representing a cause can be the independent variable, and a variable representing the effect can be a dependent variable. The closer the data points are to a diagonal line, the stronger the relationship (called the *correlation*) is between the two variables.

Histograms

A histogram is a bar chart that shows a distribution of variables. Each bar can represent an attribute, such as defects due to a specific cause, and its height can represent the frequency of the attribute, such as number of defects. This tool helps to identify and rate the causes of defects.

You might wonder how the defects can be repaired efficiently. Pareto diagrams, which are examples of histograms, have the answer for you.

Pareto Diagrams

A Pareto diagram is used to rank the importance of each error (problem) based on the frequency of its occurrence over time in the form of defects. A defect is an imperfection or deficiency that keeps a component from meeting its requirements or specifications. A defect is caused by an error (problem) and can be repaired by fixing the error. An error in a product can give rise to multiple defects, and by fixing the error you repair all the defects caused by that error.

However, all errors are not equal. Some errors cause more defects than others. According to Pareto's law, which is also known as the *80/20 rule*, 80 percent of project defects are caused by 20 percent of errors (or types of errors). Qualitatively, it means that most defects are caused by a small set of errors. The Pareto diagram lets you rank errors based on the frequency of defects they cause. You begin by having the error that causes most of the defects fixed and make your way to other errors that cause smaller numbers of defects. This way the efforts of the project team are optimized: You get the maximum number of defects repaired with minimal effort.

The advantages of a Pareto diagram are twofold:

◆ It ranks errors according to the frequency of defects they cause.

◆ It optimizes efforts to repair the defects by working on the errors that cause most of the defects.

As an example, Table 7.2 presents data on the frequency of defects caused by certain errors. The data is displayed in Figure 7.4 in the form of a Pareto diagram. In this example, 200 defects are caused by seven errors, and error A alone causes 75 defects, which is 37.5% of all the defects. Similarly, you can understand the impact of other errors by looking at Table 7.2 and Figure 7.4. The Pareto diagram tells you that you should address error A first, error B second, and so on.

Table 7.2 Example of Frequency of Defects Corresponding to Errors Causing the Defects

Error Causing the Defects	Number of Defects	Percentage of Defects Caused by This Error	Cumulative Percentage
A	75	37.5	37.5
B	50	25.0	62.5
C	30	15.0	77.5
D	20	10.0	87.5
E	15	7.50	95.0
F	7	3.5	98.5
G	3	1.5	100.0

NOTE

Pareto's Law, in its original form, was presented as an economic theory by Vilfredo Pareto, a 19th-century Italian economist, and it states that 80 percent of income is earned by 20 percent of the population. Since then, it has been applied to other fields, such as project management.

You might ask: How many defects are acceptable? To find an answer to this question, you need to understand another tool, called the *control chart*.

Control Charts

Control charts are used to monitor whether the variance of a specified variable is within the acceptable limits dictated by quality control. A variance is a measurable deviation in the value of a project variable, such as cost from a known baseline or expected value. This is a way to monitor the deviations and determine whether the corresponding variable is in or out of control. The values are taken at different times to measure the behavior of a variable over time.

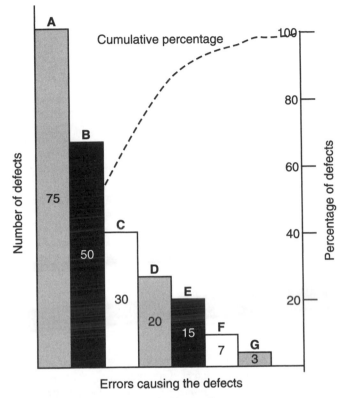

FIGURE 7.4 *An example of a Pareto diagram*

The mean value in the control chart represents the expected value, and a predetermined spread from the mean value (usually ±3) is used to define the limits within which an acceptable value can fall.

Control charts can be used to monitor the values of any type of output variables. To illustrate their main features, consider the example of a control chart shown in Figure 7.5. In this example, assume that a manufacturer produces 100 units of a product each day and it is expected that 95 out of 100 units should have no defect—that is, the expected number of defective units is equal to five. The control limits are set to ±3. In other words, 95 units out of 100 must be correct, give or take three. That puts the lower limit at 92 and the upper limit at 98. Crossing the lower limits is not acceptable to the customer, and crossing the upper limits might require an unjustifiable cost.

Controlling quality includes dealing with defects and problems that cause them. So, studying causes of a problem is critical to quality control.

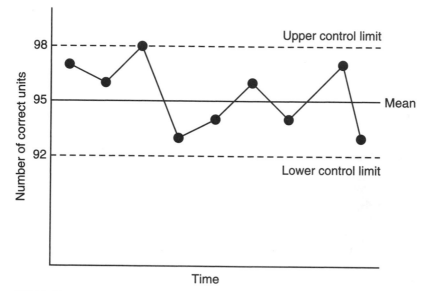

FIGURE 7.5 *An example of a control chart*

Cause and Effect Diagram

A cause and effect diagram is used to explore all the potential causes (inputs) that result in a single effect (output), such as a problem or a defect. This type of diagram is the brainchild of Kaoru Ishikawa, who pioneered quality management processes in the Kawasaki shipyards, and therefore these diagrams are also called *Ishikawa diagrams*. Due to the shape of these diagrams, they are also known as *fishbone diagrams*. To construct and use cause and effect diagrams effectively, perform the following simple steps:

1. **Identify the problem.** Write down the problem in the box drawn on the right side of a large sheet of paper. This represents the head of the fish. Starting from the box, draw a horizontal line across the paper. This represents the spine of the fish.

2. **Identify the possible areas of causes.** Identify the areas or factors from where the potential causes of the problem might come. Environment, people, materials, measurements, and methods are some examples of areas (factors) of causes. For each factor relevant to the problem under study, draw a line off the spine and label it with the name of the factor. These lines represent the fish bones.

3. **Identify the possible causes.** For each factor, identify possible causes. Represent each possible cause with a line coming off the bone that represents the corresponding factor.

4. **Analyze the diagram.** Analyzing the diagram includes narrowing down the most likely causes and investigating them further.

Figure 7.6 shows an example of a cause and effect diagram. The problem in this example is the delay in the release of a Web site. The factors considered are environment, methods, people, and time. Of course, the diagram is incomplete in the sense that more factors and related causes can be explored, and causes for each factor can be explored further. But you get the point.

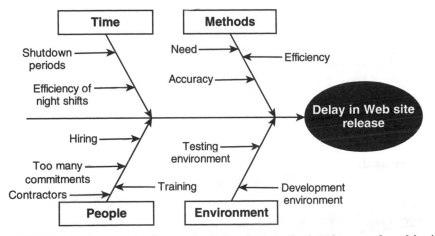

FIGURE 7.6 *An example of a cause and effect diagram: Explore the causes for a delay in a Web site release.*

TIP

While constructing the cause and effect diagram, you can use the brainstorming method for identifying the potential factors of causes and the potential causes for each factor.

A cause and effect diagram offers a structured way to think through all possible causes of a problem. You can use these diagrams to carry out a thorough analysis of a problematic situation. This kind of analysis is useful in complex situations when, to discover the real causes, you need to explore all the potential causes and not just the obvious ones.

In addition to the seven quality tools we have discussed, there are some other tools that you can use for quality control.

Other Quality Control Tools

In addition to the seven quality tools, the following tools can also be used for controlling quality:

◆ **Statistical sampling.** Statistical sampling involves randomly selecting a part of the population for study. In quality control, you can select a subset of features for inspection. This can save a substantial amount of resources.

◆ **Inspection.** This is a technique to examine whether an activity, component, product, service, or result conforms to specific requirements. Inspections can be conducted at various levels of project execution. For example, you can inspect the results of a single activity, or you can inspect the final product of the project. Nevertheless, inspection generally includes measurements. There are various forms of inspections, such as reviews, peer reviews, audits, and walkthroughs.

◆ **Defect repair review.** This review is conducted by the QC department or body to ensure that the defects are repaired to bring the defective product, service, or results in conformance with the specified requirements.

These tools can be used to make quality control measurements, which in turn can be used to recommend preventive and corrective actions: the output of quality control.

Output of Quality Control

The quality control measurements and the recommendations based on those measurements are the obvious output items of the quality control process. These and other output items are discussed in this section.

Quality control measurements. These are the results of the QC activities and are fed back to the QA process. They are also used to make recommendations for corrective and preventive actions.

Recommended items. The quality control process can generate the following kinds of recommendations:

◆ **Recommended corrective actions.** These actions are recommended as a result of the QC process to meet the established quality goals.

◆ **Recommended preventive actions.** These actions are recommended as a result of the QC process to avoid future failure to meet the established quality goals.

◆ **Recommended defect repair.** A defect is an imperfection or deficiency that keeps a component from meeting its requirements or specifications. Such a component needs to be repaired or replaced.

◆ **Requested changes.** The recommended corrective or preventive actions might require changes to the project. The changes are requested and processed through the integrated change control process.

Validated items. These are the items that have been validated through the QC process:

- ◆ **Validated defect repair.** Once a component has been repaired from a defect, it needs to be inspected so the repair will be accepted or rejected. The rejected items might need to be repaired again. The accepted repair is a validated defect repair.
- ◆ **Validated deliverables.** This refers to verifying the correctness of project deliverables. A deliverable accepted through a QC process is a validated deliverable.

Updates. The quality control process might generate updates to the following items:

- ◆ **Organizational process assets.** The completed checklists become part of the project record. Furthermore, you can update the lessons-learned database and documentation. These might include the causes of variances, the reasons for corrective and preventive actions, and the actions that worked and those that did not.
- ◆ **Project management plan.** The project management plan should be updated to reflect the changes to the quality management plan resulting from the QC process.
- ◆ **Quality baseline.** The quality baseline might need to be updated to reflect the changes to the quality plan resulting from the QC process.

High-quality projects deliver the promised product, service, or result within the planned cost, schedule, and scope. Therefore, it is necessary to monitor and control changes to these three parameters: cost, schedule, and scope.

Controlling Changes in Cost, Schedule, and Scope

Changes to cost, schedule, and scope are controlled using the cost control, schedule control, and scope control processes, respectively. These three project parameters comprise a triple constraint that is a framework for evaluating competing demands. A triple constraint is often depicted as a triangle, with each corner (or side) representing one of the three parameters. Figure 7.7 shows the triple constraint for the cost, schedule, and scope. This means if one of these parameters changes, at least one of the other two must change as well.

For example, assume you are being interviewed by a functional manager for a project manager position. Don't be surprised if you are asked a question based on the following situation:

1. The project is way behind the schedule.
2. No extra resources, such as money or project team members to perform activities, are available.
3. You have to implement all the planned features.

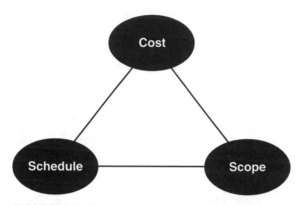

FIGURE 7.7 *Triple constraint: cost, schedule, and scope. You cannot change one side of the triangle without changing at least one of the other two sides.*

The question is, what will you do to meet the deadline that is approaching within a week? From a project management viewpoint, this situation is a good example of the triple constraint. The project is behind schedule, which means there is a schedule change (or a change in time available to finish the remaining project). Therefore, at least one of the other two parameters must change. If you want to meet the deadline, either you should be allotted more funds to hire more human resources, or the scope of the project should be changed, which means some of the features would be left out. Depending upon the knowledge level of the functional manager about project management, this answer might not get you the job, but as a project manager, you must stand your ground. Project management is not magic; it involves dealing with cold, hard reality in a realistic way, thereby establishing clear and achievable objectives.

NOTE

While considering the cost-schedule-scope constraint, you should also remember the schedule compression techniques, such as crashing and fast tracking, discussed in Chapter 5. Also remember that those techniques do not guarantee that no additional cost (or resources) will be required.

You can see the relationship of triple constraint with quality by recalling that a high-quality project delivers the required product on time and within planned scope and budget. Therefore, while balancing between these three constraints, the quality (and as a result, customer satisfaction) might be affected. The triple constraint is also a good example of how one change can give rise to other changes across the project. This highlights the importance of managing and controlling changes.

Cost control is discussed in a later section, and schedule control and scope control are discussed in the next section.

Schedule Control

Schedule control has two-pronged goal—to ensure that the project is progressing on time as planned, and to monitor any changes to this progress. As a project manager, you should be out in front of the project, performing the following tasks on regular basis:

◆ Determine the current status of the project schedule.

◆ Influence the factors that generate schedule changes.

◆ Determine whether the project schedule has changed—for example, if some activities are running late.

◆ Manage the changes as they occur.

You detect a schedule change by comparing the execution time against the time in the schedule baseline, which is a major input item to the schedule control process.

Input to Schedule Control

To control the project schedule, you need to know what the schedule baseline (that is, the expectation) is, how the project is performing from the perspective of schedule, and what the plans are to monitor the schedule. Accordingly, the input items to the schedule control process are the following:

◆ **The schedule management plan.** This plan specifies how to monitor and control the project at hand.

◆ **Schedule baseline.** This is the approved version of the schedule, against which the schedule performance of the project will be measured.

◆ **Performance reports.** These reports provide information on the schedule performance of the project, such as missed and met planned dates.

◆ **Approved change requests.** These are requests to change the schedule or other change requests that will affect the schedule. Approved change requests can update the schedule baseline.

Tools and Techniques for Schedule Control

The schedule is monitored by progress reporting and performance measurements and is controlled using the schedule control system. These and other tools and techniques are discussed in this section.

Progress reporting. Progress reports and current schedule status are key items to monitor the schedule. They can include the finished activities, the percent of in-progress activities that has been completed, and remaining durations for unfinished activities.

Schedule change control system. This is the system you use to receive, evaluate, and process schedule changes. It can include forms, procedures, approval committees, and tracking systems.

Performance measurement and analysis. The following tools and techniques can be used to measure and analyze the schedule performance of the project:

◆ **Performance measurement techniques.** These techniques are used to calculate the schedule variance and schedule performance index and are discussed in the "Measuring Performance" section later in this chapter. The schedule variance discussed there is in terms of cost, but you can also perform a barebones schedule variance analysis based on the start and end dates of the schedule activities.

◆ **Variance analysis.** Performing a barebones schedule variance analysis is crucial to schedule monitoring because it reveals the deviation of the actual start and finish dates from the planned start and finish dates of schedule activities. It might suggest corrective actions to be taken to keep the project on track.

◆ **Schedule comparison bar charts.** Bar charts can be used to facilitate the schedule variance analysis. You can draw two bars corresponding to one schedule activity— one bar shows the actual progress, and the other bar shows the expected progress according to the baseline. This is a great tool to visually display where the schedule has progressed as planned and where it has slipped.

TIP

A schedule variance does not necessarily mean that a schedule change is required. For example, a delay on a schedule activity that is not on the critical path might not trigger any schedule change.

Project management software. You can use project management software for scheduling to track planned start/finish dates versus actual dates for schedule activities. This software also enables you to predict the effects of project schedule changes. These are important pieces of information for monitoring and controlling the schedule.

Output of Schedule Control

Schedule performance measurements and recommendations for actions based on the measurements and progress reports are the important output items of the schedule control process.

Performance measurements. The results from schedule performance measurements, such as the schedule variance (SV) and schedule performance index (SPI), should be documented and communicated to the stakeholders. These measurements might trigger recommendations for corrective actions and change requests.

Recommended corrective actions. The goal of schedule-related corrective actions is to bring the future schedule performance in line with the schedule baseline—that is, the approved version of the planned schedule. To that end, the following actions can be taken:

◆ Expedite the execution to ensure that schedule activities are completed on time or with minimal delay.

◆ Perform a root cause analysis to identify the causes of the schedule variance.

◆ Make plans to recover from the schedule delay.

TIP

Remember that corrective actions are not about going back and fixing past mistakes. Rather, they're about ensuring that future results match with the plan. You can do this by influencing the future results, such as expediting the execution, or by changing the plan.

Updates. The following updates can result from the schedule control process:

◆ **Schedule updates.** Schedule changes can happen at the activity level (the start/end date of an activity has changed) or at the project level (the start/end date of the project has changed). A schedule change at the project level is called a *schedule revision*. For example, when the schedule scope is expanded, the project end date might have to be changed to allow the extra work. All significant schedule changes must be reported to the stakeholders.

◆ **Activity updates.** The schedule changes and the project progress will cause changes in the activity list and in the list of activity attributes. These changes must be documented.

◆ **Project management plan.** The schedule management plan, a component of the project management plan, is updated to reflect the changes that occur during the schedule control process.

◆ **Organizational process assets.** The lessons learned from the schedule control process can be documented to the historical database. Following are some examples:

◆ The causes of schedule variance

◆ The reasons for choosing the corrective actions that were taken

◆ The effectiveness of the corrective actions

Future projects can make use of this information.

Change requests. The schedule performance analysis and progress report review can result in requests for changes to the project schedule baseline. These changes must be processed through the integrated change control process for approval. As with any other change, you must think through whether a change to the schedule baseline has any other effect across the project. If it does, you might need to update the corresponding component of the project management plan accordingly.

The project schedule is there to execute the project work within the scope of the project. So, the project scope must be controlled as well.

Scope Control

Controlling the project scope includes influencing factors that create changes to the scope, as well as managing change requests and controlling their impact when the change actually occurs. While controlling the scope, you focus on the following tasks:

◆ Watch out for scope creep: Determine whether it has happened and correct the situation. Scope creep refers to scope changes applied without processing them though the change control process.

◆ Process the scope change requests through the integrated change control process for approval.

◆ Manage the implementation of scope changes after approval, as well as their impact across the project.

> ### TIP
>
> In real life, scope creeps occur for various reasons. For example, perhaps a development engineer thought something was a cool feature to implement, or the customer spoke directly with the engineer to make a request for a minor additional feature, or various other similar situations. If scope creep has taken your project off track, you need to take corrective actions to get the project back on track. You should also investigate how the scope creep happened and take steps to prevent it in the future—for example, by educating team members about the proper scope change process.

The obvious input items to the scope control process are the elements that define the scope, such as the project scope statement, the scope baseline, the WBS, the WBS dictionary, and a scope management plan that describes how to manage the scope. The performance reports might help to detect a scope change, and some change requests in other areas can result in scope change, as well.

The main output of the scope control process is the update to scope-related input elements, such as the project scope statement, the WBS, the WBS dictionary, and the scope baseline. The components of the project management plan affected by these changes might also need to be updated. Change requests and recommendations for corrective actions are other obvious output items from the scope control process.

The main tools used in the scope control process are the change control system and the project performance analysis, including the scope variance and the schedule variance. Schedule variance can have an effect on the scope if you want to finish the project on time and there are no additional resources available. The change control system of an organization is a collection of formal documented procedures that specify how the project deliverables and documents will be changed, controlled, and approved.

You monitor the project by watching its progress, which is a measure of its performance. Therefore, performance measurement and analysis are an important category of tools and techniques in monitoring and controlling the project.

Measuring Performance

Project performance is measured by comparing the project execution against the performance measurement baseline, which is an approved integrated plan for scope, schedule, and cost for the project, as explained here:

- **Cost baseline.** This is the planned budget for the project over a time period, used as a basis against which to measure, monitor, and control the cost performance of the project. The cost performance is measured by comparing the actual cost with the planned cost over a time period.

- **Schedule baseline.** This is a specific version of the project schedule developed from the schedule network analysis and the schedule model data, discussed in Chapter 5. This is the approved version of the schedule with a start date and an end date, and it is used as a basis against which the project schedule performance is measured.

- **Scope baseline.** This is the approved project scope that includes the approved project scope statement, the WBS based on the approved project scope statement, and the corresponding WBS dictionary.

The elaborate nature of the performance measurement analysis can be seen in the cost control process.

Performance Measurement Analysis for Cost Control

Cost control includes influencing the factors that can create changes to the cost baseline. But to detect the arising changes, you need to detect and understand variances from the cost baseline by monitoring cost performance.

In general, variance is a measurable deviation in the value of a project variable (or parameter), such as cost or schedule from a known baseline or expected value. Variance analysis is a technique used to assess the magnitude of variation in the value of a variable, such as cost from the baseline or expected value, determine the cause of the variance, and decide whether a corrective action is required. A common technique to assess the cost variance is called the *earned value technique (EVT)*; in this technique you calculate the cumulative value of the budgeted cost of work performed in terms of the originally allocated budgeted amount and compare it to the following:

1. Budgeted cost of work scheduled—that is, planned
2. Actual cost of work performed

Don't worry if these terms sound confusing right now; I will go through an example soon. However, as you will see, the greatest difficulty in understanding EVT stems from the coupling of cost and schedule. You must realize that the project cost and the project schedule are inherently related to each other. Schedule relates to performing certain work over a certain time period, whereas cost refers to the money spent to perform the work on a project (or a project activity) over a certain period of time. The relationship between cost and schedule can be realized by understanding that it costs money to perform a schedule activity. The "time is money" principle is at work here. For example, a project activity can be looked upon in terms of an amount of work that will be needed to complete it or in terms of its monetary value, which will include the cost of the work that needs to be performed to complete the activity.

The EVT involves calculating some variables where you will see the interplay of schedule (work) and cost. I will work through an example to help you understand the variables. Assume you are a project manager for the construction of a 16-mile road. Further assume that the work is uniformly distributed over 12 weeks. The total approved budget for this project is $600,000. At the end of first four weeks of work, $125,000 has been spent, and four miles of road have been completed.

I will use this example to perform the cost performance analysis and the schedule performance analysis in terms of cost.

Cost Performance

Cost performance refers to how efficiently you are spending money on the project work, measured against the expectations set in the project management plan—that is, the cost baselines. The total cost approved in the baseline is called the *budget at completion (BAC)*.

> **NOTE**
>
> The variables discussed here, such as BAC, EV, and AC, can be calculated either for the whole project or for a part of the project, such as a project activity.

Budget at completion (BAC). This is the total budget authorized for performing the project work (or a project activity), also called the *planned budget*. In other words, it is the cost originally estimated in the project management plan. You use this variable in defining almost all the following variables. In our example, the value of BAC is $600,000.

Earned value (EV) or budgeted cost of work performed (BCWP). This is the value of the actually performed work expressed in terms of the approved budget for a project or a project activity for a given time period. In this variable, you see the relationship of schedule (work) and cost in action. BAC represents the total value of the project. But when you perform some work on the project, you have earned some of that value, and the earned value is proportional to the fraction of the total work performed, as shown by the formula here:

EV = BAC * (work completed / total work required)

So, in our example, EV can be calculated as:

EV = $600,000 * (4 miles / 16 miles) = $150,000

This is the earned value of the work, which may or may not be equal to the actual money that you spent to perform this work.

Actual cost (AC) or actual cost of work performed (ACWP). This is the total cost actually incurred until a specific point on the timescale in performing the work for a project. In our running example, $125,000 has already been used up to this point. So the actual cost at this point in time is $125,000. This cost is to be compared with the earned value to calculate the cost variance and cost performance.

Cost variance (CV). This is a measure of cost performance in terms of deviation of reality from the plan, and is obtained by subtracting the actual cost (AC) from the earned value (EV), as shown in the formula here:

CV = EV − AC

So, in our example, CV can be calculated as shown here:

CV = $150,000 − $125,000 = $25,000

The expected value of CV is zero because we expect the earned value to be equal to the actual cost. The positive result indicates better cost performance than expected, whereas a negative result indicates worse cost performance than expected. Deviation is one way of comparison, and ratio is another.

Cost performance index (CPI). Earned value represents the portion of the work completed, and actual cost represents the money spent. So, the CPI indicates whether you are getting a fair value for your money. This is a measure of cost efficiency of a project calculated by dividing earned value (EV) by actual cost (AC), as shown in the formula here:

CPI = EV / AC

So, the CPI for our example can be calculated as:

CPI = $150,000 / $125,000 = 1.2

This means you are getting $1.20 worth of performance for every dollar spent. A value of CPI greater than one indicates good performance, whereas a value less than one indicates bad performance. The expected value of CPI is one.

So both the CV and the CPI indicate that you are getting more value for each dollar spent. Hold back a little before opening the champagne, though. If you read the text of our example again, note that four out of 12 weeks have already passed, and only four out of 16 miles of road have been built. That means that only one-fourth of the work has been accomplished in one-third of the total scheduled time. This means we are lagging behind in our schedule. Although cost performance is good, schedule performance needs to be investigated, too.

Schedule Performance in Terms of Cost

Schedule performance refers to how efficiently you are executing your project schedule as measured against the expectations set in the project management plan. It can be measured by comparing the earned value to the planned value, just like cost performance is measured by comparing the earned value to the actual cost. Planned value refers to the value that we planned to create in the time spent so far.

Planned value (PV) or budgeted cost for the work scheduled (BCWS). This is the authorized cost for the scheduled work on the project or a project activity up to a given point on the timescale. The planned value is also called the *budgeted cost for the work scheduled (BCWS)*. PV is basically how much you were authorized to spend in the fraction of schedule time spent so far, as shown in the formula here:

$$PV = BAC * (time\ passed\ /\ total\ schedule\ time)$$

Therefore, the planned value for the project in our example at the end of first four weeks is calculated as shown here:

$$PV = \$600,000 * (4\ weeks\ /\ 12\ weeks) = \$200,000$$

So, PV represents the planned schedule in terms of cost. You can calculate the schedule performance by comparing the planned schedule to the performed schedule in terms of cost.

Schedule variance (SV). This is the deviation of the performed schedule from the planned schedule in terms of cost. No confusion is allowed here because you already know that the schedule can be translated to cost. SV is calculated as the difference between EV and PV, as shown in the formula here:

$$SV = EV - PV$$

So, the SV in our example can be calculated as:

$$SV = \$150,000 - \$200,000 = -\$50,000$$

The negative value means we are behind schedule. Deviation represented by schedule variance is one way of comparison, and ratio represented by schedule performance index is another.

Schedule performance index (SPI). Earned value represents the portion of work completed in terms of cost, and planned value represents how much work was planned by this point in time in terms of cost. So, the SPI indicates how the performed work compared to the planned work. This is a measure of the schedule efficiency of a project calculated by dividing earned value (EV) by planned value (PV), as shown in the formula here:

SPI = EV / PV

So, the SPI for our example can be calculated as shown here:

SPI = $150,000 / $200, 000 = 0.75

This indicates that the project is progressing at 75% of the planned pace—not good.

You should note that all these performance variables except the BAC are calculated at a given point in time. As shown in Figure 7.8, you can maintain a graphic that presents the values of these variables against points in time as the project progresses. Note that the value of the BAC does not change with time because it is the cost at completion time. Further note that given the BAC, the PV can be calculated at any point in time, even before the project execution starts. EV and EC are accumulated as the project execution progresses.

By using the variables discussed so far, you can monitor the project performance as the time progresses. Not only that, you can also make predictions about the future performance based on the past performance.

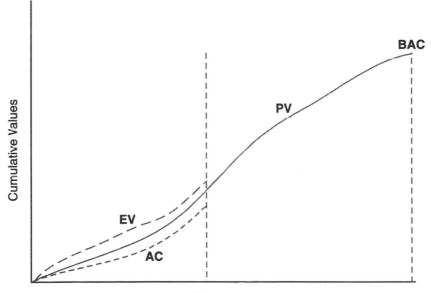

FIGURE 7.8 *The behavior of some performance variables as the project progresses in time. The variable BAC is independent of time.*

Forecasting Techniques

Forecasting refers to predicting some information about the project in the future based on the performance in the past. The forecasting is regularly updated as the project progresses and more data of the past performance becomes available.

Estimate to complete (ETC). This is the prediction about the expected cost to complete the remaining work for the project or for a project activity. This is basically how much value remains to be earned in terms of the BAC. Therefore, the value of the ETC is obtained by subtracting the earned value (EV) from the budget at completion (BAC), as shown in the formula here:

$$ETC = BAC - EV$$

So, in our example, the value of ETC can be calculated as:

$$ETC = \$600,000 - \$150,000 = \$450,000$$

The next question that can be asked about the future is how much it will cost to complete the whole project.

Estimate at completion (EAC). This is the estimate made at the current point in time for how much it will cost to complete the project or a project activity. The value of the EAC is obtained by adding the value of ETC to AC, as shown in the formula here:

$$EAC = ETC + AC$$

Accordingly, the value of EAC for our example can be calculated as:

$$EAC = \$450,000 + \$125,000 = \$575,000$$

Another useful prediction to be made is how much performance you need in the future to complete the remaining work within budget.

To complete performance index (TCPI). This is the variable to predict the future performance needed to finish the work within budget. It is calculated as the ratio of the remaining work to the remaining budget, as shown in the formula here:

$$TCPI = \text{Remaining work} \, \% \, \text{Remaining funds} = (BAC - BCWP) \, \% \, (BAC - ACWP) = (BAC - EV) / (BAC - AC)$$

Therefore, the value of TCPI in our example can be calculated as:

$$TCPI = (\$600,000 - \$150,000) / (\$600,000 - \$125,000) = 450,000 / 475,000 = 0.95 = 95 \, \%.$$

Table 7.3 summarizes all these performance variables.

So, during the executing stage, the obvious items that need to be executed are the schedule activities, and while these activities are being executed, the attached cost, schedule, and scope need to be monitored and controlled. However, there is another important component of the project that needs to be monitored and controlled—the risk.

Table 7.3 Performance Variables Used in the Earned Value Technique Analysis

Variable	Abbreviation	Description	Formula
Budget at completion	BAC	Total planned cost	None
Earned value or budgeted cost of work performed	EV or BCWP	Fraction of the completed work in terms of the planned budget at a given point in time	EV = BAC * (Work completed % / Total work required)
Actual cost	AC or ACWP	The money spent on the work until a given point in time	The sum of all the costs until a given point in time
Cost variance	CV	The difference between what you planned to spend and what is actually spent until a given point in time	CV = EV – AC
Cost performance index	CPI	The work performed per actual cost	CPI = EV / AC
Planned value or budgeted cost of work scheduled	PV or BCWS	The fraction of work planned to be completed at a given point in time	PV = BAC * (Time passed % / Total schedule time)
Schedule variance	SV	The difference between the work actually completed and the work planned to be completed at a given point in time	SV = EV – PV
Schedule performance index	SPI	The actual work performed per planned work performed in terms of cost	SPI = EV / PV
Estimate to complete	ETC	Estimate of what will be spent on the remaining project (or a project activity) based on the performance so far and the planned cost	ETC = BAC – EV
Estimate at completion	EAC	Estimate of what will be spent on the whole project (or a project activity) based on the performance so far and the planned cost	EAC = ETC + AC
To complete performance index	TCPI	Calculates the efficiency: remaining work per remaining funds	(BAC – EV) / (BAC – AC)

Monitoring and Controlling Risks

The project management plan contains the list of risks you identified during risk planning and the responses you will execute if the risks occur. You must actively monitor the identified risks and identify and respond to the new risks as they appear. The risk monitoring and controlling process is used to monitor and control risks and includes the following goals:

◆ Tracking identified risks

◆ Monitoring residual risks (the risks that remain after risk responses have been implemented)

◆ Identifying new risks and preparing responses for them

◆ Executing the risk plan and evaluating its effectiveness

Figure 7.9 shows the risk monitoring and controlling process.

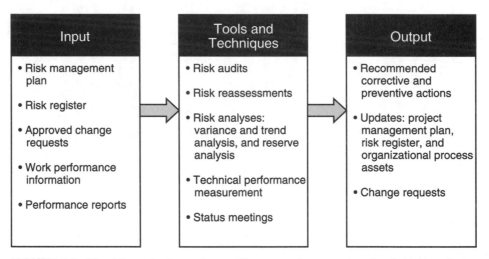

FIGURE 7.9 *The risk monitoring and controlling process: input, tools and techniques, and output*

To monitor and control risks, you must have a list of identified risks, a plan to deal with the risks, and the signs of risk occurrence. Accordingly, the input items to risk monitoring and controlling are risk management plans, risk registers, approved change requests, and work performance information. These items were discussed in Chapter 4. The tools and techniques to risk monitoring and the output from it are discussed in the following sections.

Tools and Techniques for Risk Monitoring and Controlling

There are some tools and techniques available to detect risk triggers, to respond effectively to the risks that have occurred, and to identify new risks.

Risk audits. A risk audit is conducted to examine the following:

◆ Root causes of the identified risks

◆ Effectiveness of responses to the identified risks

◆ Effectiveness of the risk management processes

Risk reassessment. The risks should be continually reassessed as the project progresses. For example, a risk on the watch list might become important enough that you might need to prepare a response plan for it.

Risk analyses. Risk analyses are necessary to effectively respond to the risks that have occurred, to detect the risk triggers, and to identify new risks. The following two kinds of analyses are appropriate for risk monitoring:

◆ **Variance and trend analysis.** Trends in the project performance should be reviewed on a regular basis as the project execution progresses. These trends can be determined by analyzing the performance data based on various performance control techniques, such as variance and earned value analysis, discussed earlier in this chapter. This analysis can help in detecting new risks.

◆ **Reserve analysis.** Recall that the contingency reserve is the amount of funds or time (in the schedule) in addition to the planned budget reserved to keep the impact of risks to an acceptable level when the project is executing. The risks occurring during the project execution can have positive or negative effects on contingency reserve. You perform the reserve analysis at a given time to compare the remaining reserve amount to the remaining risk to determine whether the remaining reserve amount is adequate.

Technical performance measurement. Technical performance measurements compare actual versus planned parameters related to the overall technical progress of the project. The deviation determines the degree to which system requirements are met in terms of performance, cost, schedule, and progress in implementing risk handling. The parameters chosen to measure technical performance could be any parameters that represent something important related to the project objectives and requirements; software performance, human resource performance, and system test performance are some examples.

Status meetings. You should always put risk management as an agenda item at project status meetings. The time spent on this item will depend on the number of identified risks, their priorities, and the complexity of the responses planned for them. Nevertheless, keeping risk on your agenda and discussing risks with the team on a regular basis help make risk management smoother and more effective.

These tools and techniques are used to monitor the risks that might generate recommendations for actions, which are part of the output of the risk monitoring and controlling processes.

Output from Risk Monitoring and Controlling

The output of monitoring risks includes recommendations for actions and requests for changes to control the risks. These and other output items are discussed in the following list.

Recommended actions. There are two kinds of actions recommended as a result of risk monitoring: corrective actions and preventive actions. Corrective actions include contingency plans and workaround plans. A workaround is a response to a negative risk that has occurred. A workaround is based on a quick solution and is not planned in advance of the risk occurrence event. Preventive actions are recommended to bring the project into compliance with the project management plan. Recommended corrective and preventive actions are input to the integrated change control process.

Updates. The risk monitoring and controlling processes might require updates to the following items:

- ◆ **Risk register.** You might need to include the following updates to the risk register:
  - ◆ Outcomes of risk reassessments, risk reviews, and risk audits
  - ◆ Outcomes of risks and responses to risks
- ◆ **Project management plan.** The project management plan might need to be updated as a result of risk monitoring and controlling. For example, the change requests might change the risk management processes, which in turn will change the project management plan.
- ◆ **Organizational process assets.** As a result of the risk monitoring and controlling processes, some organizational process assets might need to be updated, such as templates for the project management plan, the historical information database, for such information as actual costs and durations of project activities, the lessons-learned knowledge database, and checklists.

Change requests. You will need to make some change requests as a result of risk monitoring and controlling. For example, recommended actions, such as contingency plans and workarounds, might result in requirements to change some elements of the project management plan to respond to certain risks. Of course, the change requests will need to go through the integrated change control process for approval, and the approved change requests will become the input to the direct and manage project execution process for implementation.

Figure 7.10 shows the big picture of monitoring and controlling the project. The recommended actions and change requests from the monitoring processes as a result of monitoring the project go through the integrated change control process for approval. If approved, the execution of these actions and changes is managed using direct and manage project execution, a process in the executing process group.

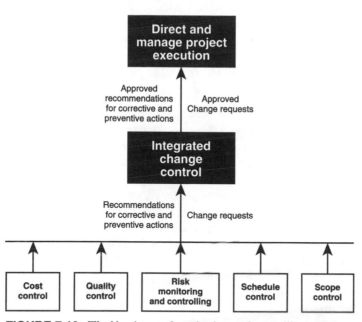

FIGURE 7.10 *The big picture of monitoring and controlling a project*

The three most important takeaways from this chapter are as follows:

◆ A project is monitored by continually measuring its performance as it progresses.

◆ Based on the performance measurements, actions can be recommended and changes can be requested to control the project and thereby bring it in line with the project management plan. These actions and changes are processed through the integrated change control process for approval and, if approved, their execution is managed using the direct and manage project execution process.

◆ The risk monitoring and controlling processes are used to monitor and control the identified risks and to look out for new risks.

Summary

You need to monitor and control your project throughout its lifecycle, which includes monitoring and controlling performance, changes, and risks. Change requests might arise from the evaluation of performance results to bring the performance in line with the project management plan, or they might originate from other sources, such as project stakeholders. Regardless of their origin, all change requests must go through the integrated change control process, which will approve them or reject them.

In an ideal world, there should be no changes to or variations from the planned baselines, such as cost, schedule, and scope baselines. A good-quality project is completed within the planned cost, schedule, and scope. However, in the real world, there are changes and variations, and therefore quality needs to be monitored and controlled, which involves monitoring certain project results by making measurements and taking actions based on those measurements.

The three project parameters—cost, scope, and schedule—are collectively known as a triple constraint because if one of them changes, at least one of the other two parameters must change. Therefore, project monitoring and controlling includes monitoring and controlling these three parameters, which involves measuring cost, schedule, and scope performance and taking actions based on performance. The most commonly used technique to measure cost and schedule performance is known as the *earned value technique (EVT)*, and it measures the performance by comparing the earned value of the actual work performed to the actual cost and to the planned value that was supposed to be earned according to the plan. In addition to monitoring and controlling the cost, schedule, and scope of the project work, you also need to monitor and control the identified risks and watch out for new risks that might appear. The recommendations for actions and change requests from monitoring and controlling the project go through the integrated change control process for approval and, if approved, go though the direct and manage project execution process for implementation.

After the execution of the last schedule activity is complete, you are not done yet. You need to give a proper closure to the project, which is the topic I discuss in the next chapter.

Exam's Eye View

Comprehend
◆ You monitor and control the project by monitoring and controlling project performance, changes, and risks.
◆ All the individual control processes, such as risk control and quality control, can generate change requests and recommended actions, which must be processed through the integrated change control process, in which each of these requests and recommendations will either be rejected or approved.
◆ The approved change requests and recommendations for actions will be processed through the direct and manage project execution process for implementation.
◆ The three project parameters—cost, schedule, and scope—form a triple constraint, which means if one of these three parameters changes, at least one of the other two must change.

Look Out

◆ Cost variance (CV) is calculated by subtracting the actual cost (AC) from the earned value (EV), and not from the planned value (PV).

◆ Schedule variance (SV) and schedule performance index (SPI) are calculated in terms of cost: EV and PV.

◆ It is possible for CV and SV to run in opposite directions—for example, CV has a positive value when SV has a negative value.

Memorize

◆ For cost performance analysis:
EV = BAC * (Work completed / Total work required)
CV = EV – AC
CPI = EV / AC

◆ For schedule performance analysis:
PV = BAC * (Time passed / Total schedule time)
SV = EV – PV
SPI = EV / PV

Key Terms

◆ **actual cost (AC).** The total cost actually incurred until a specific point on the timescale in performing the work for a project or a project activity.

◆ **budget at completion (BAC).** The total budget authorized for performing the project work. This is the planned budget for the project, the cost that you originally estimated for the project.

◆ **change control system.** A collection of formal documented procedures that specifies how the project deliverables and documents will be changed, controlled, and approved.

◆ **cost baseline.** The planned budget for the project over a time period, used as a basis against which to monitor, control, and measure the cost performance of the project. The cost performance is measured by comparing the actual cost to the planned cost over a time period.

◆ **cost performance index (CPI).** A measure of cost efficiency of a project calculated by dividing earned value (EV) by actual cost (AC).

♦ **cost variance (CV).** A measure of cost performance obtained by subtracting actual value (AV) from earned value (EV). A positive result indicates good performance, whereas a negative result indicates bad performance.

♦ **defect.** An imperfection or deficiency that keeps a component from meeting its requirements or specifications. A defect is caused by an error (problem) and can be repaired by fixing the error.

♦ **earned value (EV) or budgeted cost of work performed (BCWP).** The value of the actually performed work expressed in terms of the approved budget for a project or a project activity for a given time period.

♦ **estimate at completion (EAC).** The estimate from the current point in time of how much it will cost to complete the project or a project activity. The value of EAC is obtained by adding the value of ETC to AC.

♦ **estimate to complete (ETC).** The expected cost, estimated from CPI, to complete the remaining work for the project or for a project activity.

♦ **inspection.** A technique to examine whether an activity, component, product, service, or result conforms to specific requirements.

♦ **performance measurement baseline.** An approved integrated plan for scope, schedule, and cost for the project, against which the project execution is compared to measure the project performance.

♦ **project scope creep.** Changes applied to the project scope without going through the approval process, such as the integrated change control process.

♦ **risk trigger.** An alert that indicates a risk event has occurred or is about to occur.

♦ **schedule baseline.** A specific version of the project schedule developed from the schedule network analysis and the schedule model data. This is the approved version of the schedule with a start date and an end date, and it is used as a basis against which the project schedule performance is measured.

♦ **schedule performance index (SPI).** A measure of the schedule efficiency of a project calculated by dividing earned value (EV) by planned value (PV).

♦ **schedule revision.** An update to the project schedule that includes changing the project start date, end date, or both.

♦ **scope baseline.** The approved project scope, which includes the approved project scope statement, the WBS based on the approved project scope statement, and the corresponding WBS dictionary.

♦ **variance.** A measurable deviation in the value of a project variable, such as cost from a known baseline or expected value.

♦ **variance analysis.** A technique used to assess the magnitude of variation in the value of a variable (such as cost from the baseline or expected value), determine the cause of the variance, and decide whether a corrective action is required.

♦ **workaround.** A response to a negative risk that has occurred. A workaround is based on a quick solution and is not planned in advance of the risk occurrence event.

Review Questions

1. The integrated change control process is used to manage changes to the project at which stage?

    A. Initiating only

    B. Planning only

    C. Executing only

    D. Executing and closing only

    E. From initiating through closing

2. You are using an Ishikawa diagram to find real causes of a problem by exploring all the possible causes. Which quality process are you performing?

    A. Quality assurance

    B. Quality planning

    C. Quality control

    D. Auditing

    E. Inspection

3. You want to examine the results of a process to determine whether the process is in or out of control. Which of the following is the most suitable tool to use?

    A. Control chart

    B. Cause and effect diagram

    C. Pareto diagram

    D. Scatter diagram

4. You are managing a software project with limited development resources. The QA department has discovered a large number of defects in the product, and the project sponsor is very concerned about this. You want to get the maximum number of defects repaired with minimal efforts. Which quality-control tool are you going to use before you direct the efforts of the project team to fix specific problems?

    A. Control chart

    B. Cause and effect diagram

    C. Pareto diagram

    D. Scatter diagram

5. You are the project manager for a software development project that has limited resources. The customer is concerned with the quality of the code developed and wants you to conduct the code review. The product contains a large body of code with millions of lines. Which approach will you take?

   A. Tell the customer it's not possible.

   B. Use statistical sampling.

   C. Use automated testing tools.

   D. Arrange to review each line of the code.

6. A project manager is recommending corrective actions related to risk. Which of the following processes is the project manager involved in?

   A. Integrated change control

   B. Risk response planning

   C. Risk identification

   D. Qualitative risk analysis

   E. Risk mentoring and controlling

7. A project manager is getting the risk-related recommended corrective actions approved. Which of the following processes is the project manager involved in?

   A. Integrated change control

   B. Risk response planning

   C. Risk identification

   D. Qualitative risk analysis

   E. Risk monitoring and controlling

8. You are the project manager for a software product and your project is in the execution stage. You have learned that Maya, a developer, has started adding some new features to the deliverable she is working on. What is the best action for you to take?

   A. Tell Maya to delete the code corresponding to these features because this is a scope creep, and scope creeps are not allowed.

   B. Learn from Maya what those features are and how much time they will take, and make necessary updates to the WBS, the WBS dictionary, and the schedule. Also tell Maya that in the future she should get approval from you before adding any new features.

   C. Determine where the request for the new features came from and process the change request through the integrated change request process.

   D. Contact Maya's functional manager and ask the manager to replace Maya with another developer.

9. Which of the following is not an output of the schedule control process?

    A. Recommended corrective actions

    B. Updates to the schedule baseline

    C. Performance measurements

    D. Updates to the activity list

    E. Budget review

10. Assume that you are the project manager for the construction of a 15-mile road. Further assume that the work is uniformly distributed over 12 weeks. The total approved budget for this project is $600,000. At the end of the first three weeks of work, $160,000 has been spent, and five miles of road have been completed. What is the earned value of the project at the end of the first three weeks?

    A. $160,000

    B. $200,000

    C. $150,000

    D. $600,000

11. Assume that you are the project manager for the construction of a 15-mile road. Further assume that the work is uniformly distributed over 12 weeks. The total approved budget for this project is $600,000. At the end of the first three weeks of work, $160,000 has been spent, and five miles of road have been completed. What is the planned value of the project at this point in time?

    A. $160,000

    B. $200,000

    C. $150,000

    D. $600,000

12. Assume that you are the project manager for the construction of a 15-mile road. Further assume that the work is uniformly distributed over 12 weeks. The total approved budget for this project is $600,000. At the end of the first three weeks of work, $160,000 has been spent, and five miles of road have been completed. What is the cost variance?

    A. $40,000

    B. $50,000

    C. −$40,000

    D. $120,000

    E. −$10,000

13. Assume that you are the project manager for the construction of a 15-mile road. Further assume that the work is uniformly distributed over 12 weeks. The total approved budget for this project is $600,000. At the end of the first three weeks of work, $160,000 has been spent, and five miles of road have been completed. What is the schedule variance?

    A. $40,000

    B. $50,000

    C. Three weeks

    D. Twelve weeks

14. A CPI value of 1.25 and an SPI value of 1.33 for a project mean which of the following?

    A. The project is making slower progress and costing more than planned.

    B. The project is making faster progress and costing less than planned.

    C. The project is making slower progress and costing less than planned.

    D. The project is making faster progress and costing more than planned.

Chapter 8

Closing the Project

PMP Exam Objectives

Objective	What It Really Means
5.1 Obtain Final Acceptance for the Project	You must know that formal acceptance of the final product is an output of the close project process. You also must know that the administrative closure procedure should specify activities to define the requirements for getting approval from the stakeholders on the project deliverables and the approved changes that were supposed to be implemented.
5.2 Obtain Financial, Legal, and Administrative Closure	Understand that the project closure contains two parts: administrative closure and contract closure. You must know that the procedures for these two closures are defined during the close project process. You also must understand the close project process and the contract closure process.
5.3 Release Project Resources	You must know that releasing the project resources and turning over the project deliverables to another group are the elements of the administrative closure, and the procedure for the administrative closure is developed during the close project process. You must also know that you should follow the policies and procedures of the performing organization to release the resources.

PMP Exam Objectives

Objective	What It Really Means
5.4 Identify, Document, and Communicate Lessons Learned 5.6 Archive and Retain Project Records	You must know that documenting the lessons learned and archiving the project documents are included in the output of the close project process. You should also know that identifying the lessons learned is an essential component of project review.
5.5 Create and Distribute Final Project Report 5.7 Measure Customer Satisfaction	You must know that reviewing the project is part of administrative closure. You must also know that measuring customer satisfaction and creating and distributing the final project report are essential components of the project review.

The last deliverable on the project schedule has been completed. However, put that champagne bottle back into the refrigerator; the project has not ended yet. It has just reached another stage called the *project closing stage*, and, as a project manager, you need to continue monitoring and controlling the project through this stage. Also, recall that there are two kinds of project work—in-house and procured. The procured work involves some kind of legal agreement, such as a contract. Accordingly, there are two components of project closure—the work-related closure, called *administrative closure*, and the contract closure called, well, *contract closure*. So that nothing falls between the cracks, you should establish procedures to perform both of these closures.

The main issue in this chapter is project closure. To enable you to wrap your arms around this issue, we will explore three avenues—administrative closure, contract closure, and closure procedures.

Understanding Project Closure

Project closure refers to a set of tasks that are required to formally end the project. There are two kinds of projects that you need to close formally:

- ◆ **Completed projects.** A project that has met its completion criteria falls into this category.
- ◆ **Terminated projects.** A project that was terminated before its completion falls into this category. A project can be terminated at various stages for various reasons. Following are some examples:
    - ◆ The project management plan is not approved for whatever reason.
    - ◆ The project has been executing but you have run out of resources, and no more resources are available.
    - ◆ The project has been cancelled because it was going nowhere.
    - ◆ The project has been indefinitely postponed because there is not a large enough market for the product it would produce.

🔲 NOTE

The processes of the closing process group can be used to close a project, as well as to close a phase of a project.

The process of closure consists of two kinds of tasks:

◆ Establish procedures to coordinate the activities needed to close the project.

◆ Implement the procedures.

There are two aspects of closing a project—administrative closure and contract closure. As described in the following list, you define the procedures for carrying out both aspects of the project closure.

◆ **Administrative closure procedure.** Performing administrative closure of a project includes obtaining final acceptance for the project deliverables, analyzing the project's success or failure, gathering lessons learned, archiving project information, and releasing project resources. How will these activities be performed and coordinated, and by whom? For that, you establish an administrative closure procedure for your project that will take into account the relevant policies and procedures of the performing organization.

◆ **Contract closure procedure.** Contract closure includes settling and closing all the contracts associated with the project. To carry out and coordinate the activities needed for the contract closure, you define the contract closure procedure.

These procedures are defined and implemented using the processes in the closing process group. This process group contains the following two processes:

◆ **The close project process.** This is the process used to finalize all activities across all of the process groups to formally close the project. It's also used to establish the procedures for administrative and contract closures.

◆ **The contract closure process.** This is the process used to complete and settle each contract, which includes resolving any open item and closing each contract applicable to the project.

The relationship between these two processes is shown in Figure 8.1. The procedures for administrative and contract closure are established by using the close project process.

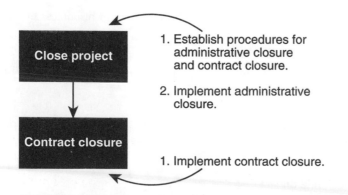

FIGURE 8.1 *The processes in the closing process group used to close a project*

Performing Project Closure

A project is closed using two processes in the closing process group—close process and contract closure. The close project process is used to close the project work portion of the project (as opposed to the contract portion). This includes finalizing all activities completed across all process groups to formally close the project. Figure 8.2 shows the close project process.

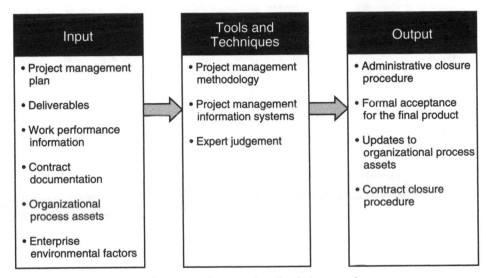

Input	Tools and Techniques	Output
• Project management plan • Deliverables • Work performance information • Contract documentation • Organizational process assets • Enterprise environmental factors	• Project management methodology • Project management information systems • Expert judgement	• Administrative closure procedure • Formal acceptance for the final product • Updates to organizational process assets • Contract closure procedure

FIGURE 8.2 *The close project process: input, tools and techniques, and output*

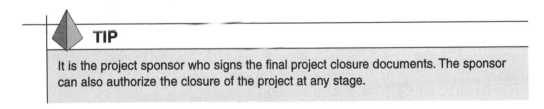

TIP

It is the project sponsor who signs the final project closure documents. The sponsor can also authorize the closure of the project at any stage.

The items that describe what the project was planned to deliver and what it has delivered are the obvious input to the close project process.

Input to the Close Project Process

You need a list of project deliverables that will go through the acceptance procedure. The project management plan contains guidelines on how to close the project. These and other input items are discussed in the following list:

◆ **Project management plan.** This defines how to close this project and will be useful in establishing the project closure procedure.

◆ **Deliverables.** These will need to go through the acceptance procedure.

◆ **Work performance information.** This has the important information for the project closure, such as deliverables that have been completed, the extent to which the quality standards have been met, authorized and incurred costs, lessons learned, and the like.

◆ **Contract documentation.** This is needed to establish the contract closure procedure.

◆ **Organizational process assets.** These can include project closure guidelines or requirements—for example, product validation and acceptance criteria, final project audits, and project evaluations.

◆ **Enterprise environmental factors.** These include tools, such as a project management information system used to perform tasks involved in closing the project, such as updating the lessons learned database.

These input items provide information about what the project was supposed to deliver and what it has delivered. You use this input and some tools and techniques to carry on the project closure.

Tools and Techniques for the Close Project Process

The tools and techniques available to develop and implement the project closure procedures are discussed in the following list:

◆ **Project management methodology.** This is used to define a process (or set of processes) that will help the project management team execute both the administrative and the contract closure procedures for the project.

◆ **Project management information system.** This system, owned by the performing organization, can include tools that will help the project management team perform the administrative and contract closure of the project.

◆ **Expert judgment.** Help from relevant experts can be used to both develop and implement the closure procedures.

You use these tools to carry on the project closure.

▲ **TIP**

Although the fundamental project processes are the same for each organization, the manners in which they are implemented might be different for different organizations. Each organization can have its own project management methodology that consists of items such as detailed steps for how to carry on the project processes, templates, meetings, and procedures. However, the name "project management methodology," given to this tool/technique used for various processes in the PMBOK, might be confusing for some folks for whom the whole PMBOK is the project management methodology.

Output of the Close Project Process

The output of the close project process contains three kinds of elements—closing procedures, acceptance of the project deliverables by the customer, and archival of project-related documents. These elements are described in this section.

Administrative closure procedure. This procedure specifies the step-by-step methodology for the administrative closure of the project, which includes specifying all the necessary activities, roles, and responsibilities of the project team members who will participate in the closure process. The activities defined by this procedure include the following:

- Activities to define the requirements for getting approval from the stakeholders, such as customers and the sponsor on the project deliverables, and the approved changes which were supposed to be implemented
- Activities that are necessary to satisfy the project completion or exit criteria
- Activities related to the project completion, such as:
  - Confirm that the project has met all requirements
  - Verify that all deliverables have been provided and accepted
  - Verify that the completion or exit criteria have been met

Formal acceptance for the final product. This includes handing over the final product to the customer and getting formal acceptance for it—for example, in the form of a receipt that contains a formal statement to the effect that the requirements of the project have been met, including the terms of the contracts.

Updates to organizational process assets. The closure process will add the following documents to the organizational process assets:

- **Acceptance documentation.** This is the documentation that proves that the fulfillment of the project requirements have been confirmed, completion of the project has been verified, and the product has been formally accepted by the customer. In the case of a project termination, of course, the documentation should show that the exit criteria have been met.
- **Project closure documentation.** In addition to the acceptance documentation, you should also archive the other project closure documents, such as the closure procedure and the handing-over of project deliverables to an operation group. If the project was terminated, then the formal documentation indicating why the project was terminated should be included in the archive.
- **Project files archive.** This includes the documents from the project's lifecycle, such as the project management plan, risk registers, planned risk responses, and baselines for cost, schedule, scope, and quality.
- **Lessons-learned database.** The documentation on lessons learned should be saved in the organization's knowledge database so that future projects can benefit from it.

Contract closure procedure. This procedure is developed to formally close all contracts associated with the project. It specifies a step-by-step methodology to execute activities needed to close the contracts. The roles and responsibilities of the team members who will be involved in the closure process are also specified.

NOTE

A procedure and a process are not the same thing. For example, the administrative closure procedure and contract closure procedure are two of several output items of the close project process.

The contract closure procedure established by using the close project process becomes an input item to the contract closure process.

Performing Contract Closure

A project might include work that was procured, and that's where legal agreements, such as contracts, come into the picture. The contracts are closed at the end of a project or a phase by using the contract closure process. Strictly speaking, the contract closure process is used to accomplish the following two goals:

◆ Close all the contracts applicable to the project.
◆ Receive verification (if you are a seller) or issue verification (if you are a buyer) that all the procured deliverables were received and accepted. In this respect, the contract closure process supports the administrative closure of the project.

If the project terminates without completion, you still need to go through the contract closure process, if there is a contract. Usually a contract contains the contract termination clause, which contains the terms of the project termination, including the rights and responsibilities of the parties in case of the project's early termination.

Figure 8.3 shows the contract closure process. The contract closure procedure that you established in the close project process becomes an input item to the contract closure process.

Input to the Contract Closure Process

The input items to the contract closure process are what you need to close the contract. They are discussed in the following list:

◆ **Contract closure procedure.** This is needed to close the contract in an effective manner.
◆ **Contract management plan.** This contains the requirements for formal contract closure.

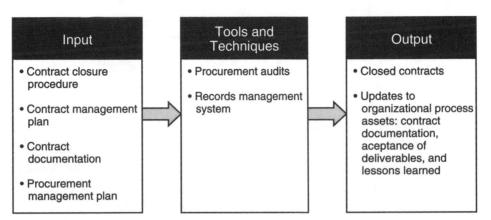

FIGURE 8.3 *The contract closure process: input, tools and techniques, and output*

- ◆ **Contract documentation.** This is obviously needed to close the contract.
- ◆ **Procurement management plan.** This is needed to check whether the procurement requirements are met; it might have some procedures that you need to follow during closure.

You implement the contract closure procedure by using the available tools and techniques, discussed in the next section.

Tools and Techniques for the Contract Closure Process

The tools and techniques for the contract closure process are the items you need to facilitate the contract closure. They are discussed in this section.

Procurement audits. This is a structured review of the procurement process with the purpose of identifying successes and failures from the planning through the executing stage of the project. The lessons learned from the audit can be applied to other phases of the same project (if it is a phase closeout) or to other projects within the same performing organization.

Records management system. This is a part of the project management information system and can be used to manage contract documentation and records. For example, you can use this system to archive documents, maintain an index of contract and communication documents, and retrieve documents.

Now, I'll ask you the easiest question in this book: What is the output of the contract closure process?

Output of the Contract Closure Process

Yes, you are right. The output of the contract closure process is the closed contract. But you also need to get the acceptance notice and save some documents, as discussed in this section.

Closed contracts. Closing the contract means the procured work is completed with all its requirements and is accepted. Generally, it is accomplished by a formal notice from the buyer to the seller, which might come, for example, through the buyer's authorized administrator. The requirements for the formal contract closure are usually defined in the terms of the contract and are included in the contract management plan, an input item to the contract closure process.

Updates to organizational process assets. The following items should be added to the organizational process assets:

◆ Contract documentation, including the closed contract with the closure notice

◆ Acceptance of deliverables through a notice from the buyer to the seller, notifying that the procurement deliverables have been accepted

◆ Lessons learned from this procurement that can be used in the future projects

Note that the contract closure process supports the close project process in the sense that it includes the administrative activities, such as acceptance of (procured) deliverables and additions to the documentation archive, including the lessons learned database.

Some elements of the administrative closure demand a closer look.

The Finishing Touch

Reviewing the project, releasing the project resources, and turning over the project deliverables to another group are the elements of the administrative closure that need to be explored further.

Reviewing the Project

Part of the administrative closure is to analyze project success or failure. You can accomplish this by collecting and generating the project evaluation information, such as what went well and what did not. Some of this information already exists in the work performance (status) reports. However, the final information can be gathered in various ways, such as a post-project review meeting with the team or a questionnaire. The most important output (and the whole purpose) of the review are the lessons learned. The review should be comprehensive and should cover the following:

◆ Both the technical and non-technical components

◆ Both positive and negative aspects—that is, the things that went well and the things that did not go well

◆ All stages and phases of the project

> ◆ **TIP**
>
> The purpose of the post-project review, also called the *post-project assessment*, is to learn lessons that can be applied to future projects to run them more effectively. Do not let the review turn into a finger-pointing show.

As part of the project review, you should also measure customer satisfaction from the customer feedback collected by using techniques such as interviews and surveys. This will help the organization establish and maintain a long-term relationship with the customer.

The findings of the review should be recorded in a document that might have different names in different organizations, such as the post-project review report or the project assessment report. Your organization might even have a template or standard for such a report. Depending upon the size of the project, the review report might be a part of the project closure report or a separate report. The report will be distributed among the stakeholders and will be added to the project archive. The project closure report can also include the final project performance as compared to the baselines, as well as a description of the final project product.

Releasing the Resources

For the effective and efficient use of the organization's resources, it is imperative that they be released in an efficient and proper manner. The release procedure might be included in the resource planning—for example, the staff management plan should address the issue of releasing the human resources. Well-planned release or transfer of team members reflects managerial professionalism, which requires that employees be treated with respect and dignity. By ensuring a well-planned release and a smooth transition to other projects, you are helping the employees focus wholeheartedly on the project toward the very end, rather than worrying about the next assignment. This will obviously improve the productivity of the team members and the efficiency of the project. Following are some suggestions to consider for properly releasing the human resources:

◆ Although it is possible that different team members will be released at different times, at the project closure you should organize some closure event to honor and thank the project team members, including the contractors, for their contributions. However, you must check your company policy regarding including the contractors in company-sponsored events and giving them rewards.

◆ Plan ahead, and do not wait until the last minute. Communicate with the functional manager ahead of time about when a staff member is going to be released.

◆ Work closely with your organization's human resources department, which might have some guidelines or procedure that you need to follow.

◆ Write (or offer to write) recommendation letters for team members who have made outstanding contributions to the project.

Once all the closure tasks are completed and the documents are finalized, the project might need to be turned over to another group in the organization—for example, to the maintenance or operations group.

Saying Goodbye: The Project Turnover

Depending upon the project, you might need to coordinate the turnover of the project deliverables to another group, such as a maintenance or operations group. The turnover requirements, such as training the help-desk employees, should have been included in the project management plan.

The three most important takeaways from this chapter are as follows:

◆ The administrative closure refers to closing the work part of the project, and it includes obtaining product acceptance, compiling project records, reviewing the project for lessons learned, and archiving all this information so future projects can benefit from it.

◆ Contract closure refers to closing all the contracts applicable to the project; it is performed using the contract closure process.

◆ The administrative closure procedure and the contract closure procedure are both established using the close project process.

Summary

All projects, big or small, terminated or completed, should go through the closure stage, which involves administrative closure and contract closure. The administrative closure accomplishes closure of the work portion of the project and includes obtaining final acceptance for the project deliverables, analyzing the project's success or failure, gathering lessons learned, archiving project information, and releasing project resources. The contract closure includes settling and closing all the contracts associated with the project.

You use the close project process to perform the administrative closure as well as to establish the procedures for the administrative and contract closures. The contract closure process is used to close the contracts associated with the project.

Like every other profession, project management has its integrity and ethics that you need to uphold. You'll explore this topic in the next chapter.

Exam's Eye View

Comprehend

◆ You, the project manager, manage the project closure. You can even recommend the project closure to the project sponsor—for example, if you run out of resources and no more resources are available, but the authorization for the project closure must come from the sponsor.

◆ The project, in general, can have two kinds of work—in-house and procured. Accordingly there are two components of closure—administrative closure and contract closure.

◆ The contract closure process also has some administrative closure elements, such as acceptance of the (procured) product and additions to the documents archive and the lessons-learned database.

Look Out

◆ Not only the completed projects, but also the terminated projects, should be formally closed using the processes of the closing process group.

◆ Administrative closure procedure is an output of the close project process, not an input to it.

◆ The contact closure procedure is the output of the close project process, not of the contract closure process. However, it is an input into the contract closure process.

Memorize

◆ The project sponsor signs the final project closure documents. The sponsor can also authorize the closure of the project at any stage.

◆ The product acceptance is carried out using the close project process.

◆ The contracts are closed using the contract closure process.

◆ The contributions to the documentation archive, including the lessons learned database, are made by both the close project and the contract closure processes.

Key Terms

◆ **administrative closure.** Part of the project closure that includes obtaining final acceptance for the project deliverables, analyzing the project's success or failure, gathering lessons learned, archiving project information, and releasing project resources.

◆ **administrative closure procedure.** A procedure, developed during the close project process, used to carry out and coordinate the activities needed for the administrative closure.

◆ **close project.** A process used to finalize all activities across all of the process groups to formally close the project. It's also used to establish the procedures for administrative and contract closures.

◆ **contract closure.** The process used to complete and settle each contract, which includes resolving any open item and closing each contract applicable to the project.

◆ **contract closure procedure.** A procedure developed during the close project process, used to carry out and coordinate the activities needed for the contract closure.

Review Questions

1. Which of the following scenarios will not trigger the closure stage of the project?

    A. The project plan was not accepted, and therefore the project never went to the execution stage.

    B. All the project work has been completed successfully.

    C. The project was cancelled when it was in the middle of the executing stage.

    D. The project sponsor has withdrawn support for the project.

    E. A schedule activity on a critical path is way behind schedule, and there is no way you can meet the project finish date.

2. Your project has entered the closing stage, and you are planning for the project review. Which of the following guidelines will you follow for the review?

    A. Cover all the stages of the project and both its positive and negative aspects.

    B. The emphasis in the review should be on the schedule.

    C. The focus should be on the positive aspects of the project, where the team performed well. This will boost the morale of the team, and the team will even perform better in the future projects, and it will also help get funding for future projects.

    D. The focus of the review should be on the risk management.

3. At which stage has a successful project arrived when the closing process starts?
   A. Initiating
   B. Planning
   C. Executing
   D. Closing
   E. Completing

4. For which kind of projects it is appropriate to skip the closing stage?
   A. Technical projects
   B. Small and simple projects
   C. Large and complicated projects
   D. No projects
   E. All projects

5. Which of the following stakeholders can authorize the closure of a project?
   A. Project manager
   B. Customer
   C. Project sponsor
   D. Any stakeholder
   E. Functional manager

6. Which of the following is not an activity of the administrative closure of a project?
   A. Establishing an administrative closure procedure
   B. Obtaining formal acceptance for the final product
   C. Closing all the contracts associated with the project
   D. Archiving lessons-learned documents

7. Which of the following is not an input to the close project process?
   A. Administrative closure procedure
   B. Project management plan
   C. Project deliverables
   D. Work performance information

8. Which of the following is not an output of the close project process?
   A. Administrative closure procedure
   B. Contract closure procedure
   C. Closed contracts
   D. Project closure documentation

9. Which of the following processes is used to close out the project work portion of a project?

   A. Administrative closure

   B. Contract closure

   C. Activity closure

   D. Close project

10. The lessons learned are an output of which closing processes? (Choose two.)

    A. Close project

    B. Contract closure

    C. Work closure

    D. Administrative closure

Chapter 9

Performing Professional Responsibility

PMP Exam Objectives

Objective	What It Really Means
6.1 Ensure Individual Integrity	You must know that as a project manager you need to ensure personal integrity and professionalism by adhering to ethical standards, legal requirements, and social norms of the locality of your project.
6.2 Contribute to the Project Management Knowledge Base	You must know that you are expected to contribute to the project management knowledge base by sharing research, best practices, and lessons learned. The goal here is to advance the project management profession by improving the quality of project management and improving the capabilities of colleagues.
6.3 Enhance Personal Professional Competence	You must know that you are expected to continually improve your professional competence by acquiring and applying knowledge of project management, and thereby improving the project management services you offer.
6.4 Promote Interaction among Stakeholders	You must know that you are expected to promote a collaborative project management environment by facilitating interaction among the project team members and other stakeholders. You accomplish this in a professional and cooperative manner by showing respect for personal and cultural differences. For all these objectives, you must understand the Project Management Institute PMP Code of Professional Conduct.

As the name of the certification suggests, you are going to become a project management professional, if you are not one already. A professional is an individual who practices an occupation with professionalism, which is a bond that binds a professional with the code of conduct for that occupation.

Professionalism is not Einstein's theory of relativity. You might need to learn a few things in the beginning, but during the course of practicing a profession, professional conduct (that is, professionalism) becomes common sense. All professions share the essence of professionalism. It is as simple as doing the right thing. As a project manager, remember one golden rule: Deal with unprofessional situations directly, openly, and fairly, rather than ignoring them. Professionalism starts with individual integrity, which is based on truth, honesty, and openness.

Therefore, the key question in this chapter is, how can you practice project management with professional responsibility? In search of an answer, we will explore three avenues—individual integrity, interaction with clients and project stakeholders, and professional competence and contribution to the project management knowledge base.

Ensuring Individual Integrity

Professionalism begins with individual integrity, which is a state of being complete and incorruptible. You can look at integrity as a point of reference based on truth and honesty, and you can maintain your integrity by using this point of reference as a guideline for your behavior and decision-making. Integrity identifies you as who you are. If you don't have integrity, people won't know who you really are and they won't trust you. So, individual integrity is a very significant part of professionalism in any profession.

In project management, you maintain your integrity by being honest and truthful everywhere—in the PMP exam, as well as while working in the project management field.

Dealing with the PMP exam and PMI. While going through the process of obtaining PMP certification, individual integrity demands that it is your responsibility to adhere to the following practices:

◆ While going through the process of obtaining PMP certification, provide accurate and true information.

◆ Maintain the confidentiality of the content of the PMP examination. For example, do not disclose the questions in the exam to other PMP candidates.

◆ Cooperate with PMI concerning any ethical violation and in collecting the related information.

The same honesty, truthfulness, and openness that you exhibit during the process of obtaining PMP certification also applies while you are working in the field of project management.

Working in the project management field. The activities that you perform as a PMP include representing yourself as a PMP, advertising your organization and your services, and running projects. To maintain your individual integrity during these activities, it is your responsibility to adhere to the following practices:

◆ Be accurate and truthful in advertising and representing your qualifications, experience, and the services you can perform.

◆ Be accurate and truthful to the public in advertising and public statements. For example, if your project is going to damage the environment, don't say it's going to help the environment.

◆ Maintain and satisfy the scope and objectives of the services promised to the customer.

◆ Follow the applicable laws, regulations, and ethical standards of the city, state, and country of your workplace. For example, don't say something like, "This is not how we do it back in Texas."

◆ Neither offer nor accept inappropriate payments in any form, such as gifts, which might qualify as bribery.

TIP

When you are in a foreign country, sometimes it can be tricky to figure out the right thing to do in a given situation. The trick here is if you are being asked to do something, such as pay some money to an official for getting something done, that is not legal or ethical in your country and culture, first investigate whether it is legal and ethical in the country you are in now. If you find it to be illegal and unethical there as well, but you are told it's a common practice, do not do it.

As you practice project management, you will learn lessons you can share with the community of project managers—that is, you can contribute to the project management knowledge base.

Contributing to the Knowledge Base

Professionalism demands (or encourages) that project managers (or PMPs) contribute to the project management knowledge base by publishing, teaching, and sharing lessons learned during practice.

While doing so, you should adhere to the following practices:

◆ Share the information in an accurate, truthful, and complete manner.

◆ Recognize and honor the intellectual property developed or owned by others, and give credit where credit is due when you use it.

◆ Follow the PMP Code of Professional Conduct and disseminate it among the PMP community.

TIP

PMI expects a PMP to stay engaged and help advance the project management profession by completing tasks such as contributing to the knowledge base. So participating in project management training, mentoring, sharing lessons learned, and promoting best practices are all recommendations by PMI that might appear in some exam questions, even if you think they have nothing to do with running projects.

Contributing to the knowledge base is one side of the coin; the other side is obtaining the knowledge, or enhancing your individual professional competence.

Enhancing Individual Professional Competence

Professionalism in project management, as in any other field, demands that while practicing your profession you continue to learn and grow professionally. This is important for your individual success and for the advancement of the profession.

Project management is a very involved and growing field. PMP certification and this book only introduce you to the field. For example, you can focus on any of the nine knowledge areas, such as risk management or quality management, and explore it further. Exploring the existing dimensions further is one area of learning, and adding new dimensions is another. For example, how about managing virtual teams—that is, teams that are spread out geographically? This new dimension in project management is quickly becoming an important and integral part of the project management profession, even faster than PMI can digest.

Exploring existing dimensions further and practicing new dimensions enhances your individual professional competence, as well as enables you to contribute to the knowledge base. Working in the field will also expose your professional weaknesses, which you will need to work on. This is also an integral part of enhancing your individual professional competence.

Whether you are enhancing your individual professional competence or contributing to the knowledge base, you are interacting with other members of your professional community. During the course of a project, the most important interaction is the interaction among the project stakeholders.

Promoting Interaction among Stakeholders

A project manager needs to have a host of skills, and all of them are important. However, if I'm forced to name the most important skill a project manager has and the most important activity a project manager should perform, the answer would be communication. On that note, as a project manager, it is your responsibility to facilitate interaction among the project stakeholders. You use communication for various purposes, such as to keep everybody on the same page regarding the status and issues of the project so there is no confusion or misunderstanding.

While dealing with stakeholders and facilitating interaction among them, professionalism demands that you adhere to the following practices:

- ◆ Treat the stakeholder with respect and show respect for cultural diversity.
- ◆ Be accurate and truthful when presenting services and preparing estimates for costs and expected results.
- ◆ Be open and honest in your dealings with stakeholders, especially when you are resolving an issue.
- ◆ Honor confidentiality for the information you collect during your interactions with stakeholders.
- ◆ Disclose to stakeholders (clients, customers, owners, or contractors) significant circumstances that could be construed as conflicts of interest. It is your responsibility to ensure that a conflict of interest does not compromise the legitimate interests of a stakeholder and does not influence your professional judgments.

The material in this chapter is largely based on the PMP Code of Professional Conduct statement by PMI.

Getting It Straight from the Horse's Mouth

The PMI's philosophy on professional responsibility is not covered in the project management book of knowledge (PMBOK). However, you sign the PMP Code of Professional Conduct statement by PMI when you apply to take the PMP exam. I recommend that you study this statement carefully because most of the questions based on this topic will be directly or indirectly based on this statement. The statement is presented here in its entirety.

Project Management Institute PMP Code of Professional Conduct

As a PMI Project Management Professional (PMP) I agree to support and adhere to the responsibilities described in the PMI PMP Code of Professional Conduct.

I. **Responsibilities to the Profession**

    A. **Compliance with all organizational rules and policies**

        1. Responsibility to provide accurate and truthful representations concerning all information directly or indirectly related to all aspects of the PMI Certification Program, including but not limited to the following examination applications, test item banks, examinations, answer sheets, candidate information and PMI Continuing Certification Requirements Program reporting forms.

        2. Upon a reasonable and clear factual basis, responsibility to report possible violations of the PMP Code of Professional Conduct by individuals in the field of project management.

        3. Responsibility to cooperate with PMI concerning ethics violations and the collection of related information.

        4. Responsibility to disclose to clients, customers, owners or contractors, significant circumstances that could be construed as a conflict of interest or an appearance of impropriety.

    B. **Candidate/Certificant Professional Practice**

        1. Responsibility to provide accurate, truthful advertising and representations concerning qualifications, experience and performance of services.

        2. Responsibility to comply with applicable laws, regulations and ethical standards governing professional practice in the state/province and/or country when interacting with PMI and when providing project management services.

        3. Responsibility to act in an honest and ethical manner when interacting with PMI and when providing project management services.

        4. Responsibility to maintain and respect the confidentiality of the contents of the PMP Examination.

   C. **Advancement of the Profession**

      1. Responsibility to recognize and respect intellectual property developed or owned by others, and to otherwise act in an accurate, truthful and complete manner, including all activities related to professional work and research.

      2. Responsibility to support and disseminate the PMP Code of Professional Conduct to other PMI certificants.

II. **Responsibilities to Customers and the Public**

   A. **Qualifications, experience and performance of professional services**

      1. Responsibility to provide accurate and truthful representations to the public in advertising, public statements and in the preparation of estimates concerning costs, services and expected results.

      2. Responsibility to maintain and satisfy the scope and objectives of professional services, unless otherwise directed by the customer.

      3. Responsibility to maintain and respect the confidentiality of sensitive information obtained in the course of professional activities or otherwise where a clear obligation exists.

   B. **Conflict of interest situations and other prohibited professional conduct**

      1. Responsibility to ensure that a conflict of interest does not compromise legitimate interests of a client or customer, or influence/interfere with professional judgments.

      2. Responsibility to refrain from offering or accepting inappropriate payments, gifts or other forms of compensation for personal gain, unless in conformity with applicable laws or customs of the country where project management services are being provided.

III. **Administration of Code of Conduct**

By becoming a PMP certificant, you agree to abide by this Code of Conduct. PMI reserves the right to suspend or revoke the credential of any PMP certificant who is determined to have committed a violation of this Code or otherwise failed to adhere to the tenets of this Code.

Dealing with Unprofessional Conduct

Working as a project manager, you will encounter minor to serious unprofessional conduct from time to time. The key here is, again, to be honest, truthful, and open.

TIP

You might encounter small ethical violations, which might be painful to resolve. However, as a professional, you should choose to address them instead of ignoring them, and you should address them openly, fairly, and in a timely fashion.

As you already know, we live in a world of duality—good and bad, pleasure and pain, professionalism and unprofessionalism, and the like, all living side by side. Scary! However, if you stick to *your* professionalism, then you do not need to be afraid of a lack of professionalism in others. Do not focus on the person; focus on the conduct and remember that the only weapon you have to defeat a lack of professionalism is professionalism. If you are unprofessional, you cannot defeat a lack of professionalism; you can only promote it.

So, when you encounter a lack of professionalism, stay professional, focus on the issue and not on the person, maintain a smile on your face, and deal with the situation honestly, openly, and truthfully.

The three most important takeaways from this chapter are as follows:

◆ You should practice your profession with professionalism, supported by individual integrity based on honesty, truthfulness, and openness.

◆ You should interact with your clients and project stakeholders with respect, truthfulness, and openness. Show your respect to diversity in cultures, and follow the law of the land for your workplace.

◆ You should continue enhancing your professional competence and contributing to the project management knowledge base.

Summary

As a PMP, you must practice project management with professionalism—that is, with professional responsibility—which includes following the rules and policies of the certification process and of the organization for which you are managing the project. The key to professionalism is individual integrity based on honesty, truth, and openness. Professionalism requires that you interact with your client and with the project stakeholders with mutual dignity and respect, and show respect to diversity of cultures and beliefs. If you encounter an unprofessional situation, rather than ignoring it, you deal with it honestly, openly, and truthfully. Your professional responsibility as a PMP also demands that you continue enhancing your professional competence and contributing to the project management knowledge base.

Keep in mind that while honesty, truth, and openness are essential elements of individual integrity regardless of where you are, the definitions of right versus wrong, acceptable versus unacceptable, and to some extent ethical versus unethical might vary across cultures. Sometimes you will need to think hard to do the right thing when faced with tricky situations. For example, just because bribery is a common and acceptable practice in a country, that does not make it the right thing to do, especially if it is illegal. When you are not sure which option is the right one, investigate whether it is legal and ethical in that country.

Exam's Eye View

Comprehend

◆ Honesty, truthfulness, and openness define integrity, which is the key to professionalism.

◆ While managing a project, you will perform the selected process for the project and will not cut corners—for example, to save money. A process is in place for the overall efficiency of the project, not as a formality.

◆ If an option sounds sneaky, manipulative, and as if it favors one stakeholder against another, it is not the option you want to choose.

◆ Disclose any conflict of interest to the relevant client and don't let this conflict influence your professional judgment.

Look Out

◆ Do not do something that is illegal, unethical, or both in the country and culture of your workplace, even if it is legal and ethical back home.

◆ Do not do something that is illegal, unethical, or both, even if you are told that it is a common and acceptable practice.

◆ When you encounter an unprofessional attitude or situation, deal with it quickly, honestly, and openly even when it is hard to do so and easy to ignore the problem.

◆ Beware of the options that offer you easier ways out or shortcuts. Those options are usually wrong.

◆ Showing respect to other cultures does not mean getting involved in something illegal.

Memorize

◆ Follow the law of the land for your workplace.

◆ Show respect to other individuals and cultures.

◆ Honor the confidentiality of information that you learn during the course of getting certified, dealing with customers, and managing projects.

◆ Help advance the profession of project management by enhancing your individual professional competence and by contributing to the project management knowledge base.

Review Questions

1. You have applied for the PMP exam, and you are attending a training session for the exam offered by a PMP who proudly poses a number of questions to the audience and claims that these are the questions in the real exam. What should you do? (Choose one.)

    A. Immediately leave the classroom and never take another course from the same training agency.

    B. Write to the president of the training agency.

    C. Report this trainer to the police.

    D. Contact PMI and inform them of the situation.

2. You are managing a project in a country foreign to you. The project sponsor asks you to write a check to a city official to get some paperwork required for the project moving forward. Such an activity in your home country would be considered bribery, which is illegal. What should you do?

    A. Investigate whether what the sponsor is suggesting is legal and ethical in this country.

    B. Report the sponsor to the police.

    C. Write the check to the city official because the project sponsor asked you to do so.

    D. Tell the sponsor that he's an unethical person and you are leaving the project.

3. You are managing a project in a country foreign to you. The project sponsor asks you to write a check to a city official to get some paperwork required for the project moving forward. She confesses that it is, as a matter of fact, bribery and is technically illegal, but it is a very common and acceptable practice in this country. What should you do?

    A. Go ahead and do it.

    B. Tell the project sponsor politely that because it is illegal you cannot do it.

    C. Write an e-mail to the project sponsor's boss.

    D. Tell the sponsor that she's an unethical person and you are leaving the project.

    E. Report the project sponsor to the police.

4. You are managing a project in a country foreign to you and the project is in the planning stage. The project sponsor asks you to inflate the cost estimate by 30 percent. He says, "We're not in Kansas anymore, buddy; if you want to get the license for a pistol here, you would have to apply for a machine gun." He insists that this is the only way he can get the required money because the management always reduces the estimate before allotting the money. Which of the following is the best step you could take?

A. Report the project sponsor to PMI.

B. Inflate the cost estimate as the sponsor said; after all, he is the sponsor.

C. Prepare an accurate estimate along with a risk report that explains the risks involved if the adequate funds are not available.

D. Prepare two cost estimates—one for the management and another one for actual implementation.

E. Quit the project.

5. You are the project manager of a project that needs to procure a bunch of activities as a subproject due to the lack of skills in the organization. Your sister-in-law owns a firm that specializes in the area of the activities that need to be procured. She has shown an interest in this procurement. Which of the following steps would be the best to take?

A. Allot this work to your sister-in-law. After all, her firm specializes in this area.

B. Allot this work to your sister-in-law and make sure you don't let your relationship affect your professional judgment.

C. Disclose your relationship with your sister-in-law to the stakeholders and allow multiple vendors to bid for the opportunity. Excuse yourself from the final decision-making.

D. Insist that this is part of networking and you can get the best deal from your sister-in-law.

6. Which two of the following are not expected by the PMP Code of Professional Conduct? (Remember, choose two.)

A. Making publications based on your experience or research in project management

B. Taking classes to improve your professional weaknesses in project management

C. Going to church or temple as often as you can to learn about ethics

D. Cooperating with PMI concerning ethics violations

E. Reporting possible violations of the PMP Code of Professional Conduct by individuals in the field of project management

F. Keeping an eye on your PMP colleagues if they are involved in unethical conduct, such as taking drugs or watching X-rated movies, and reporting to PMI any PMP involved in such activities.

7. You are the project manager for a project that involves procurement. Multiple vendors bid for the work to be procured. The cost estimate from Best Deals is significantly higher than from any other vendor. Which of the following is an appropriate action to take?

   A. Be open and ask Best Deals why their estimate is higher than that of all other vendors.

   B. Communicate with Best Deals to find out exactly how they reached this estimate and what statement of work they are using to make the estimate.

   C. Talk to other bidders to find out what's going on with Best Deals. Why are their estimates so high?

   D. Write to the CEO of Best Deals to complain about this outrageously high estimate.

8. You are the project manager for the Peace in the City project. You have learned that three of the stakeholders have started fighting over the scope of the project. What step will you take?

   A. Contact the stakeholders and check whether they have any questions about the scope of the project. Starting this way, you will resolve the conflict.

   B. Contact the senior management and report the conflict to them so they can resolve it.

   C. Contact the project sponsor and inform him of the conflict among the stakeholders so the sponsor can resolve it.

   D. Don't do anything; just keep your focus on the actual work of the project.

9. You have taken over a project which is already in the executing stage. You discover that some of the milestones still in progress have been reported as completed to the senior management by the previous project manager in the status reports. Which of the following is the best first step to take?

   A. There is no need to inform the stakeholders about it; just use schedule compression techniques to make up the difference.

   B. Immediately inform stakeholders and senior management of the discrepancy and provide them with the accurate project status.

   C. Report the previous manager to PMI.

   D. Ask the sponsor what to do now.

10. You are hired as a project manager for a company. Which of the following is not your responsibility?

    A. Ensuring that no project activity violates the law of the land

    B. Honoring the confidentiality of the information you collected while managing the project

    C. Determining whether company procedures are legal

    D. Contributing to the project management knowledge base

Appendix A

Answers to Chapter Review Questions

Learning Objectives

◆ Understand why the correct answers are correct

◆ Understand why the incorrect answers are incorrect

Chapter 1

1. Answer: D and E

    D and **E** are the correct answers because the defining characteristics of a project are that it must be temporary (with a start and finish date), and it must produce a unique (new) product.

    A and **B** are incorrect because it's possible to have a project that will involve only one person, and there could be a project without an individual called the project manager. The only two defining characteristics of a project are that it is temporary and unique.

    C is incorrect because an operation can have a budget too.

2. Answer: B

    B is the correct answer because building a library is temporary—that is, it will have a start and a finish date, and it will be new library.

    A, C, and **D** are incorrect because running a donut shop, keeping a network up and running, and running a warehouse are all ongoing operations.

3. Answer: C

    C is the correct answer because there is no process group in project management called implementing. The five process groups representing the five stages of the project lifecycle are initiating, planning, executing, monitoring/controlling, and closing.

    A, B, D, and **E** are incorrect because the five process groups representing the five stages of the project lifecycle are initiating, planning, executing, monitoring/controlling, and closing.

4. Answer: D

    D is the correct answer because team management is part of the knowledge area called human resource management.

    A, B, C, and **E** are incorrect because all these are four of the nine project management knowledge areas.

5. Answer: A

   A is the correct and the best answer because the project plan is developed starting from the concept and going through progressive elaboration.

   B and **C** are incorrect because B includes project lifecycle and C is the lifecycle. Progressive elaboration does not include the lifecycle of the project; its goal is to plan the project. Because the project planning can develop (or change) throughout the project lifecycle, progressive elaboration can continue through the project lifecycle, but it does not include the work of the lifecycle.

   D is incorrect because decomposing the project into smaller, more manageable work pieces is a technique used in creating the WBS.

6. Answer: C

   C is the correct answer because the matrix organization provides the greatest authority for the project manager.

   A and **B** are incorrect because the authority of the project manager is none to low in a functional organization and low to high in a matrix organization.

   D is incorrect because there is no organizational structure called leveled.

7. Answer: A

   A is the correct answer because the authority of the project manager is none to low in a functional organization.

   B and **C** are incorrect because the authority of the project manager is high to full in a projectized organization and low to high in a matrix organization.

   D is incorrect because there is no organizational structure called leveled.

Chapter 2

1. Answer: A

   A is correct because the management of the performing organization issues the project charter.

   B is incorrect because issuing a project charter is the responsibility of the performing organization, and a stakeholder does not have to be even a member of the performing organization.

   C is incorrect because issuing a project charter is the responsibility of the performing organization, and a customer does not have to be even a member of the performing organization.

   D is incorrect because the charter authorizes the project manager and not vice versa.

2.   Answer: B and D

    B and **D** are correct because the project charter and preliminary statement of work are two documents that are the output of the initiation process group.

    A is incorrect because the statement of work is an input to the initiation process group and not a result (output) of it.

    C is incorrect because the scope plan document does not belong to the initiation phase.

3.   Answer: B and C

    B and **C** are correct because the project charter names the project manger and provides the project manager the authority to use organizational resources to run the project.

    A is incorrect because the sponsor is not authorized by the project charter; the opposite might be true.

    D is incorrect because it will be your responsibility to identify all the stakeholders.

    E is incorrect because the project team is not formed in the initiation phase.

4.   Answer: D

    D is correct because the initial defined risks item is part of the preliminary project statement, not a part of the project charter.

    A, B, C, and **E** are incorrect because all these items may be included in the project charter.

5.   Answer: F

    F is correct because the statement of work is an input into developing the preliminary project statement, not a part of it.

    A, B, C, D, and **E** are incorrect because all these items may be included in the preliminary project scope statement.

6.   Answer: A

    A is correct because the statement of work is an input to the project charter and the preliminary scope statement, and the project charter is an input to the preliminary scope statement.

    B is incorrect because the statement of work is an input to the project charter, so it must be available before the project charter.

    C is incorrect because both the statement of work and the project charter are input to the preliminary scope statement, so they must be developed before the scope statement can be.

    D is incorrect because the project charter is an input to the preliminary scope statement and not vice versa.

7. Answer: B

   B is correct because a hard deadline imposed on a project is an example of a constraint.

   A is incorrect because an assumption is a factor that you believe to be true; it is not a condition such as a hard deadline.

   C is incorrect because a hard deadline tells very little about the actual schedule.

   D is incorrect because crashing is the process of assigning more resources to finish a project by a given deadline. Just because a deadline is given does not necessarily mean that you need crashing.

8. Answer: B

   B is correct because assumptions represent uncertainty and hence risk. Assumptions must be validated and analyzed as part of the risk management at various stages of the project.

   A is incorrect because assumptions by definition represent uncertainty, and as a project manager, it is your responsibility to validate the assumptions at various stages of the project.

   C is incorrect because it is not the correct definition of assumption.

   D is incorrect because you can start the project with the assumptions. All you have to do is validate them at various stages of the project and analyze them as part of the risk management.

9. Answer: E

   E is correct because enterprise environmental factors are an input to the project charter and the preliminary project statement, not a project selection method.

   A, B, C, and **D** are incorrect because expert judgment, scoring models, benefit cost ratio, and constrained optimization methods are all project selection methods.

10. Answer: A

    A is correct because adding parental guide notices is a business (legal) requirement.

    B is incorrect because adding these notices is not an opportunity to make revenues; it is a requirement that must be met to keep the Web site up without offending the customers or the legal system.

    C and **D** are incorrect because the project at hand does not solve any organizational problem and is not launched to meet any internal organizational need.

Chapter 3

1. Answer: D

   D is the correct answer because the work packages don't have to appear in the order the work will be performed. This sequencing will be done later.

   A, B, and **C** are the incorrect answers because theses are the characteristics of the WBS.

2. Answer: D

   D is correct because the project charter is created in the initiation stage and it is an input item to creating the preliminary project scope statement.

   A is incorrect because the project charter and the preliminary project scope statement are input items into creating the project scope statement.

   B is incorrect because the project scope statement is an input item into creating the WBS.

   C is incorrect because the project charter is an input item into creating the preliminary project scope statement.

3. Answer: A

   A is correct because the create WBS process is used to create the WBS.

   B is incorrect because the scope definition process is used to create the project scope statement.

   C is incorrect because there is no such process named creating project scope.

   D is incorrect because project initiation is a process group that includes two processes to develop the project charter and the preliminary project scope statement.

4. Answer: B

   B is correct because the scope definition process is used to create the project scope statement.

   A is incorrect because the create WBS process is used to create the WBS.

   C is incorrect because there is no such process named creating project scope.

   D is incorrect because project initiation is a process group that includes two processes to develop the project charter and the preliminary project scope statement.

5. Answer: C

   C is the correct answer because the scope statement, the WBS document, and the WBS dictionary combined make the scope baseline against which all the change requests will be evaluated.

   A, B, and **D** are incorrect because all these are true statements about the project scope management plan.

6. Answer: A

    A is correct because the components in the lowest level of the WBS hierarchy are called *work packages*.

    B is incorrect because a milestone might consist of more than one work package.

    C is incorrect because if a phase is represented in the WBS it will be represented at a much higher level.

    D is incorrect because a feature does not necessarily correspond to one work package.

7. Answer: E

    E is correct because the four constraints common across all the projects are resources, scope, time, and quality.

    A, B, C, and **D** are incorrect because the four constraints common across all the projects are resources, scope, time, and quality. Cost (resources), scope, and schedule (time) are the constraints collectively called a *triple constraint* because if one of them changes, at least one of the other two must change.

8. Answer: D

    D is correct because the detailed scope statement, the WBS document, and the WBS dictionary combined make the scope baseline for the project.

    A is incorrect because the preliminary scope statement does not need to be included in the baseline, whereas you must include the WBS document and the WBS dictionary.

    B is incorrect because you must include the WBS document and the WBS dictionary in the scope baseline.

    C is incorrect because you must include the scope statement and the WBS dictionary in the scope baseline.

    E is incorrect because you must include the scope statement in the scope baseline.

9. Answer: D

    D is correct because you, the project manager, create the WBS with help from the project team.

    A is incorrect because the project manager creates the WBS with help from the team.

    B is incorrect because the project manager creates the WBS with help from the team; however, the project sponsor can help as part of the team.

    C and **E** are incorrect because neither the customer nor the upper management of the performing organization creates the WBS.

10. Answer: B

    B is correct because the WBS is not part of the project statement; it is an output of the create WBS process, to which the scope statement is an input item.

    A, C, D, and **E** are incorrect because all these items are parts of the scope statement.

Chapter 4

1. Answer: B

   B is the correct answer because a risk can have a negative or a positive effect on a project.

   A, C, and **D** are incorrect answers because these are true statements about project risks.

2. Answer: A

   A is correct because the risk register is the output of the risk identification process, but it is not used as an input because it does not exist before this process.

   B, C, and **D** are incorrect because the risk register is an input item to qualitative risk analysis, quantitative risk analysis, and risk response planning, whereas the updated risk register is an output from each of these processes.

3. Answer: D

   D is the correct answer because you cannot identify risks in your specific project based on the information collected from the Web.

   A, B, and **C** are incorrect answers because brainstorming, Delphi technique, and SWOT analysis are valid information-gathering techniques used for identifying risks.

4. Answer: A

   A is the correct answer because depending upon the experience of the team, a risk can be moved directly after the identification process to the quantitative process without performing the qualitative analysis.

   B, C, and **D** are incorrect answers because these are true statements.

5. Answer: B

   B is correct because building redundancy into a system is an example of mitigating the risk.

   A is incorrect because the risk can still happen because you have not changed the plan, such as moving the server center to some other city.

   C is incorrect because accepting a risk means no action or conditional action.

   D is incorrect because you have not transferred the risk to a third party.

6. Answer: D

   D is correct because you have transferred the risk to a third party.

   A is incorrect because the risk can still happen because you have not changed the plan, such as eliminating the need for that part of the system.

   B is incorrect because mitigating the risk does not involve transferring the risk to a third party.

   C is incorrect because accepting a risk means no action or conditional action.

7. Answer: C

   C is correct because the numerical analysis of a risk is called *quantitative analysis.*

   A is incorrect because assigning numbers does not necessarily mean you are performing a Monte Carlo simulation, although it is one of the tools to perform quantitative analysis.

   B is incorrect because qualitative analysis does not involve numerical analysis, such as EMV calculations.

   D is incorrect because risk response planning will be based on the results of risk analysis.

8. Answer: D

   D is correct because the probability of the risk is 50% and the probability of the positive impact is 40%, so the total probability for the positive impact to happen is $0.5 * 0.4 = 0.2$.

   > EMV = Probability * Value of the outcome = 0.2 * $200, 000 = $40,000

   A, B, and **C** are incorrect because they show wrong values for EMV.

9. Answer: A

   A is correct because the probability of the risk is 50%, and the probability of the positive impact is 40%, so the total probability for the positive impact to happen is $0.5 * 0.4 = 0.2$.

   > EMV = Probability * Value of the outcome = 0.2 * $200, 000 = $40,000
   > Similarly, EMV for threat = 0.3 * $50,000 = –$15,000
   > Therefore, EMV for the risk = $40,000 – $15,000 = $25,000

   B, C, and **D** are incorrect because they show wrong values for EMV.

10. Answer: E

    E is correct because secondary risks are those risks that arise as a result of risk responses.

    A is incorrect because a residual risk is a risk that remains after a response has been performed.

    B is incorrect because depending upon the nature of the secondary risk, it may have any priority.

    C and **D** are incorrect because the risk response will depend upon the analysis results of the risk.

11. Answer: E

    E is the correct answer because there is no such risk response named risk rejection.

    A, B, C, and **D** are all incorrect answers because these are valid risk responses.

12. Answer: A

    A is correct because SWOT is a risk identification technique that identifies the risks by examining the strengths, weaknesses, opportunities, and threats (SWOT) of a given project.

    B is incorrect because this is a wrong statement about SWOT.

    C and **D** are incorrect because SWOT is a technique used in risk identification, not in risk response planning, nor in quantitative risk analysis.

13. Answer: C

    C is the correct answer because you need to perform quantitative risk analysis to create a list of risks prioritized based on the total effect of each risk on the overall project objectives.

    A, **B**, and **D** are incorrect because these are the possible output items from the qualitative risk analysis.

14. Answer: E

    E is the correct answer because a risk-related contractual agreement can be an output of the risk response planning, not the quantitative risk analysis.

    A, **B**, **C**, and **D** are incorrect because all these are the possible output items from the quantitative risk analysis.

15. Answer: B

    B is the correct answer because benchmarking is a quality planning technique that compares practices, products, or services of a project with those of some reference projects for the purpose of learning, improving, and creating the basis for measuring performance.

    A is incorrect because you can always brainstorm, but it does not have to compare the results of similar activities.

    C is incorrect because although it is a quality planning technique, it involves striking a balance between cost and benefit (which are not similar).

    D and **E** are incorrect because quality metrics and quality checklists are not quality planning techniques; these are the output items of the quality planning process.

Chapter 5

1. Answer: C

   C is the correct answer because the precedence diagramming method is the most commonly used network diagramming method that can be used in the activity sequencing process to represent any of the four kinds of dependencies.

   A and **B** are incorrect because CPM and CCM are the network diagram analysis methods that are used in the schedule development process.

   D is incorrect because the arrow diagramming method is not the popular method, and it can only be used to represent one of the four kinds of dependencies: the finish-to-start dependency.

2. Answer: B

   B is the correct answer because crashing is used to compress the schedule by adding more resources to the project.

   A and **D** are incorrect because the network diagramming method and the sequencing method do not need crashing.

   C is incorrect because crashing does not reduce cost. It may well increase cost when you commit additional resources.

3. Answer: E

   E is the correct answer because the critical path is the longest sequence in the network diagram, and therefore it controls the finish date for a given start date; also, each activity on the critical path has a zero float time.

   Because both **A** and **B** are true, and you are allowed to choose only one, you choose E.

   C is incorrect because the critical path controls the finish date for a given start date.

   D is incorrect because the critical path is the longest sequence, not the shortest.

4. Answer: B

   B is the correct answer because an activity has external dependency when it relies on factors outside the project.

   A is incorrect because activity Y has a mandatory dependency on activity X when Y inherently depends on X.

   C is incorrect because there is no such dependency called internal.

   D is incorrect because we have an external dependency here.

   E is incorrect because the finish-to-start relationship is not relevant to this dependency.

5. Answer: B and E

   B and **E** are correct because finish-to-start dependency means that the successor (B) activity cannot start until the predecessor (A) activity is finished.

   A is incorrect because the start-to-finish relationship means that the successor activity cannot finish until the predecessor activity is started.

   C is incorrect because we do not have enough information to say that this dependency is mandatory.

   D is incorrect because just because there is a dependency between two activities, that does not mean they are on the critical path.

6. Answer: A

   A is the correct answer because each activity on the critical path has a zero float time, and therefore if an activity is delayed it will delay the entire project.

   B, C, and **D** are incorrect because these are incorrect statements about the activities on the critical path.

7. Answer: C

   C is the correct answer because the analogous estimating technique estimates the duration of an activity based on the duration of a similar activity in a previous project.

   A is incorrect because parametric estimating uses parameters such as the productivity rate of the resource assigned to the activity.

   B is incorrect because the individual in this example used the analogous method and not the expert judgment method, even though he happened to be an expert.

   D is incorrect because the Delphi technique is used for risk identification, not for activity duration estimating, and also there are multiple experts involved in the Delphi technique.

8. Answer: C

   C is correct because the team member is offering a valid reason for the change, and it does not affect the finish date of the project. However you must change the schedule to reflect the new duration estimate.

   A and **F** are incorrect because you do not need to consult with the functional manager or the project sponsor in making this decision because the team member is offering a valid reason for the change, and it does not affect the finish date of the project.

   B is incorrect because the schedule should reflect the current reality. Because you accepted the schedule change, the schedule must reflect it.

   D is incorrect because this change does not qualify to be processed through the integrated change control process.

   E is incorrect because the proposed change does not mean that the team member does not have the skills to perform the activity.

9. Answer: A

   A is the correct answer because float time is the positive difference between the allowed late start date and the early start date of a schedule activity, without changing the schedule finish date.

   B, C, and **D** are incorrect because these are not the valid terms used to describe delaying an activity without changing the schedule finish date.

10. Answer: B

    B is the correct answer because by doing some activities in parallel (fast tracking) you might be able to compress the schedule without adding cost.

    A is incorrect because crashing usually results in increased cost because it involves adding extra resources.

    C is incorrect because the project sponsor is sponsoring (paying for) the project. So, asking for a new sponsor does not make sense; it can only trigger the sponsor to ask for a new project manager.

    D is incorrect because you do not want to bypass the sponsor on budgetary matters because the budget will need the sponsor's approval.

    E is incorrect because your role is of a project manager, and that's what you should do. By performing the activities yourself, you might be stepping on other people's toes—and, how many projects can you finish in time by applying this technique?

11. Answer: C

    C is the correct answer because it has the longest sequence: 8 + 6 + 8 = 22.

    A is incorrect because this path is only 20 units long.

    B is incorrect because there is no such path as Start-I-G-E-Finish in this network diagram.

    D is incorrect because this path is only 21 units long, which is less than 22.

    E is incorrect because there is no such path as Start-I-G-H-E-Finish in this network diagram.

12. Answer: D

    D is the correct answer because the float time for G is zero because it is on the critical path.

    A, B, and **C** are incorrect because G is on the critical path and must have a float time of zero.

13. Answer: C

    C is the correct answer because if you consider all the paths in the network diagram, the path Start-F-G-H-Finish adds up to 22, which is longer than any other path in the diagram.

    A, B, D, and **E** are incorrect because they do not add up to the correct total for the path.

14. Answer: A

A is the correct answer because in the three-point method the duration estimate is calculated as the average of the three values: (9 + 18 + 12) / 3 = 13.

B is incorrect because the average should be taken of the three points, not just between the smallest and the largest number.

C, D, and **E** are incorrect because the duration estimate is the average of the three points.

15. Answer: B

B is the correct answer because the activity duration is calculated after an activity has been defined.

A, C, and **D** are incorrect because the WBS, project scope statement, and WBS dictionary are valid input items to the activity definition process.

16. Answer: D

D is the correct answer because a chart that displays the resource requirements for each activity is an example of a resource assignment matrix (RAM).

A is incorrect because a project organization chart represents the relationships between the different roles in the project, and that is not what the management wants.

B is incorrect because the WBS contains the work packages, not the activities and the resource requirements.

C is incorrect because the management wants the resource requirements for each activity, not just a list of roles and responsibilities.

17. Answer: C

C is the correct answer because the project schedule is the output of the schedule development process.

A, B, and **D** are incorrect because all these items are the output of the human resource planning process.

18. Answer: C

C is the correct answer because the project manager (along with the project management team) is responsible for the staff management plan, and it is created as an output of the human resource planning process.

A, B, and **D** are incorrect because these are the false statements about the staff management plan.

Chapter 6

1. Answer: D

   D is the correct answer because corrective actions are recommended by the QA process.

   A, B, and **C** are incorrect answers because deliverables and work performance information (status) are generated, and defect repairs are implemented by the direct and manage project execution process.

2. Answer: D

   D is the correct answer because corrective actions are an output item of the QA process.

   A, B, and **C** are incorrect answers because quality metrics are generated by quality planning, work performance information (status) is generated, and defect repairs are implemented by the direct and manage project execution process, and they all become input to the QA process.

3. Answer: C

   C is the correct answer because cost overrun is paid by the buyer, and the fee increases with the increase in cost as well.

   A is incorrect because the firm fixed price presents risk to both buyer and seller because the fixed price might turn out to be above or below the actual cost.

   B and **D** are incorrect because the fee in these cases does not rise with the rise of the actual cost.

   E is incorrect because in a time and material contract, there could be a cost overrun to be paid by the buyer, but unlike a contract, in the category of cost plus percentage of cost there is no increasing fee attached to the increasing cost.

4. Answer: A

   A is the correct answer because a firm fixed price presents a risk to the seller if the fixed price turns out to be lower than the actual cost.

   B, C, D, and **E** are incorrect because only the firm fixed price can present risk to the seller.

5. Answer: C

   C is the correct answer because the buy or make analysis is a technique used in the procurement planning process called *plan purchases and acquisitions*.

   A, B, and **D** are incorrect because you must know if you are going to buy or make before you start implementing the procurement.

6. Answer: A

A is the correct answer because you can fairly estimate the cost for one program, and you do not know the number of programs required.

B and **C** are incorrect because the reimbursable cost does not make sense in this case, and you don't have to add a fee to the cost.

D is incorrect because you cannot correctly estimate the total price because you do not know how many programs are required.

7. Answer: D

D is the correct answer because the procurement documents should be rigorous enough to ensure consistent responses from different sellers that could be fairly compared with one another, and flexible enough to allow the sellers to offer suggestions on better ways to satisfy the requirements.

A is incorrect because it does not allow the sellers to be creative in offering solutions.

B is incorrect because the documents must be rigid enough that each seller understands the requirements.

C is incorrect because the requirements are set by the buyer and not by the seller.

8. Answer: C

C is the correct answer because the amount of work, and hence the cost, cannot be determined at this point.

A is incorrect because the amount of work, and hence the cost, cannot be determined at this point.

B is incorrect because a time and material contract is used when the cost of an item can be fairly estimated but the number of needed items is unknown. This is not the case here.

D is incorrect because there is no such contract type as cost plus time.

9. Answer: E

E is the correct answer because collaboration offers a win/win resolution.

A is incorrect because avoidance ignores the problem rather than solving it.

B is incorrect because in compromising both parties give up something and might look at the resolution as a lose/lose proposition.

C is incorrect because accommodation offers a win/lose resolution; one party gives up something to accommodate the interests of the other party.

D is incorrect because in competition one party attempts to get its way at the expense of the other party, and it could cause the conflict to escalate. Even using this technique from a power position (forcing) is not a good idea, when you have a choice.

10. Answer: B

B is the correct answer because quality planning is the process to plan for quality, which is the degree to which the project requirements are met.

A is incorrect because quality control is the process to monitor the specific project results to ensure they meet the planned quality standards.

C is incorrect because quality assurance is the process of applying (not planning) the planned quality activities to ensure (and verify) that the requirements are met.

D is incorrect because this answer is not relevant to the given scenario.

11. Answer: A

A is the correct answer because the quality audit is a technique for performing quality assurance.

B and **C** are incorrect because the quality audit is a technique for performing quality assurance, whereas quality planning is about determining which quality standards are relevant to the project, and how to satisfy them. Quality assurance is about applying the planned quality activities.

D is incorrect because there is no such quality management process as quality inspection.

12. Answer: D

D is the correct answer because you are forcing your way on the other party.

A and **B** are incorrect because you are neither ignoring the problem nor compromising.

C is incorrect because you are not accommodating the other side.

13. Answer: E

E is the correct answer because change in budget has very little to do directly with the team development.

A and **B** are incorrect answers because the project kickoff meeting is an indirect method to start team development, and an effective resolution of a conflict does contribute to team building.

C and **D** are also incorrect answers because during the times when the team is in a low-morale mode, you should be able to lift the team morale and thereby contribute to team development. Also, during the organizational changes, some team members might start wondering what it means to them, which might disrupt the project work. So, it is your responsibility to help the team keep their eyes on the ball, and this way you contribute to the team development.

Chapter 7

1. Answer: E

    E is the correct answer because changes can happen and need to be managed throughout the lifecycle of a project.

    A, B, C, and **D** are incorrect because changes can happen and need to be managed throughout the lifecycle of a project.

2. Answer: C

    C is the correct answer because the Ishikawa diagram is a tool used in the perform quality control process to explore all the potential causes of a problem.

    A and **B** are incorrect because the Ishikawa diagram is a tool used in the quality control process.

    D is incorrect because auditing is a technique used in the QA process.

    E is incorrect because inspection is another tool used in the quality control process.

3. Answer: A

    A is the correct answer because a control chart is used to plot the results to determine whether they are within the acceptable limits.

    B is incorrect because a cause and effect diagram, also called an *Ishikawa diagram* or a *fishbone diagram*, is used to explore all the possible causes of a problem.

    C is incorrect because a Pareto diagram is used to identify and rank the errors based on the frequency of defects caused by them.

    D is incorrect because a scatter diagram is used to find the relationship between two variables, such as cause and effect, or two causes.

4. Answer: C

    C is the correct answer because a Pareto diagram can be used to rank the problems based on the frequency of defects caused by them. Then, you will direct the team effort to fix those problems that caused most of the defects.

    A is incorrect because a control chart is used to plot the results to determine whether they are within the acceptable limits.

    B is incorrect because a cause and effect diagram, also called an *Ishikawa diagram* or a *fishbone diagram*, is used to explore all the possible causes of a problem.

    D is incorrect because a scatter diagram is used to find the relationship between two variables, such as cause and effect, or two causes.

5. Answer: B

B is the correct answer because by using statistical sampling, you will pick up a few samples of the code at random and get them reviewed. The results will represent the quality of the whole code, statistically speaking.

A is incorrect because this is not an unreasonable demand.

C is incorrect because testing tools cannot serve the purpose of a code review, and the customer wants the code review.

D is incorrect because you have limited resources.

6. Answer: E

E is the correct answer because the risk-related recommendations for corrective actions are the output of the risk controlling and monitoring process.

A, B, C, and **D** are incorrect because the outputs of these processes do not include recommended corrective actions.

7. Answer: A

A is the correct answer because the recommendations for corrective and preventive actions and change requests must be processed through the integrated change control process for approval.

B, C, D, and **E** are incorrect because changes and recommendations are approved through the integrated change control process.

8. Answer: C

C is the correct answer because the right action here is to find the source of the change requests and process the request through the integrated change control process.

A is incorrect because you are taking action without doing your homework: investigation.

B is incorrect because you should not let anyone apply the changes without the changes having been approved.

D is incorrect because the right course of action here is to find out the source of the change request and ensure that the request goes through the approval process.

9. Answer: E

E is the correct answer because budget review is not an output item from the schedule control process.

A, B, C, and **D** are incorrect because all these items are the output of the schedule control process.

10. Answer: B

    B is the correct answer because the formula for earned value is:

    $$EV = BAC \times (\text{work completed \% total work required})$$

    which means

    $$EV = \$600,000 \times (5 \text{ miles \% } 15 \text{ miles}) = \$200,000$$

    A is incorrect because $160,000 is the actual cost (AC) and not the earned value (EV).

    C is incorrect because earned value is proportional to the fraction of work performed and not the fraction of time passed.

    D is incorrect because $600,000 is the budget at completion (BAC), not EV.

11. Answer: C

    C is the correct answer because the formula for planned value is:

    $$PV = BAC \times (\text{time passed \% total schedule time})$$

    which means

    $$PV = \$600,000 \times (3 \text{ weeks \% } 12 \text{ weeks}) = \$150,000$$

    A is incorrect because $160,000 is the actual cost (AC) and not the planned value (EV).

    B is incorrect because planned value is proportional to the fraction of time passed, not the fraction of work performed.

    D is incorrect because $600,000 is the budget at completion (BAC), not PV.

12. Answer: A

    A is the correct answer because the formula for cost variance is:

    $$CV = EV - AC$$

    which means

    $$CV = \$200,000 - \$160,000 = \$40,000$$

    B is incorrect because CV is equal to EV – AC, not EV – PV.

    C is incorrect because it calculates the total cost for 12 weeks based on AC for three weeks and then subtracts it from BAC, which is the wrong method to calculate CV.

    D is incorrect because it calculates the total cost for 15 miles based on AC for five miles and then subtracts it from BAC, which is the wrong method to calculate CV.

    E is incorrect because CV is not equal to PV – AC.

13. Answer: B

    B is the correct answer because the formula for schedule variance is:

    $$SV = EV - PV$$

    which means

    $$SV = \$200,000 - \$150,000 = \$50,000$$

    A is incorrect because SV is equal to EV − PV, not EV − AC.

    C and **D** are incorrect because SV is measured in units of cost, not in units of time.

14. Answer: B

    B is the correct answer because a CPI value greater than one means the cost performance of the project is better than planned, and an SPI value of greater than one means the schedule performance of the project is better than planned.

    A, C, and **D** are incorrect because a CPI value greater than one means the cost performance of the project is better than planned, and an SPI value of greater than one means the schedule performance of the project is better than planned.

Chapter 8

1. Answer: E

    E is the correct answer because if the project is behind the planned schedule, it does not mean it should be closed. You can bring it back on schedule or you can change the plan accordingly.

    A, B, C, and **D** are incorrect because all these scenarios will cause the project to close, and when a project is closed it must be closed by using the processes in the closing process group.

2. Answer: A

    A is the correct answer because the future projects can benefit the most from the review if all the stages of the project are covered with both positive and negative aspects.

    B and **D** are incorrect because all the stages and aspects of the project should be reviewed.

    C is incorrect because both positive and negative aspects should be covered with equal emphasis.

3. Answer: D

    D is the correct answer because if the project is to be successful, it must have been executed and controlled successfully before the closure begins.

    A, B, and **C** are incorrect because if a project has not made it to the closing stage by the time closing begins, the project is being terminated without completion.

    E is incorrect because there is no such project stage called completing.

4. Answer: D

    D is the correct answer because no project, small or large, should skip the closing stage.

    A, B, C, and **E** are incorrect because no project should skip the closing stage. Each project must go through a proper closure.

5. Answer: C

    C is the correct answer because it is the project sponsor who signs the final closure documents and can send the project to closure at any stage of the project.

    A is incorrect because the project manager is responsible for managing all the activities needed to close the project, but the closure must be authorized by the sponsor.

    B and **E** are incorrect because neither the customer nor the functional manager can authorize the project closure.

    D is obviously incorrect because it is almost equivalent to saying that any person on the street can close your project, because the definition of the stakeholder is so wide.

6. Answer: C

    C is the correct answer because closing contracts is part of the contract closure, not the administrative closure.

    A, B, and **D** are incorrect because all these activities are part of the administrative closure.

7. Answer: A

    A is the correct answer because the administrative closure procedure is the output of the close project process, not the input.

    B, C, and **D** are incorrect because all these items are valid input to the close project process.

8. Answer: C

    C is the correct answer because the closed contracts are the output of the contract closure process.

    A and **B** are incorrect because both administrative and contract closure procedures are the output of the close project process.

    D is incorrect because project closure documentation should be archived as an output of the close project process.

9. Answer: D

    D is the correct answer because the work portion of the project, also called the *administrative closure*, is closed by using the close project process.

    A and **C** are incorrect because these are not the valid process names.

    B is incorrect because the contract closure process is used to close the contracts.

10. Answer: A and B

A and **B** are the correct answers because you can review the project work as well as the procurement work and procedure and learn from both.

C and **D** are incorrect because these are no closing processes with these names.

Chapter 9

1. Answer: D

D is the correct answer because the PMP code of professional conduct states that upon a reasonable and clear factual basis, it is your responsibility to report possible violations of the PMP Code of Professional Conduct by individuals in the field of project management.

A and **B** are incorrect because you can do it if you feel like it, but this is not the best answer.

C is incorrect because you don't know whether a law was violated, and according to the code of conduct statement, D is the best answer.

2. Answer: A

A is the correct answer because if in a foreign land you are being asked to do something that is unethical and illegal, you are supposed to investigate whether it is illegal and unethical there as well.

B and **D** are incorrect because you don't know yet whether the sponsor is asking you to do something illegal.

C is incorrect because you think it is unethical and illegal, so you must investigate it.

3. Answer: B

B is the correct answer because you should share your findings that this is an illegal activity with the project sponsor.

A is incorrect because it clearly disobeys the law of the land.

C, **D**, and **E** are incorrect because B is the best answer.

4. Answer: C

C is the correct answer because honesty, openness, and truthfulness are part and parcel of professional behavior, and this is true inside and outside of Kansas. Regardless of where you are, the professional code of conduct is the same.

A is incorrect because you do not have enough information to take this step.

B and **D** are both incorrect because you are not being truthful, honest, and open.

E is incorrect because it's not necessary to quit the project at this stage.

5. Answer: C

   C is the correct answer because this is a case of possible conflict of interest, and option C is the right thing to do.

   A and **B** are incorrect because you are not disclosing a possible conflict of interest.

   D is incorrect because this is a possible conflict of interest or can be looked upon as such by others, rather than as mere networking.

6. Answer: C and F

   C and **F** are the correct answers because these are not part of the PMP Code of Professional Conduct.

   A, B, D, and **E** are all incorrect because these activities are included in the PMP Code of Professional Conduct.

7. Answer: B

   B is the correct answer because you want to make sure that Best Deals is making the estimate based on the same information about the work that the other vendors are.

   A and **C** are incorrect because you are violating the confidentiality.

   D is incorrect because it is an unnecessary activity.

8. Answer: A

   A is the correct answer because as a project manager it is your responsibility to facilitate interaction among the stakeholders and resolve conflicts.

   B, C, and **D** are incorrect because it is your responsibility to resolve this conflict.

9. Answer: B

   B is the correct answer because as a project manager it is your responsibility to keep the stakeholders informed of the project status.

   A is incorrect because you are not performing your responsibility to provide true project status to the stakeholders.

   C is incorrect because you don't have enough information to take this action.

   D is incorrect because it is your responsibility to investigate the situation and propose a solution.

10. Answer: C

    C is the correct answer because it is not your job to investigate the legality of the company procedures.

    A, B, and **D** are incorrect because all these are parts of the professional responsibility of a project manager.

Appendix B

Final Exam

Questions

1. Which of the following is not a project selection method?

   A. Expert judgment

   B. Scoring models

   C. Benefit/cost ratio

   D. Cash flow

   E. Cost variance

2. You are starting a project in your company and are identifying the stakeholders. The CEO of your company is not directly involved in the project. Which of the following is not a key stakeholder in this project?

   A. Investor

   B. Project sponsor

   C. PMO

   D. Project manager

   E. CEO of your company

3. Which of the following statements is true about the initiating process group?

   A. Establish the need for the feasibility study about the project.

   B. Put together a project schedule.

   C. Facilitate the formal approval for starting the new project or a project phase.

   D. Develop a complete project management plan.

4. Which of the following officially starts a project?

   A. The project charter

   B. The preliminary project scope statement

   C. The process initiation plan document

   D. The project management plan

5. You are the project manager of the Golden Arches project, which will generate a software product. A critical bug is discovered in the software by the QA team. You meet with the experts and determine a workaround for this bug to keep the project on track. Which process were you performing to make this determination?

   A. Testing

   B. Quality planning

   C. Risk response planning

   D. Perform quality control

   E. Executing

6. Which of the following best defines a project?

   A. A set of schedule activities performed by a team that has a project manager

   B. A set of sequential activities performed by using project management processes

   C. A temporary endeavor undertaken to create a unique product, service, or result

   D. An ongoing operation being performed to meet customer requirements

7. Which of the following statements best defines a program?

   A. A project with a large budget exceeding a minimum threshold value

   B. A set of processes used to perform a sophisticated project

   C. A set of projects coupled together to save money

   D. A set of related projects managed in a coordinated way to gain benefits and control not available by managing them individually

8. You are the project manager of Mind the Gap project that involves providing Internet access to an underprivileged community in your city. You have to get some of the schedule activities of the project finished by an external vendor. You have written the statement of work and you have gathered or prepared all the documents that will be given to the bidders. What process were you performing while you were engaged in these activities?

   A. Plan purchases and acquisitions

   B. Procurement planning

   C. Solicitation planning

   D. Human resource planning

9. You are the project manager of Mind the Gap project that involves providing Internet access to an underprivileged community in your city. You have to get some of the schedule activities of the project finished by an external vendor. You have written the statement of work and you have gathered or prepared all the documents that will be given to the bidders. What process will you perform next?

   A. Request seller responses

   B. Procurement planning

   C. Solicitation planning

   D. Select sellers

10. In which of the following organization types does the project manager have the highest level of authority?

   A. Functional

   B. Strong matrix

   C. Weak matrix

   D. Projectized

11. In which of the following organization types does the project manager have the lowest level of authority?

   A. Functional

   B. Strong matrix

   C. Weak matrix

   D. Projectized

12. You are the project manager of a project and you are evaluating the project performance measured against the project baseline on a regular basis. In doing so, you are performing processes that belong to which of the following process groups?

   A. Planning

   B. Executing

   C. Monitoring/controlling

   D. Evaluating

13. You are the project manager of a project that is already executing. You have just discovered that there are differences among the stakeholders over what the project objectives are and what their expectations of the project are. As a project manager, which of the following actions will you take? (Choose one.)

    A. Report the differences to the project sponsor because it is the sponsor's responsibility to resolve the differences.

    B. People are entitled to their points of view, so you should ignore the differences and honor them.

    C. You should encourage the differences because different opinions will result in the best end product.

    D. You must manage the stakeholders' expectations on regular basis and ensure that everyone is on the same page about the scope of the project.

14. Which of the following are the five process groups in project management? (Choose one answer.)

    A. Initiating, planning, executing, monitoring, and controlling

    B. Initiating, planning, executing, monitoring, and closing

    C. Initiating, scoping, executing, monitoring, and closing

    D. Initiating, planning, executing, testing, and closing

15. Which of the following should always be included in a project charter? (Choose one.)

    A. Business case for the project

    B. Statement of work

    C. Project scope statement

    D. Project management plan

16. Which of the following statements about the project management process groups is true? (Choose one.)

    A. Process groups are always executed in a serial fashion without any overlap.

    B. The execution of processes from various process groups can overlap in time.

    C. A given process group is executed with equal intensity at each phase of a project.

    D. Process groups are one-time events: You execute them only once in a project.

    E. When you execute a process group, you execute all the processes in the group.

17. You are the project manager of a project that has finished its first phase. What is your approach toward reviewing the initiating processes at the beginning of the second phase and all subsequent phases?

    A. It should be done because it will keep the project team members employed for a longer time.

    B. It should be done to ensure that the project stays the course even if the business need for which the project is being performed changes.

    C. It should be done because it helps keep the project focused on the business need for which the project is being performed.

    D. It should not be done because it's a waste of time and human resources.

18. You are the project manager in a functional organization. One of your team members, Lou Dobb, is falling behind in completing the schedule activities assigned to him. When you talked to him, he told you that too many people were asking him to do things. You want to look into this matter further. Who do you think has the authority to give assignments to Lou Dobb?

    A. A functional manager

    B. Project managers

    C. The project team

    D. The project management team

19. A project phase is authorized by using a process in which of the following process groups?

    A. Initiating

    B. Phase initiating

    C. Planning

    D. Executing

20. Which two of the following are not the project management process groups? (Choose two.)

    A. Initiating

    B. Designing

    C. Planning

    D. Executing

    E. Closing

    F. Testing

    G. Controlling

21. Which two of the following are not project management knowledge areas? (Choose two.)

    A. Integration management

    B. Team management

    C. Cost management

    D. Risk management

    E. Outsource management

    F. Procurement management

    G. Quality management

22. You are the project manager of a project that is executing. Several defects have been discovered in the project product. The project team does not have time to repair all the defects. Which tool will you use to prioritize the defects?

    A. Control chart

    B. Pareto diagram

    C. Decision tree analysis

    D. Variance analysis

23. You are identifying which quality standards are relevant to your project and determining how to meet those standards. To accomplish this task you are using processes from the:

    A. Planning process group

    B. Executing process group

    C. Controlling process group

    D. Quality planning process group

24. Which two of the following processes are not included in project time management? (Choose two.)

    A. Schedule control

    B. Activity definition

    C. Activity sequencing

    D. Time estimating

    E. Human resource planning

    F. Activity resource estimating

25. You are the project manager of a project that is executing and being controlled. You want to measure the performance of the project against the baseline. Which of the following tools will you use? (Choose one.)

    A. Control chart

    B. Pareto diagram

    C. Decision tree analysis

    D. Variance analysis

26. What is the purpose of the schedule control process?

    A. To ensure that no changes to the schedule happen

    B. To ensure that only the approved changes to the schedule are implemented

    C. To prevent scope creep

    D. To control schedule activities on the critical path

27. Which of the following statements is not true about the project charter?

    A. It determines the scope of the project.

    B. It names the project manager for the project.

    C. It authorizes the project manager to use organizational resources to perform project activities.

    D. It provides a high-level product description.

28. Which of the following is not true about the preliminary project scope statement?

    A. It includes project assumptions and constraints.

    B. It includes an initial list of risks.

    C. It may include an initial WBS.

    D. It is an output of the scope planning process.

29. Which of the following is an output of the scope definition process?

    A. Project charter

    B. Project scope statement

    C. Preliminary project scope statement

    D. Project schedule

30. You are the project manager of a project that is executing and being controlled. You want to make a decision on one part of the project product—whether to build it or to update an existing version. Which of the following tools will you use? (Choose one.)

   A. Control chart

   B. Pareto diagram

   C. Decision tree analysis

   D. Variance analysis

31. Which of the following is an example of a constraint?

   A. A milestone that must be met by a certain date due to a marketing window depending on the beginning of a shopping season

   B. A quality standard

   C. A schedule activity on a critical path

   D. The threat of a strike at the external vendor from whom you are going to procure some items

32. Which of the following is not true about the project scope management plan?

   A. It describes how the project scope will be defined.

   B. It describes how the project scope will be controlled.

   C. It is the output of a process that takes the WBS as an input.

   D. It describes how the project scope will be verified.

33. Which of the following is an output of the scope planning process?

   A. Project scope management plan

   B. Project management plan

   C. Project scope statement

   D. WBS

34. Which of the following is not an input item to the scope definition process?

   A. Project charter

   B. Preliminary project scope statement

   C. Project scope management plan

   D. Detailed project scope statement

35. Which of the following is not an output item to the detailed project scope statement?

   A. Project assumptions and constraints

   B. WBS

   C. Product scope description

   D. Cost estimate

36. While walking down the hallway, you accidentally hear Mike, your project team member, declaring to another team member that he is not going to be able to finish his assignment on time because there was a problem he could not solve. The assignment that Mike is working on involves a schedule activity on the critical path. Which of the following actions will you take?

    A. You won't take any action until Mike speaks directly with you.

    B. You will raise this issue in the next project team meeting.

    C. You will raise the issue with Mike's functional manager.

    D. You will tell Mike that you overheard him and discuss the issue with him directly.

    E. You will start making plans to minimize the impact of delay on the completion of the activity that Mike is working on.

37. Which of the following statements correctly defines the statement of work?

    A. A type of contract used to procure a product, service, or result

    B. A document that describes a product, service, or result that will be procured

    C. A document that describes each schedule activity

    D. A document written by the seller in the procurement

38. Which of the following is a tool used in the scope planning process?

    A. Expert judgment

    B. Product analysis

    C. Stakeholder analysis

    D. Project charter

39. Which of the following is not a tool used in the scope definition process?

    A. Expert judgment

    B. Product analysis

    C. Stakeholder analysis

    D. Project charter

40. Which of the following is a true statement about the WBS?

    A. It is a deliverable-oriented hierarchical decomposition of the project work to be performed by the project team.

    B. It's a hierarchically organized set of resources needed by the project.

    C. It's a hierarchically organized set of risks identified for the project.

    D. It represents the reporting hierarchy in the performing organization.

41. The WBS is an input to which two of the following processes?

    A. Activity definition process

    B. Cost estimating process

    C. Scope definition process

    D. Human resource planning process

    E. Schedule development process

42. You are the project manager of a project that is being planned. Which of the following techniques can you use to develop the WBS?

    A. Pareto chart

    B. Analogous estimating

    C. Decomposition

    D. Bottom-up estimating

43. Variance analysis is a technique used for which of the following?

    A. To measure the deviation of the actual project performance from the planned baseline and determine the cause of this variance

    B. To determine how different schedule activities vary in their importance to the final objectives of the project

    C. To determine the difference between the cost estimates for various schedule activities

    D. To determine the variance between the available resources and the required resources for a project and how this variance will affect the project results

44. You are the project manager of a project that is being executed. You are actively monitoring and controlling changes to the project. Which of the following is not an output of the scope control process?

    A. Updates to the scope statement

    B. Updates to the scope baseline

    C. Updates to the WBS

    D. Updates to cost estimates

45. You are in the process of creating the WBS for your project. Which process group are you using?

    A. Initiating

    B. Planning

    C. Executing

    D. Scoping

46. Which of the following does not affect the duration of a schedule activity?

    A. Resources assigned to the activity

    B. Availability of the assigned resources

    C. Whether the activity is on a critical path

    D. Experience of the human resource assigned

47. You are the project manager of a project that is running behind schedule, and the customer is not happy about the delay. You can put a limited amount of additional resources on the project. However, you want to obtain the greatest amount of schedule compression for the least increase in cost. Which schedule compression technique will you be using?

    A. Fast tracking

    B. PDM

    C. Crashing

    D. Critical path elimination

48. Which of the following is not an input to the activity definition process?

    A. Project scope statement

    B. WBS

    C. Project management plan

    D. Risk breakdown structure (RBS)

49. You are the project manager of a project that is running behind schedule, and the customer is not happy about the delay. You are planning to run two phases of the project in parallel that were originally scheduled to be run in sequence. In doing so, which schedule compression technique will you be using?

    A. Fast tracking

    B. PDM

    C. Crashing

    D. Critical path elimination

50. Parametric estimating is used in:

    A. Estimating the resources for an activity

    B. Assessing the duration for an activity

    C. Sequencing the schedule activities

    D. Controlling the schedule

51. Which of the following is not an input to the activity sequencing process?

    A. Project scope statement

    B. Project schedule network diagrams

    C. Activity list

    D. Milestone list

52. The project manager of the Blue Sky project has left, and you have been appointed the new project manager for this project. You have discovered that there are some unaddressed change requests. You have evaluated these requests, and they all tend to change the scope of the project. You want to know who has the authority to approve these requests. Which of the following sources will you check first?

    A. The customer

    B. The project sponsor

    C. The project scope management plan

    D. The project charter

    E. The project scope statement

53. Which of the following is an output of the activity sequencing process?

    A. PDM

    B. ADM

    C. WBS

    D. Project schedule network diagrams

54. You are the project manager of the project World Dominance. The project is almost complete when you get a request from a stakeholder for a minor change to the project that apparently will not change the schedule or the cost. The requester is not a key stakeholder. Which of the following is the appropriate action that you should take?

    A. Tell the stakeholder that this is not the time to make any changes to the project.

    B. Investigate the impact of this change across the project.

    C. Tell the appropriate team member to make the change.

    D. Submit the change request for approval.

55. Which of the following is an output of the resource estimating process?

    A. Resource breakdown structure

    B. Risk breakdown structure

    C. WBS

    D. Activity list

56. The Delphi technique is used for:
  - **A.** Resolving conflicts
  - **B.** Analyzing performance
  - **C.** Estimating resources
  - **D.** Gathering information

57. Which of the following sets of processes belongs to time management?
  - **A.** Monitor and control project work, activity duration estimating, and schedule development
  - **B.** Activity definition, activity resource estimating, and schedule compression
  - **C.** Activity definition, activity resource estimating, and schedule control
  - **D.** Develop project team, schedule development, and schedule control

58. Which of the following is the correct sequence in which the processes will be performed?
  - **A.** Create WBS, activity definition, activity resource estimating, activity duration estimating, and schedule development
  - **B.** Activity definition, create WBS, activity resource estimating, activity duration estimating, and schedule development
  - **C.** Create WBS, activity definition, activity duration estimating, activity resource estimating, and schedule development
  - **D.** Create WBS, activity definition, activity duration estimating, schedule development, and activity resource estimating

59. You are the project manager of the Good Will project. The WBS has been created, activities have been defined, and resources have been estimated. It's time to estimate the duration for each activity. Which of the following should perform the activity duration estimate?
  - **A.** The project manager
  - **B.** The individual or the team that will do the work
  - **C.** The customer
  - **D.** The senior management
  - **E.** The project management team

60. Which of the following is not true about the critical path?

   A. The float time for each activity on the critical path is zero.

   B. The critical path is the longest of all the paths in the network diagram on the time scale.

   C. If an activity on the critical path is delayed, the finish date for the project will be delayed.

   D. Any change request for an activity on the critical path will automatically be rejected.

61. The project manager of the Mother Nature project has left during the project execution, and you have been appointed the new project manager for this project. The project sponsor has asked you to give her a copy of the document that contains the work package descriptions. Which of the following documents will you look for?

   A. The project scope statement

   B. The WBS dictionary

   C. The project schedule

   D. The project charter

62. Which of the following is true about the critical chain method?

   A. It is a technique used in the activity duration estimating process.

   B. It is a technique used in the cost estimating process.

   C. It is a schedule development technique that involves adding duration buffers, which are not actual activities.

   D. It is a technique that involves adding duration buffers, which are actual work activities, to change the interdependencies of the activities.

63. Which of the following is true about the three-point estimating technique?

   A. It determines three values from three scenarios: optimistic, pessimistic, and most likely. The most likely value is taken as the final value.

   B. This method is used to determine the uncertainty in estimating the activity duration.

   C. It is a technique that uses the float time in duration estimating.

   D. It is a method that calculates the activity duration by taking the average of three estimates provided by the customer, the project manager, and the team member who will do the work.

64. Which of the following is true about the analogous estimating technique?
    A. It is used to assess the probability of success for a project based on the success rate for similar projects executed previously.
    B. It is bottom-up estimating: You estimate the duration for the components of an activity and sum them up.
    C. It estimates the duration of an activity based on the duration of a similar activity in the same project.
    D. It estimates the duration of an activity based on the duration of a similar activity in a previous project.

65. Which of the following is a true statement about the earned value technique?
    A. It is used in the scope control process.
    B. It is used in the project performance measurements.
    C. It is used in the planning for procurement.
    D. It is a project selection technique.

66. The rolling wave planning technique is used in the:
    A. Activity definition process
    B. Activity sequencing process
    C. Activity resource estimating process
    D. Schedule development process

67. Parametric estimating involves:
    A. Taking the average of duration estimates for similar activities
    B. Using a statistical relationship between historical data and other variables to calculate quantities such as activity duration estimate and cost estimate
    C. Using the previous cost estimates on similar activities to calculate the cost of an activity in the current project
    D. Performing quantitative risk analysis

68. Which of the following items is not used in calculating the earned value (EV)?
    A. Actual cost of the work performed: budget at completion (BAC)
    B. Originally approved budget
    C. Work completed
    D. Total work required to be completed

69. Recall actual cost (AC), planned value (PV), earned value (EV), and cost variance (CV) in the earned value technique. The CV is calculated as:

   A. PV – EV

   B. AC – EV

   C. EV – AC

   D. PV – AC

70. Recall actual cost (AC), planned value (PV), earned value (EV), cost variance (CV), budget at completion (BAC), and cost performance index (CPI) in the earned value technique. The CPI is calculated as:

   A. EV / PV

   B. EV / AC

   C. CV / AC

   D. EV / BAC

71. The activity list is an input to:

   A. Activity sequencing

   B. Activity definition

   C. WBS

   D. Scope planning

72. Given:

   AC = 100
   BAC = 300
   EV = 90

Assuming that the variations that have occurred so far in the project will not occur in the future, the estimate to complete (ETC) is:

   A. 290

   B. 200

   C. 210

   D. 10

73. Given:

AC = 100
BAC = 300
EV = 90

Assuming that the variations that have occurred so far in the project will not occur in the future, the EAC is:

A. 290

B. 310

C. 110

D. 400

74. You are the project manager of a project that is executing 17% under budget. Which of the following does this mean?

A. EV is 100 and AC is 120.

B. PV is 100 and EV is 120.

C. PV is 120 and AC is 100.

D. AC is 100 and EV is 120.

75. Which of the following is not an input to the schedule control process?

A. Activity list

B. Schedule baseline

C. Performance reports

D. Schedule management plan

76. In project management, the term "float" is synonymous with the term:

A. Lag

B. Lead

C. Slack

D. Critical

77. Which of the following processes uses a technique called *adjusting leads and lags?*

A. The activity definition process

B. The schedule control process

C. The activity sequencing process

D. The schedule development process

78. Which of the following is an input to quality planning?

    A. Project scope statement

    B. Quality checklists

    C. Quality metrics

    D. Cost of quality

79. Which of the following is not an output of the quality planning process?

    A. Quality baseline

    B. Quality checklists

    C. Quality metrics

    D. Recommended preventive actions

80. Which of the following quality processes is performed first?

    A. Quality definition

    B. Quality planning

    C. Perform quality control

    D. Perform quality assurance

81. You are the project manager of a project that is executing. You are monitoring and controlling the quality of the project. Which of the following is not an input to quality control?

    A. Quality metrics

    B. Quality checklists

    C. Pareto chart

    D. Work performance information

82. You are the project manager of a project that is executing. You are working on ensuring the application of systematic quality activities that were planned in the quality planning process, and ensuring that the project will employ all the processes needed to meet the requirements. Which process are you performing?

    A. Quality control

    B. Quality planning

    C. Quality assurance

    D. Testing

83. You are the project manager of a project that is executing. You are monitoring and controlling the quality of the project. Which of the following is not a technique for quality control?

    A. Flowcharting

    B. Control charts

    C. Pareto chart

    D. Benchmarking

84. You are the project manager of a project that is executing. You are working on ensuring the application of systematic quality activities that were planned in the quality planning process, and ensuring that the project will employ all the processes needed to meet the requirements. Which of the following is not an output of the process you are performing?

    A. Recommended corrective actions

    B. Quality metrics

    C. Change requests

    D. Updates to the quality management plan

85. You are using a cause and effect diagram to find real causes of a problem by exploring all the possible causes. Which quality process are you performing?

    A. Quality assurance

    B. Quality planning

    C. Quality control

    D. Auditing

    E. Inspection

86. Which of the following is not a characteristic of a control chart?

    A. It reflects the expected variation of the data.

    B. It is used to monitor whether the variance of a specified variable is within the acceptable limits dictated by quality control.

    C. It is used to illustrate the behavior of a variable over time.

    D. It predicts the amount of risk associated with a variance.

87. Which two of the following are not tools of quality control?

    A. Regression diagram

    B. Run chart

    C. Scatter diagram

    D. Benchmarking

    E. Pareto diagram

    F. Ishikawa diagram

88. Which of the following is a characteristic of benchmarking?

    A. It is used to prepare a response to an identified risk.

    B. It compares practices, products, or services of a project with those of some reference projects.

    C. It is a managerial technique used to manage the stakeholder expectations.

    D. It is used only to compare the performance of two software programs.

89. Which of the following processes will be performed first?

    A. Create WBS

    B. Activity sequencing

    C. Quality control

    D. Schedule control

90. Which of the following is not a process of quality management?

    A. Perform quality control

    B. Perform quality assurance

    C. Quality planning

    D. Procurement quality planning

91. You are the project manager of the ABC project. You are in the process of identifying the project risks. Which of the following is an output of risk identification?

    A. Recommended corrective actions

    B. Risk register

    C. Response plan

    D. Risk dictionary

92. You are looking into strategies to deal with the negative risks in your project. Which of the following is not a strategy that you can use to deal with negative risks?

    A. Avoid

    B. Transfer

    C. Mitigate

    D. Audit

93. You are looking into strategies to deal with the negative risks in your project. Which of the following statements is not true about the risk mitigation strategy?

    A. Mitigation is used only after the risk occurs.

    B. Mitigation involves taking action to reduce the impact of the risk if it occurs.

    C. Mitigation involves taking action early on to reduce the probability of risk occurrence.

    D. Designing redundancy into a system is an example of mitigation.

94. Which of the following is not an input to risk identification?

    A. Project scope statement

    B. Risk register

    C. Risk management plan

    D. Project management plan

95. Which of the following is a set of risk management processes?

    A. Risk management planning, risk identification, qualitative risk analysis, quantitative risk analysis, risk response planning, and risk monitoring and controlling

    B. Risk management planning, risk evaluation, qualitative risk analysis, quantitative risk analysis, risk response planning, and risk monitoring and controlling

    C. Risk management planning, risk identification, risk evaluation, risk mitigation, risk response planning, and risk monitoring and controlling

    D. Risk management planning, risk transference, risk assessment, quantitative risk analysis, risk response planning, and risk monitoring and controlling

96. Activities are further decomposition of:

    A. Work packages

    B. Project charter

    C. Project scope statement

    D. Schedule network diagrams

97. You are the project manager of a project that is executing. You are looking at different ways to maximize the opportunities and minimize the threats presented by the project risks. Which process are you performing?

    A. Risk identification

    B. Quantitative risk analysis

    C. Qualitative risk analysis

    D. Risk response planning

    E. Risk monitoring and control

98. You are the project manager of a project that is executing. You are looking at different options to respond to the risks. Which of the following is not an output of risk response planning?

    A. Risk-related contractual agreements

    B. Recommended corrective actions

    C. Project management plan updates

    D. Risk register updates

99. The acceptance strategy in risk response planning means the project team has decided to:

    A. Purchase insurance for the product to which the risk belongs.

    B. Take no action or take an action only if a particular event happens in the future.

    C. Take action to eliminate the risk.

    D. Accept whatever response the project manager comes up with.

100. You are the project manager of a project that is executing. You are actively monitoring and controlling the risks. Which of the following is not an output of the risk monitoring and control process?

    A. Risk register updates

    B. Change requests

    C. Performance reports

    D. Recommended corrective actions

101. You are the project manager of a construction project. The project team has identified some project risks and wants to analyze them. Which of the following is a set of tools and techniques that can be used in the quantitative risk analysis?

    A. Data-gathering techniques, quantitative risk analysis and modeling techniques, and mitigation techniques

    B. Sensitivity analysis, expected monetary value analysis, decision tree analysis, and expert judgment

    C. Data-gathering techniques, quantitative risk analysis and modeling techniques, and checklist analysis

    D. Sensitivity analysis, expected monetary value analysis, decision tree analysis, and contingency planning

102. You have joined a project as a project manager. The project was already executing. Just before leaving, the previous project manager handed you the risk management plan and told you that the team has just finished the risk management planning. Which of the following don't you expect to see in this document?

    A. Probability and impact matrix

    B. Risk response plan for each risk

    C. Risk categories

    D. Risk reporting and tracking

103. You are the project manager of a project that is in the planning stage. You are using a probability and impact matrix and other tools and techniques to prioritize the risks. Which process are you performing?

    A. Quantitative risk analysis

    B. Qualitative risk analysis

    C. Risk response planning

    D. Risk monitoring and control

104. You are using different tools and techniques to prioritize the risks in your project. Which of the following tools will you not be using?

    A. Probability and impact matrix

    B. Risk urgency assessment

    C. Risk audits

    D. Assessment of the risk data quality

105. You, with your project team, are performing the risk response planning process. You update the risk register as a result of this process. Which of the following is not going to be an item in the risk register after you make the updates?

    A. Risk owners and assigned responsibilities

    B. Agreed-upon risk response strategies

    C. Results from qualitative and quantitative risk analyses

    D. WBS

106. A project team member has asked you what the progressive elaboration is. Which of the following is the best definition of progressive elaboration that you can give to her?

    A. Taking the project from initiating to closing

    B. Taking the project from conception to completion

    C. Taking the project from concept to the project management plan

    D. Decomposing the project objectives into smaller, more manageable work pieces

107. The project charter is important due to which of the following reasons?

    A. It authorizes the sponsor.

    B. It names the project manager.

    C. It identifies all the stakeholders.

    D. It authorizes the project manager to use the organization's resources.

    E. It identifies the project team members.

108. Which of the following is true about assumptions in the project planning?

    A. Because assumptions are a part of the project charter that you did not write, you don't need to validate them. Just assume the assumptions are true, and if the project fails, it's not your fault.

    B. The project charter may include assumptions.

    C. An assumption is a condition that has been verified to be true, so you don't need to validate it.

    D. You must not start a project until all the assumptions have been proven to be true.

109. Which of the following is done first?

    A. Creating the preliminary scope statement

    B. Creating the project charter

    C. Developing the schedule

    D. Creating the WBS

110. Which of the following is not an output of human resource planning?

   A. Project staff assignments

   B. Staffing management plan

   C. List of roles and responsibilities

   D. Project organization chart

111. You are in the process of planning the scope for your project. Which of the following is a false statement about the project scope management plan?

   A. It describes how to verify the scope.

   B. It serves as the baseline for the project scope.

   C. It describes how to control the scope.

   D. It describes how to create the WBS.

112. You have joined the Project Rainbow project because the previous project manager left. The previous project manager handed you the project charter and the project scope statement before leaving. The next step, he said, is to develop the WBS. Who will do that?

   A. The project manager alone

   B. The project manager and the project sponsor

   C. The project manger with help from the project team

   D. The customer

   E. The upper management in the performing organization

113. Which of the following are not tools and techniques for the project human resource planning?

   A. Resource assignment matrix (RAM)

   B. Networking

   C. Organizational theories

   D. Benchmarking

114. Which of the following is a false statement about a project risk?

   A. A project can only have a negative effect on a project.

   B. A risk arises out of uncertainty.

   C. Identified risks are usually listed in a document called the *risk register*.

   D. Risks can be categorized by developing the Risk Breakdown Structure (RBS).

115. Which of the following is not a process of human resource management?

    A. Human resource planning

    B. Acquire project team

    C. Train project team

    D. Develop project team

116. You are the project manager of the Golden Arches project. With the help of the project team, you are identifying the project risks. Which of the following is not an information-gathering technique used in the risk identification process?

    A. Interviewing

    B. Delphi technique

    C. Decision tree analysis

    D. SWOT analysis

117. Which of the following is a correct statement about secondary risks?

    A. These are the residual risks.

    B. These are the risks that have medium or low priority.

    C. These are the risks that can result from responses to the identified risks.

    D. These are the risks that have been transferred.

    E. These are the risks that will be avoided.

118. In your moviemaking project, you must shoot a scene on a ski resort with many people skiing around. This project activity has which of the following kinds of dependencies?

    A. External

    B. Mandatory

    C. Internal

    D. Discretionary

    E. Finish-to-start

119. You are the project manager for a software development project in a matrix organization. You have an influence on making the staff assignments. Which of the following characteristics will you not consider during these assignments?

    A. Competency

    B. Availability

    C. Lifestyle

    D. Salary requirement

120. Conflict management is a technique used in which of the following processes?

   A. Human resource planning

   B. Acquire project team

   C. Develop project team

   D. Manage project team

121. Co-location is a technique used in which of the following processes?

   A. Human resource planning

   B. Acquire project team

   C. Develop project team

   D. Manage project team

122. You are the project manager of the Dream Big project. The project is executing. Which of the following tools and techniques are you not going to use to manage the project team?

   A. Observations and conversations

   B. Bonuses

   C. Conflict management

   D. Issue log

123. Virtual team is a tool for which of the following processes?

   A. Human resource planning

   B. Acquire project team

   C. Develop project team

   D. Manage project team

124. Which of the following does not belong to the set of characteristics that makes a good recognition and reward strategy?

   A. Clear the reward criteria.

   B. Any member should be able to win the reward.

   C. Keep the reward standard high so that only the cream of the crop can reach the reward.

   D. Cultural diversity should be considered and respected.

125. Which of the following conflict resolution strategies provides a win/win resolution?

    A. Avoidance

    B. Collaboration

    C. Accommodation

    D. Compromise

126. The activity list that will be used to develop network diagrams is an output of which process?

    A. Activity definition

    B. Create WBS

    C. Scope planning

    D. Schedule development

127. The list of risks that could affect the project is created by using which of the following processes?

    A. Risk definition

    B. Risk identification

    C. Risk management planning

    D. Risk response planning

128. Quality audits are part of which of the following quality management processes?

    A. Quality planning

    B. Perform quality control

    C. Perform quality assurance

    D. Quality inspection

129. A project team member asks you why you should monitor the activities on the critical path more closely. Which of the following will be your answer?

    A. Because the activities on the critical path need to be performed before the activities on other paths.

    B. Because each activity on the critical path has a zero float time, and thereby poses a schedule risk.

    C. Because the activities on the critical path are very critical to the organization's strategy.

    D. Because the activities on non-critical paths depend upon the activities on the critical path.

130. Which of the following is not an output of the request seller responses process?

   A. Selected sellers list

   B. Procurement documents package

   C. Proposals

   D. Qualified sellers list

131. Which of the following is not a process of project procurement management?

   A. Select sellers

   B. Request seller responses

   C. Contract closure

   D. Monitor and control procurement

132. Which of the following is not a type of contract that can be used in procurement?

   A. Cost reimbursable

   B. Fixed price

   C. Profit shared

   D. Time and material

133. You are a project manager of a project that is executing. You need to procure a well-defined product. Which of the following will be the most suitable contract type for this procurement?

   A. Cost reimbursable

   B. Fixed price

   C. Profit shared

   D. Time and material

134. You are a project manager of a project that is executing. You need to procure a product that is not well-defined. There are many grey areas. Which of the following contract types presents the highest risk?

   A. Firm fixed price

   B. Cost plus percentage of cost

   C. Cost plus fixed fee

   D. Cost plus incentive fee

   E. Time and material

135. You are the project manager of a construction project. Your company is procuring a part of your project and therefore preparing the procurement documents. Which of the following is true about the procurement documents?

    A. The documents should have a rigidly fixed format so that there are no variations in the responses from different sellers.

    B. The documents should be completely open-ended so that each seller has the complete freedom to suggest the requirements and present their solutions.

    C. Documents should be flexible enough allow the sellers to be creative in offering solutions for meeting the requirements.

    D. The documents should follow the standards required by the sellers.

136. Which of the following is not true about conflict management?

    A. Successful conflict management results in an increased productivity and positive working relationships among the team members.

    B. Communication planning and clarity of roles and responsibilities can reduce the amount of conflict.

    C. Differences of opinion are harmful for the project.

    D. A conflict should be addressed in private by using a direct collaborative approach.

137. You are the project manager of a government project and you want to procure a few items. You are looking at the possibility of advertising for this procurement. Which of the following is not true about using advertising as a tool in the request seller responses process?

    A. Advertising causes extra headaches and opens you up for lawsuits from the bidders, so stick with your company's list of sellers.

    B. Advertising can be placed in public newspapers or in professional journals.

    C. Advertising is sometimes required in government projects.

    D. Advertising can help you find a better seller by expanding the current list of sellers.

138. You are managing the execution of a Department of Defense project. Which of the following is not an output item of the direct and manage project execution process?

    A. Implementation of corrective and preventive actions

    B. Deliverables

    C. Approved change requests

    D. Implementation of defect repairs

139. Which of the following processes does not belong to integration management?
  A. Develop project charter
  B. Manage project team
  C. Close project
  D. Monitor and control project work

140. Negotiation is a tool in which of the following processes?
  A. Schedule development
  B. Acquire project team
  C. Conflict management
  D. Perform quality control

141. When should administrative closure be performed?
  A. Before the product is accepted by the customer
  B. When there are risks involved in the project
  C. At the end of each project or each phase of a project
  D. At the time of signing the contracts for a procurement

142. You are about to release the project resources. Which process are you performing?
  A. Resource release
  B. Administrative closure
  C. Close project
  D. Monitor and control project work

143. You are using a Pareto diagram to rank the importance of each error in the product of your project. Which quality process are you performing?
  A. Quality control
  B. Quality planning
  C. Quality assurance
  D. Auditing
  E. Inspection

144. You are a project manager for the construction of a 30-mile road. Further assume that the work is uniformly distributed over 12 weeks. The total approved budget for this project is $600,000. At the end of first three weeks of work, $150,000 has been spent, and 10 miles of road have been completed. What is the cost variance?

    A. $40,000

    B. $50,000

    C. −$40,000

    D. $120,000

    E. $0

145. A CPI value of 1.20 and an SPI value of 1.30 for a project mean which of the following?

    A. The project is making faster progress and costing less than planned.

    B. The project is making slower progress and costing more than planned.

    C. The project is making slower progress and costing less than planned.

    D. The project is making faster progress and costing more than planned.

146. The close project process belongs to which of the following knowledge areas?

    A. Time management

    B. Human resource management

    C. Monitoring and controlling

    D. Integration management

147. You are in the process of closing a completed project. Which of the following is not an output of the close project process?

    A. Administrative closure procedure

    B. Implementation of recommended actions

    C. Contract closure procedure

    D. Final product

148. Which of the following is not an input to the close project process?

    A. Contract documentation

    B. Project management plan

    C. Contract closure procedure

    D. Work performance information

149. You have been appointed project manager for a project that is already executing. The previous project manager handed you the risk register. Which of the following do you not expect to see in this document?

   A. List of identified risks

   B. Risk probability and impact matrix

   C. List of potential responses

   D. Root causes of risks

150. Which of the following is not included in the benefit measurement methods for project selection?

   A. Scoring models

   B. Comparative approaches

   C. Dynamic programming

   D. Economic models

   E. Benefit contribution

151. You have just been appointed the project manager of the Go Get Them project. You have started identifying the project stakeholders. Which of the following is not a true statement about the project stakeholders?

   A. Individuals and organizations directly involved in the project are the project stakeholders.

   B. All project stakeholders are supposed to be supportive of the project.

   C. Individuals and organizations that can impact the project are the project stakeholders.

   D. Individuals and organizations that will use the project product are the project stakeholders.

152. You have just gotten an approval for a change request made by the customer. Which process have you performed to get this change request approved?

   A. Change approval

   B. Schedule control

   C. Integrated change control

   D. Quality control

153. Which two of the following processes are included in the initiating process group? (Choose two.)

    A. Develop project charter

    B. Develop preliminary project scope statement

    C. Develop project management plan

    D. Develop a project schedule

154. In which of the following project process groups is a project manager assigned to the project?

    A. Controlling

    B. Initiating

    C. Planning

    D. Staffing

155. You are the project manager of the Golden Arches project, which will generate a software product. An unpredicted risk event has happened during the executing stage of the project. You meet with the experts and determine a workaround for this risk. Which process are you performing to make this determination?

    A. Testing

    B. Risk response planning

    C. Risk monitoring and control

    D. Quantitative risk analysis

    E. Executing

156. Which is not a characteristic of a program?

    A. Projects in a program are related to each other.

    B. Projects in a program are managed in a coordinated fashion.

    C. A program can include work that is not part of any individual project in the program.

    D. A program is a sophisticated project that is broken into smaller projects just for the ease of executing it.

157. Which of the following is not an output of the integrated change control process?

    A. Approved change requests

    B. Requested change requests

    C. Approved preventive actions

    D. Implementation of changes

158. You are the project manager of the Mind the Gap project, which involves providing Internet access to an underprivileged community in your city. You have to get some of the schedule activities of the project finished by an external vendor. You have written the statement of work and gathered or prepared all the documents that will be given to the bidders. Which process will you perform next?

    A. Plan purchases and acquisitions

    B. Request seller responses

    C. Select sellers

    D. Request bidders

159. You are the project manager of the Multiple Voices project, which is already executing. You have just discovered that there are differences among the stakeholders over what the project objectives are and what the stakeholders' expectations of the project are. Which of the following is true about these differences? (Choose one.)

    A. Report the differences to the project sponsor because it is the sponsor's responsibility to resolve the differences.

    B. People are entitled to their points of view, so you should ignore the differences and honor them.

    C. You should encourage the differences because different opinions will result in the best end product.

    D. The differences about the project objectives and different expectations of the project make the project manager's job difficult.

160. You are the project manager of a project that is executing. The project is making progress in accordance with the baseline, and the project team morale is quite high as a result. A member of the project management team who has returned from a meeting tells you that the customer is very disappointed at the poor progress the project is making and that he is planning to talk to the CEO of your organization about it. What is the first action that you will take?

    A. Talk to the CEO before the customer does.

    B. Contact the customer and find out the detailed information from him.

    C. Call a project team meeting and invite the customer to the meeting.

    D. Talk to the project sponsor about this problem.

161. You are the project manager of a project that is about to be complete. You get a call from the customer to add a feature to the project product that is not part of the project scope, but without it the product will not be very useful, according to the customer. What is the first action will you take?

    A. Tell the customer that the project is almost complete and this is not the time to make any changes.

    B. Process the change request through the integrated change control process.

    C. Ask the sponsor to allocate more funds to accommodate this change.

    D. Accept the change and use the contingency reserve funds to implement the change.

162. Which of the following is not included in the mathematical models used to select projects?

    A. Linear programming

    B. Nonlinear programming

    C. Integer programming

    D. Project-oriented programming

    E. Multi-objective programming

163. You are on the committee that makes the final selection for sellers for procurement. You have just noticed that in the procurement for a current project, the Everest Consultant Group is on the list of sellers. This company is run by your brother. What will you do?

    A. It's unnecessary to say anything; just excuse yourself from the committee.

    B. You don't need to say anything; just make sure you stay impartial in the seller selection process.

    C. Disclose this fact to the committee.

    D. Vote against this company just to stay fair.

164. You have just been appointed the project manager of the ABC project. You have started identifying the project stakeholders. You must do all of the following *except*:

    A. Identify all the stakeholders.

    B. Manage stakeholder expectations.

    C. Create conflicts among the stakeholders whenever possible in order to get a better deal for the project team.

    D. Understand stakeholders' expectations and requirements.

    E. Manage the influence of the stakeholders.

165. Which of the following is not expected by the PMP Code of Professional Conduct? (Choose two.)

A. Satisfy the scope and objectives of your professional services.

B. Respect the confidentiality of sensitive information obtained in the course of professional activities.

C. Take courses to learn about ethics.

D. Cooperate with PMI concerning ethics violations.

E. Refrain from offering or accepting inappropriate payments.

F. Keep an eye on your PMP colleagues if they are involved in unethical conduct, such as advocating atheist philosophy.

166. Which two of the following are the documents that are produced in the initiating stage of a project? (Choose two.)

A. The project charter

B. The preliminary project scope statement

C. The process initiation plan document

D. The project management plan

E. The project schedule

167. You are managing a project in a country foreign to you. The CEO of the performing organization asks you to write a check to a city official to get some paperwork required for the project moving forward. Such an activity in your home country would be considered bribery, which is illegal. What will you do?

A. Investigate whether what the CEO is suggesting is legal and ethical in this country.

B. Report the CEO to the police.

C. Write the check to the city official because the CEO asked you to do so.

D. Tell the CEO that he's an unethical person and you are leaving the project.

168. Which two of the following processes are included in the initiating process group? (Choose two.)

A. Develop project charter

B. Develop preliminary project scope statement

C. Develop project management plan

D. Develop project schedule

169. You are the project manager of a project that has just been cancelled by the sponsor. What should you do?

    A. Write an e-mail to the manager of the sponsor telling him how unfair it was to cancel the project.

    B. Put this project behind you and focus on the next project.

    C. Properly close the project, including documenting the lessons learned and performing the administrative closure.

    D. Schedule a meeting of the project team and invite the project sponsor to the meeting to discuss the issue.

170. Which of the following is not the purpose of the integrated change control process?

    A. Ensure, if possible, that no changes are made to the project scope.

    B. Influence the factors that cause change.

    C. Approve or reject a change request.

    D. Identify whether a change has occurred.

171. You have just prepared a list of activities. What is the next process that you should perform?

    A. Schedule development

    B. Schedule control

    C. Activity sequencing

    D. Create WBS

172. Which of the following processes will be performed first?

    A. Qualitative risk analysis

    B. Quantitative risk analysis

    C. Direct and manage project execution

    D. Risk monitoring and control

173. You have been appointed the project manager for a project that is already being planned. The project sponsor has handed you the WBS and asked you to come up with a project schedule. Which of the following processes don't you need to perform before you can develop the project schedule?

    A. Activity definition

    B. Activity sequencing

    C. Schedule control

    D. Activity resource estimating

    E. Activity duration estimating

174. The approved baseline should be changed when:
- **A.** You spent more than planned on a number of activities.
- **B.** An activity on the critical path has taken longer than scheduled.
- **C.** Some changes to the scope, cost, or schedule have been approved.
- **D.** The project is running ahead of schedule.

175. Which of the following is a correct statement about project management?
- **A.** It guarantees maximum profit with minimum efforts.
- **B.** It is the application of knowledge, skills, and tools and techniques to perform project activities in order to meet project requirements.
- **C.** It consists of the processes determined by the functional managers in a given organization.
- **D.** It is only useful for very complex and large projects.

Answers and Explanations

1. Answer: E

   E is the correct answer because cost variance is not a project selection method. In fact, you will not be able to determine the cost variance until the project starts executing.

   A, B, C, and **D** are incorrect because these are valid project selection methods.

2. Answer: A

   A is the correct answer because internal and external investors can be the stakeholders in your project, but they are not the key stakeholders.

   B, C, D, and **E** are incorrect because these are the key stakeholders. The CEO of your company is an influencer.

3. Answer: C

   C is the correct answer because the project charter, which is an output of a process of the initiating process group, must be approved before the project can start.

   A, B, and **D** are incorrect because these are not the outputs of the processes in the initiating process group.

4. Answer: A

   A is the correct answer because the project charter approval officially starts the project.

   B is incorrect because the project scope statement determines the scope of the project, whereas the project charter must be approved before you start the project.

   C is incorrect because there is no such document as the project initiation plan document.

   D is incorrect because the project management plan is produced in the planning stage of the project, and the project does not move to the planning stage until the project charter is approved.

5. Answer: D

   D is the correct answer because the perform quality control process is used to recommend corrective or preventive actions to meet quality standards.

   A is incorrect because testing is not a project management process.

   B is incorrect because quality planning is used to identify the quality standards relevant to the project and to determine how to satisfy them.

   C is incorrect because the risk response planning process is used during the planning stage for the identified risks, not during the control stage.

   E is incorrect because executing is not a process; it is a process group.

6. Answer: C

C is the correct answer because the two defining characteristics of a project are that it has a beginning and an end, and it creates a unique product, service, or results.

A, B, and **D** are incorrect because they exclude two defining characteristics of a project: It has a beginning and an end, and it creates a unique product, service, or results.

7. Answer: D

D is the correct answer because a program is a set of related projects that are managed in a coordinated way to obtain the optimal results.

A is incorrect because a large budget does not make a project a program.

B is incorrect because a set of processes is called a *process group*.

C is incorrect because the projects in a program should be related to each other.

8. Answer: A

A is the correct answer because the plan purchases and acquisitions and plan contracting processes are used to plan the procurement.

B and **C** are incorrect because neither of these is a correct name for any of the project management processes.

D is incorrect because the human resource planning process is used to plan the human resources in the performing organization; it is not part of procurement planning.

9. Answer: A

A is the correct answer because the next step after planning is to request seller responses.

B and **C** are incorrect because neither of these is a correct name for any of the project management processes.

D is incorrect because the select sellers process is performed after the request seller responses process.

10. Answer: D

D is the correct answer because the project manager has the highest level of authority in a projectized organization.

A is incorrect because the project manager has the lowest level of authority in a functional organization.

B is incorrect because project manager's authority in a strong matrix organization is not higher than that in a projectized organization.

C is incorrect because project manager's authority in a weak matrix organization is lower than that in a projectized organization.

11. Answer: A

A is the correct answer because the project manager has the lowest level of authority in a functional organization.

B is incorrect because project manager's authority in a strong matrix organization is higher than that in a functional organization.

C is incorrect because project manager's authority in a weak matrix organization is higher than that in a functional organization.

D is incorrect because the project manager has the highest level of authority in a projectized organization.

12. Answer: C

C is the correct answer because performance evaluations belong to the monitoring/controlling process group.

A and **B** are incorrect because performance evaluations belong to the monitoring/controlling process group.

D is incorrect because there is no project management process group named evaluating.

13. Answer: D

D is the correct answer because it is the project manager's responsibility to manage the project stakeholders' expectations.

A is incorrect because it is the project manager's responsibility to manage the project stakeholders' expectations.

B and **C** are incorrect because the differences about objectives (and conflicts among the team members) must be resolved. Different expectations for the project mean that the stakeholders are not on the same page about the project scope, and that can be damaging for the project.

14. Answer: B

B is the correct answer because the five process groups are initiating, planning, executing, monitoring and controlling, and closing. Note that monitoring and controlling is the name of one process group; it is also called *monitoring* or *controlling*.

A is incorrect because monitoring and controlling is one process group.

C and **D** are incorrect because scoping and testing are not valid names for the project management process groups.

15. Answer: A

A is the correct answer because the project charter must make the business' case to justify the project.

B is incorrect because the SOW is an input to the develop project charter process.

C is incorrect because the project scope statement is not part of the project charter.

D is incorrect because the scope of the project management plan is much wider than the project charter.

16. Answer: B

B is the correct answer because process groups usually involve overlapping activities. For example, you monitor and control the project at the same time as you are executing it.

A and **D** are incorrect because process groups are seldom either discrete or one-time events.

C is incorrect because the level of involvement for a given process group might be different for different phases of a project; it depends upon the needs.

E is incorrect because it's silly—the processes that will be executed from a process group are determined by the needs of the project.

17. Answer: C

C is the correct answer because reviewing the initiating processes at the beginning of each phase helps keep the project focused on the business need for which the project was started.

A is incorrect because it's the wrong reason for reviewing the initiating processes.

B is incorrect because one of the purposes of reviewing the initiating processes is to determine whether the project should continue. If the business needs have changed, either the project should be cancelled or its scope should be changed.

D is incorrect because reviewing the initiating process is not a waste of time; it is a very important task.

18. Answer: A

A is the correct answer because in functional organizations, the functional managers are the bosses who assign the work to the employees.

B is incorrect because employees do not report to the project managers in a functional organization.

C and **D** are incorrect because the project teams and project management teams do not make the work assignment decisions.

19. Answer: A

A is the correct answer because the initiating group is used to authorize a project or a phase of a project.

B is incorrect because there is no project management process group named phase initiating.

C and **D** are incorrect because the planning and executing process groups are not used to authorize a project.

20. Answer: B and F

B and **F** are the correct answers because the five project management process groups are initiating, planning, monitoring and controlling, executing, and closing.

A, C, D, E, and **G** are incorrect because these are the valid names for the project management process groups.

21. Answer: B and E

B and **E** are the correct answers because team management and outsource management are not valid names for the project management knowledge areas recognized by PMI.

A, C, D, F, and **G** are incorrect because these are valid names for the project management knowledge areas.

22. Answer: B

B is the correct answer because a Pareto diagram is used to prioritize defects by displaying the frequencies of their occurrences. It is a tool used in the perform quality control process.

A is incorrect because a control chart is used to determine whether an output variable is within the control limits. It is a tool used in the perform quality control process.

C is incorrect because the decision tree analysis is a technique used in the quantitative risk analysis to choose between alternative capital strategies, such as to build or upgrade.

D is incorrect because variance analysis is a technique used to measure the project performance by comparing the actual performance with the planned performance. The performance metrics are generally the schedule, scope, and cost. So, variance analysis can be used in cost control, scope control, and schedule control.

23. Answer: A

A is the correct answer because the quality planning process is part of the planning process group.

B and **C** are incorrect because identifying the quality standards and determining how to satisfy them is part of planning, not executing or controlling.

D is incorrect because there is no process group named quality planning process group.

24. Answer: D and E

D and **E** are the correct answers because there is no process named time estimating, and the human resource planning process belongs to the human resource management.

A, B, C, and **F** are incorrect because all these processes belong to time management.

25. Answer: D

D is the correct answer because variance analysis is a technique used to measure the project performance by comparing the actual performance to the planned performance in terms of scope, cost, and schedule. So, variance analysis can be used in cost control, scope control, and schedule control.

A is incorrect because a control chart is used to determine whether an output variable is within the control limits. It is a tool used in the perform quality control process.

B is incorrect answer because a Pareto diagram is used to prioritize defects by displaying the frequencies of their occurrences. It is a tool used in the perform quality control process.

C is incorrect because decision tree analysis is a technique used in the quantitative risk analysis to choose between alternative capital strategies, such as to build or upgrade.

26. Answer: B

B is the correct answer because the purpose of the schedule control process is to manage (monitor and control) the schedule changes and make sure the changes go through an approval system before implementation.

A is incorrect because schedule control does not mean no change.

C is incorrect because scope creep is an issue that belongs to scope control.

D is incorrect because the schedule control process is to control all schedule-related changes, not just those related to the activities on the critical path.

27. Answer: A

A is the correct answer because the scope is determined by the project scope statement, not by the project charter.

B, C, and **D** are incorrect answers because these are correct statements about project charter.

28. Answer: D

D is the correct answer because the preliminary scope statement is an output of the process called develop preliminary project scope statement.

A, **B**, and **C** are incorrect answers because these are all valid items to be included in the preliminary project scope statement.

29. Answer: B

B is the correct answer because the project scope statement, also called the *detailed project scope statement*, is the major output of the scope definition process.

A and **C** are incorrect because the project charter and the preliminary project statement are input items to the project definition process.

D is incorrect because you need to perform many other processes after the project definition process before you can develop the project schedule.

30. Answer: C

C is the correct answer because decision tree analysis is a technique used in the quantitative risk analysis to choose between alternative capital strategies, such as to build or upgrade.

A is incorrect because a control chart is used to determine whether an output variable is within the control limits. It is a tool used in the perform quality control process.

B is incorrect because a Pareto diagram is used to prioritize defects by displaying the frequencies of their occurrences. It is a tool used in the perform quality control process.

D is incorrect answer because variance analysis is a technique used to measure the project performance by comparing the actual performance to the planned performance in terms of scope, cost, and schedule. So, variance analysis can be used in cost control, scope control, and schedule control.

31. Answer: A

A is the correct answer because a constraint is a state of being restricted to a given course of action (or inaction). It limits the team's options. Hard deadlines and predefined budgets are examples of constraints.

B and **C** are incorrect because quality standards and activities on the critical path are not constraints.

D is incorrect because the possibility of a strike is a risk, not a constraint.

32. Answer: C

C is the correct answer because the project scope management plan is an output of the scope planning process, which does not take the WBS as an input.

A, **B**, and **D** are incorrect answers because all these are true statements about the project scope management plan.

33. Answer: A

A is the correct answer because the output of the scope planning process is the project scope management plan.

B is incorrect because the project scope management plan is only a part of the project management plan.

C and **D** are incorrect because the project scope management plan, the output of the scope planning, only describes how to define the scope and create the WBS.

34. Answer: D

D is the correct answer because the detailed project scope statement is an output of the scope definition process.

A, **B**, and **C** are incorrect because all these are the input items to the scope definition process.

35. Answer: B

B is the correct answer because the project scope statement is used to create the WBS, but it does not already contain the WBS.

A, **C**, and **D** are incorrect answers because these items are included in the project scope statement.

36. Answer: D

D is the correct answer because when you, the project manager, anticipate or see a potential problem, you should deal with it head on.

A is incorrect because this option ignores the problem. You should not sit and let the problem happen before you act.

B and **C** are incorrect answers because these options do not deal with the problem directly.

E is incorrect because you are not confronting the problem, you are simply accepting it.

37. Answer: B

B is the correct answer because the SOW is written by the buyer to describe the product to be procured.

A is incorrect because the SOW is not a contract.

C is incorrect because the SOW is only written for the activities or the products to be procured.

D is incorrect because the SOW is written by the buyer to describe the product to be procured.

38. Answer: A

    A is the correct answer because expert judgment, templates, forms, and standards are the tools used in the scope planning process.

    B and **C** are incorrect because product analysis and stakeholder analysis are the tools for the scope definition process used to develop the project scope statement.

    D is incorrect because the project charter is an input to the scope planning process, not a tool.

39. Answer: D

    D is the correct answer because the project charter is an input to the scope definition process, not a tool.

    A, B, and **C** are incorrect answers because expert judgment, product analysis, and stakeholder analysis are all tools for the project definition process.

40. Answer: A

    A is the correct answer because the work breakdown structure (WBS) is a deliverable-oriented hierarchical decomposition of the project work to be performed by the project team.

    B is incorrect because the hierarchy of resources is called the *resource breakdown structure* (RBS).

    C is incorrect because the hierarchy of risks is called the *risk breakdown structure* (RBS).

    D is incorrect because the organization structure is called the *organizational breakdown structure* (OBS).

41. Answer: A and B

    A and **B** are the correct answers because the WBS is a direct input to the activity definition process and the cost estimating process.

    C is incorrect because the scope definition process is used to develop the project scope statement, which is an input to the create WBS process.

    D and **E** are incorrect because the WBS is not a direct input to these processes.

42. Answer: C

    C is the correct answer because the WBS is created by decomposing the project deliverables into smaller components.

    A and **B** are incorrect because a Pareto chart is used in the perform quality control process, and analogous estimating is a technique used in cost estimating.

    D is incorrect because the bottom-up estimating technique is used in the activity resource estimating process.

43. Answer: A

A is the correct answer because the purpose of the variance analysis is to measure the deviation of the actual project performance from the planned baseline and determine the cause of this variance.

B, C, and **D** are incorrect because these are false statements about the variance analysis.

44. Answer: D

D is the correct answer because updates to cost estimates are an output of the cost control process.

A, B, and **C** are incorrect answers because these are all valid output items for the scope control process.

45. Answer: B

B is the correct answer because the create WBS process is part of the planning process group.

A and **C** are incorrect because the WBS is created by using the create WBS process, which is part of the planning process group.

D is incorrect because there is no process group named scoping.

46. Answer: C

C is the correct answer because the critical path results from sequencing of activities and their durations.

A, B, and **D** are incorrect answers because all these affect the activity duration.

47. Answer: C

C is the correct answer because crashing is the schedule compression technique that involves analyzing a number of alternatives and choosing the one that lets you get the maximum schedule compression for the minimum cost increase.

A is incorrect because fast tracking is the schedule compression technique that involves obtaining the schedule compression by executing activities (or phases) in parallel that would normally be executed in sequence.

B is incorrect because PDM (precedence diagramming method) is a technique to develop the network diagram; it's not a schedule compression technique.

D is incorrect because there is no schedule compression technique named critical path elimination.

48. Answer: D

D is the correct answer because the RBS is not an input to the project definition process.

A, B, and **C** are incorrect because the project scope statement, WBS, and project management plan are all input items to the activity definition process.

49. Answer: A

A is the correct answer because fast tracking is the schedule compression technique that involves obtaining the schedule compression by executing activities (or phases) in parallel that would normally be executed in sequence.

B is incorrect because PDM (precedence diagramming method) is a technique to develop the network diagram; it's not a schedule compression technique.

C is incorrect because crashing is the schedule compression technique that involves analyzing a number of alternatives and choosing the one that lets you get the maximum schedule compression for the minimum cost increase.

D is incorrect because there is no schedule compression technique named critical path elimination.

50. Answer: B

B is the correct answer because parametric estimating is a technique used in the activity duration estimating process.

A, C, and D are incorrect because parametric estimating is not used for these tasks (or processes).

51. Answer: B

B is the correct answer because a project schedule network diagram is an output item of the activity sequencing process.

A, C, and D are incorrect answers because all these are input items to the activity sequencing process.

52. Answer: C

C is the correct answer because the project scope management plan specifies how the proposed changes to the project will be managed.

A and B are incorrect because you should check the scope management plan first.

D and E are incorrect because these documents are not meant to contain the change management information.

53. Answer: D

D is the correct answer because the network diagrams are the output of the activity sequencing process.

A and B are incorrect because PDM (precedence diagramming method) and ADM (arrow diagramming method) are techniques used in the activity sequencing process.

C is incorrect because the WBS is an output of the create WBS process.

54. Answer: B

    B is the correct answer because once a change request is made, it is your responsibility to evaluate the impact of the change across the project.

    A, **C**, and **D** are incorrect because you are taking an action without investigating.

55. Answer: A

    A is the correct answer because the resource breakdown structure is an output of the resource estimating process.

    B is incorrect because the risk breakdown structure is not an output of the resource estimating process.

    C is incorrect because the WBS is an output of the create WBS process.

    D is incorrect because the activity list is an input item to the resource estimating process.

56. Answer: D

    D is the correct answer because the Delphi technique is an information-gathering technique used to solicit expert opinions anonymously by hiding the identities of the experts to prevent the domination of one expert.

    A, **B**, and **C** are incorrect because the Delphi technique is basically an information-gathering technique.

57. Answer: C

    C is the correct answer because all these processes belong to time management.

    A is incorrect because the monitor and control project work process belongs to integration management.

    B is incorrect because schedule compression is not a process.

    D is incorrect because the develop project team process belongs to human resource planning.

58. Answer: A

    A is the correct answer because this is the correct order of process execution.

    B is incorrect because the WBS is an input to the activity definition process, so the WBS must be created before performing the activity definition process.

    C is incorrect because resource requirements are an input to the activity duration estimating process, so the activity resource estimating process must be performed before the activity duration estimating process.

    D is incorrect because you need the resource requirements and the activity durations before you can develop the schedule.

59. Answer: B

B is the correct answer because the person or the team that will perform the work will have more realistic understanding of what is involved and how long it will take.

A is incorrect because the project manager might not know the technical details of the work involved. Of course, the project manager will facilitate the estimate and make sure it happens in a timely fashion.

C, D, and **E** are incorrect because the customer, senior management, and sponsor generally will not know the technical details of the work involved.

60. Answer: D

D is the correct answer because this is the wrong statement about the critical path.

A, B, and **C** are incorrect because these are the defining statements for the critical path.

61. Answer: B

B is the correct answer because the work breakdown structure (WBS) dictionary contains the description of each work package in the WBS.

A, C, and **D** are incorrect because these documents do not contain the work package descriptions.

62. Answer: C

C is the correct answer because the critical chain method adds duration buffers that are not work schedule activities to maintain focus on the planned activity durations.

A, B, and **D** are incorrect because these are not true statements about the critical chain method.

63. Answer: B

B is the correct answer because the three-point estimating technique determines the uncertainty on the activity duration, which is taken as the average of optimistic, most likely, and pessimistic values.

A is incorrect because the final value is the average value of the optimistic, most likely, and pessimistic values.

C and **D** are incorrect because these are the false statements about the three-point estimating technique.

64. Answer: D

D is the correct answer because analogous estimating is the duration estimating technique used to determine the duration of an activity based on the duration of a similar activity in a previous project.

A, B, and **C** are incorrect because these are the false statements about the analogous estimating technique.

65. Answer: B

B is the correct answer because the earned value technique, in its various forms, is used to measure the performance of a project.

A, C, and **D** are incorrect because these are the false statements about the earned value technique.

66. Answer: A

A is the correct answer because rolling wave planning is a technique used in the activity definition process to plan the project work at various levels of detail depending upon the availability of information.

B, C, and **D** are incorrect because these are false statements about the rolling wave planning technique.

67. Answer: B

B is the correct answer because parametric estimating uses historical values and other variables to estimate activity duration and cost.

A, C, and **D** are incorrect because these are the false statements about the parametric estimating technique.

68. Answer: A

A is the correct answer because the actual cost of the completed work is not required to calculate EV according to the following equation:

$$EV = BAC * (work\ completed) / (total\ work\ required)$$

B, C, and **D** are incorrect answers because each of these items is used in calculating EV.

69. Answer: C

C is the correct answer because the cost variance is calculated as the earned value minus the actual cost.

A, B, and **D** are incorrect because these are wrong representations of cost variance.

70. Answer: B

B is the correct answer because CPI is calculated as the ratio of the earned value and the actual cost of the performed work.

A, C, and **D** are incorrect because these are wrong representations of CPI.

71. Answer: A

A is the correct answer because the activity list is an input to a number of processes, including activity sequencing, activity resource estimating, activity duration estimating, and schedule development.

B is incorrect because the activity list is an output of activity definition.

C is incorrect because the WBS is an input to the activity definition process that generates the activity list.

D is incorrect because the activity list is not there yet when you are planning the scope.

72. Answer: C

C is the correct answer because

$$ETC = BAC - EV = 300 - 90 = 210$$

A, B, and D are incorrect because the formula for the given values does not provide these results.

73. Answer: B

B is the correct answer because

$$ETC = BAC - EV, \text{ and}$$
$$EAC = ETC + AC = 300 - 90 + 100 = 310$$

A, C, and D are incorrect because the formula for the given values does not provide these results.

74. Answer: D

D is the correct answer because:

Cost performance index (CPI) = EV / AC
From the given data, 1 / CPI = AC / EV = 0.83
Therefore AC = EV * 0.85 = 120 * 0.83 = 99.6

A, B, and C are incorrect because the formula for the given values does not provide these results.

75. Answer: A

A is the correct answer because the activity list is an input to schedule development, but it is not an input item to schedule control.

B, C, and D are incorrect answers because all these items are input to the schedule control process.

76. Answer: C

C is the correct answer because the term "float" is synonymous with the term "slack," which is the time by which you can delay an activity without affecting the early start date of the next activity in the sequence.

A, B, and **D** are incorrect because they do not mean the same in project management as the term float does.

77. Answer: D

D is the correct answer because the schedule development process uses the leads and lags technique to adjust when the successor activity should start relative to the finish date of the predecessor activity.

A, B, and **C** are incorrect because the leads and lags technique is irrelevant to these processes.

78. Answer: A

A is the correct answer because the project scope statement is a major input item to the quality planning process.

B and **C** are incorrect because quality checklists and quality metrics are the output of the quality planning process.

D is incorrect because cost of quality is a technique used in quality planning.

79. Answer: D

D is the correct answer because recommended preventive actions are usually the output of a control process, such as the quality control process.

A, B, and **C** are wrong answers because all of these are valid output items for the quality planning process.

80. Answer: B

B is the correct answer because you must have a quality management plan generated by the quality planning process before you perform any other quality process.

A is incorrect because quality definition is not a valid name for any process recognized by PMI.

C and **D** are incorrect because quality control and quality assurance need to be performed according to the quality management plan generated by the quality planning process.

81. Answer: C

C is the correct answer because a Pareto chart is a technique used in the quality control process.

A, B, and **D** are incorrect answers because these are all input items to the quality control process.

82. Answer: C

C is the correct answer because quality assurance is the process used to apply the planned quality activities and standards to ensure that the project employs all processes needed to meet the project requirements.

A and **B** are incorrect because quality control is used to monitor the results to determine whether they comply with the quality standards, and quality planning is used to determine which quality standards are relevant to the project and how to meet them.

D is incorrect because there is no PMI process called testing.

83. Answer: D

D is the correct answer because benchmarking is a technique for quality planning, not for quality control.

A, **B**, and **C** are incorrect answers because all these represent the techniques that can be used in quality control.

84. Answer: B

B is the correct answer because quality metrics is the output of the quality planning process, and you are performing the quality assurance process.

A, **C**, and **D** are incorrect answers because all these items are valid outputs of the quality assurance process.

85. Answer: C

C is the correct answer because a cause and effect diagram, also called an *Ishikawa diagram*, is a tool used in the perform quality control process to explore all the potential causes of a problem.

A and **B** are incorrect because an Ishikawa diagram is a tool used in the quality control process.

D is incorrect because auditing is a technique used in the QA process.

E is incorrect because inspection is another tool used in the quality control process.

86. Answer: D

D is the correct answer because the control chart is a technique used in quality control, not in risk management.

A, **B**, and **C** are incorrect answers because all these are characteristics of a control chart.

87. Answer: A and D

A and **D** are the correct answers because there is no such quality control tool as a regression diagram, and benchmarking is a tool used for quality planning.

B, **C**, **E**, and **F** are the incorrect answers because all these represent valid tools and techniques for quality control.

88. Answer: B

B is the correct answer because benchmarking is a quality planning technique that compares practices, products, or services of a project with those of some reference projects for the purpose of learning, improving, and creating the basis for measuring performance.

A, C, and **D** are incorrect because these are false statements about the benchmarking technique.

89. Answer: A

A is the correct answer because creating the WBS is necessary to understand and finalize the scope of the project and to determine the schedule activities.

B, C, and **D** are incorrect because creating the WBS is necessary to understand and finalize the scope of the project and to determine the schedule activities.

90. Answer: D

D is the correct answer because there is no PMI process called procurement quality planning.

A, B, and **C** are incorrect answers because all these processes belong to quality management.

91. Answer: B

B is the correct answer because the risk register is the only output of the risk identification process.

A is incorrect because the recommended corrective actions could be the output of the risk monitoring and control process, but not of the risk identification process.

C and **D** are incorrect because these are not the output items of the risk identification process.

92. Answer: D

D is the correct answer because there is no risk response strategy named audit.

A, B, and **C** are incorrect because avoid, transfer, and mitigate are the strategies to respond to negative risks (threats).

93. Answer: A

A is the correct answer because a good mitigation strategy is to take action early on to first reduce the probability of the risk happening, and then plan for reducing its impact if it does occur, rather than letting it occur and then trying to reduce the impact or repair the damage.

B, C, and **D** are incorrect answers because these are correct statements about mitigation.

94. Answer: B

B is the correct answer because the risk register is the output of the risk identification process.

A, C, and **D** are incorrect because all these items are input to the risk identification process.

95. Answer: A

A is the correct answer because the processes in risk management are risk management planning, risk identification, qualitative risk analysis, quantitative risk analysis, risk response planning, and risk monitoring and controlling.

B is incorrect because risk evaluation is not a risk management process.

C is incorrect because risk evaluation and risk mitigation are not risk management processes.

D is incorrect because risk transference and risk assessment are not risk management processes.

96. Answer: A

A is the correct answer because work packages, the components at the lowest levels of the WBS, are decomposed into activities. The activities eventually make it into the project schedule.

B, C, and **D** are incorrect because activities are derived from the work packages of the WBS.

97. Answer: D

D is the correct answer because risk response planning is used to develop options to maximize opportunities and minimize threats from the risks that have already been identified and analyzed.

A, B, and **C** are incorrect because the risks are identified and analyzed before you look at the options to enhance opportunities and reduce risks from them.

E is incorrect because the risk monitoring and control process is used to execute risk response plans rather than develop them.

98. Answer: B

B is the correct answer because recommended corrective actions are an output of the risk monitoring and control process but not of the risk response planning process.

A, C, and **D** are incorrect answers because these items are outputs of the risk response planning process.

99. Answer: B

B is the correct answer because an acceptance strategy is used to accept the risk—that is, either take no action or take action contingent upon a condition that might become true in the future.

A, C, and **D** are incorrect because these are false interpretations of the acceptance strategy.

100. Answer: C

C is the correct answer because performance reports are input to the risk monitoring and control process.

A, B, and **D** are incorrect answers because all these items are output of the risk monitoring and control process.

101. Answer: B

B is the correct answer because all the listed items are techniques that can be used in quantitative risk analysis.

A is incorrect because mitigation is a risk response planning strategy.

C is incorrect because checklist analysis is a technique used in the risk identification process.

D is incorrect because contingency is a risk response strategy.

102. Answer: B

B is the correct answer because risk response planning is performed in the risk response planning process.

A, C, and **D** are incorrect because these are valid output items that can be included in the risk management plan document.

103. Answer: B

B is the correct answer because the risks are prioritized in the qualitative risk analysis.

A, C, and **D** are incorrect because the probability and impact matrix is a technique used in the qualitative risk analysis.

104. Answer: C

C is the correct answer because risk audits are used in the risk monitoring and control process.

A, B, and **D** are incorrect because all these are tools and techniques for the qualitative risk analysis process that can be used to prioritize risks.

105. Answer: D

D is the correct answer because the WBS is not part of the risk register.

A, B, and **C** are incorrect answers because all these items are part of the risk register after the updates from the risk response planning process.

106. Answer: C

C is the correct and the best answer because the project plan is developed starting from the concept and going through progressive elaboration.

A and B are incorrect because A is the lifecycle and B includes the project lifecycle. Progressive elaboration does not include the lifecycle of the project; its goal is to plan the project. Because the project planning may develop (or change) throughout the project lifecycle, progressive elaboration may continue through the project lifecycle, but it does not include the work of the lifecycle.

D is incorrect because it is the technique to create the WBS.

107. Answer: B and D

B and D are correct because the project charter names the project manger and provides the project manager the authority to use organizational resources to run the project.

A is incorrect because the sponsor is not authorized by the project charter; the opposite might be true.

C is incorrect because it will be your responsibility to identify all the stakeholders.

E is incorrect because the project team is not formed in the initiation phase.

108. Answer: B

B is correct because the project assumptions should be included in the project charter.

A is incorrect because assumptions by definition represent uncertainty, and as a project manager, it is your responsibility to validate the assumptions at various stages of the project.

C is incorrect because it is not the correct definition of assumption.

D is incorrect because you can start the project with the assumptions. All you have to do is validate them at various stages of the project and analyze them as part of the risk management.

109. Answer: B

B is correct because the project charter is created in the initiation stage and it is an input item to creating the preliminary project scope statement.

A is incorrect because the project charter is input to the develop preliminary project scope process used to create the preliminary project scope statement.

C is incorrect because the WBS is created before schedule development, and the project charter is created before the WBS.

D is incorrect because the project scope statement is an input item into creating the WBS.

110. Answer: A

A is the correct answer because the project staff assignments are the output of the acquire project team process.

B, C, and **D** are incorrect because all these items are output of the human resource planning process.

111. Answer: B

B is the correct answer because the scope statement, the WBS document, and the WBS dictionary combined make the scope baseline against which all the change requests will be evaluated.

A, C, and **D** are incorrect because all these are true statements about the project scope management plan.

112. Answer: C

C is correct because, you, the project manager, create the WBS with help from the project team.

A is incorrect because the project manager creates the WBS with the help from the team.

B is incorrect because the project manager creates the WBS with the help from the team. The project sponsor can help as part of the team, however.

D and **E** are incorrect because neither the customer nor the upper management of the performing organization creates the WBS.

113. Answer: D

D is correct because benchmarking can be used in quality planning but not in human resource planning.

A, B, and **C** are incorrect answers because all these are tools and techniques that can be used in human resource planning.

114. Answer: A

A is the correct answer because a risk can have a negative or a positive effect on a project.

B, C, and **D** are incorrect answers because these are true statements about project risks.

115. Answer: C

C is the correct answer because there is no PMI process named train project team.

A, B, and **D** are incorrect answers because all these processes are part of the project human resource management.

116. Answer: C

C is the correct answer because decision tree analysis is the technique used in the quantitative risk analysis.

A, B, and **D** are incorrect answers because brainstorming, the Delphi technique, and SWOT analysis are the valid information-gathering techniques used for identifying risks.

117. Answer: C

C is correct because secondary risks are those risks that arise as a result of risk responses.

A is incorrect because a residual risk is a risk that remains after a response has been performed.

B is incorrect because depending upon the nature of the secondary risk, it can have any priority.

D and **E** are incorrect because the risk response will depend upon the analysis results of the risk.

118. Answer: A

A is the correct answer because an activity has external dependency when it relies on factors outside the project.

B is incorrect because an activity Y has a mandatory dependency on activity X when Y inherently depends on X.

C is incorrect because there is no such dependency called internal.

D is incorrect because we have an external dependency here.

E is incorrect because a finish-to-start relationship is not relevant to this dependency.

119. Answer: C

C is the correct answer because personal choices, such as lifestyles or political and religious beliefs, should not be considered during these assignments.

A, B, and **D** are incorrect answers because competency, availability, and salary requirements (cost) are valid factors to be considered for staff assignments.

120. Answer: D

D is the correct answer because conflict management is the technique used in the manage project team process.

A, B, and **C** are incorrect because the conflict management technique is not used in these processes.

121. Answer: C

C is the correct answer because co-location is the technique used in the develop project team process.

A, B, and **D** are incorrect because the conflict management technique is not used in these processes.

122. Answer: B

B is the correct answer because a bonus is not a tool available for project team management.

A, C, and **D** are incorrect answers because these are the tools available for the manage project team process.

123. Answer: B

B is the correct answer because a virtual team is a tool for the acquire project team process.

A, C, and **D** are incorrect answers because a virtual team is a tool for the acquire project team process.

124. Answer: C

C is the correct answer because the goal here is to develop a team that might consist of members with various levels of preparation and experience.

A, B, and **D** are incorrect answers because these are good characteristics for a sound reward strategy.

125. Answer: B

B is the correct answer because collaboration provides a win/win resolution.

A is incorrect because avoidance provides a lose/lose resolution.

C is incorrect because accommodation provides a lose/win resolution.

D is incorrect because compromise provides a lose-win/lose-win resolution, and both parties might look at it as a lose/lose resolution.

126. Answer: A

A is the correct answer because the main purpose of the activity definition process is to prepare the activity list and determine attributes for each activity.

B is incorrect because the WBS contains work packages, not activities.

C is incorrect because scope planning determines how the project scope will be defined, verified, and controlled, and how the WBS will be created.

D is incorrect because the activity list is an input to schedule development.

127. Answer: B

B is the correct answer because the main purpose of the risk identification process is to create the risk register, which contains a list of risks.

A is incorrect because there is no PMI process with the name risk definition.

C is incorrect because the risk management planning process determines how to plan and execute the risk management activities.

D is incorrect because risk response planning takes a list of risks (risk register) as input.

128. Answer: C

C is the correct answer because the quality audit is a technique for performing quality assurance.

A and **B** are incorrect because the quality audit is a technique for performing quality assurance.

D is incorrect because there is no such quality management process called quality inspection.

129. Answer: B

B is the correct answer because the each activity on the critical path has a zero float time, and therefore if an activity is delayed it will delay the entire project.

A, C, and **D** are incorrect because these are incorrect statements about the activities on the critical path.

130. Answer: A

A is the correct answer because the selected sellers list is an output of the select sellers process.

B, C, and **D** are incorrect because all these items are the output of the request seller responses process.

131. Answer: D

D is the correct answer because there is no PMI process named monitor and control procurement.

A, B, and **C** are incorrect answers because all these processes belong to procurement management.

132. Answer: C

C is the correct answer because there is no contract type named profit shared.

A, B, and **D** are incorrect answers because all these are valid contract types.

133. Answer: B

B is the correct answer because fixed price (or lump sum) is the most suitable contract type for a well-defined product.

A, C, and **D** are incorrect because the product to be procured is well-defined.

134. Answer: B

B is the correct answer because cost overrun is paid by the buyer, and the fee increases with the increase in cost as well.

A is incorrect because the firm fixed price presents risks to both buyer and seller because the fixed price might turn out to be above or below the actual cost.

C and **D** are incorrect because the fee in these cases does not rise with the rise of the actual cost.

E is incorrect because in a time and material contract, there could be a cost overrun to be paid by the buyer, but unlike a contract in the category of cost plus percentage of cost, there is no increasing fee attached to the increasing cost.

135. Answer: C

C is the correct answer because the procurement documents should be rigorous enough to ensure consistent responses from different sellers that can be fairly compared with one another, and flexible enough to allow the sellers to offer suggestions on better ways to satisfy the requirements.

A is incorrect because it does not allow the sellers to be creative on offering solutions.

B is incorrect because the documents must be rigid enough that each seller understands the requirements.

D is incorrect because the requirements are set by the buyer, not by the seller.

136. Answer: C

C is the correct answer because when managed properly, differences in opinion can lead to better decisions and increased productivity.

A, B, and **D** are incorrect answers because these are true statements related to conflict management.

137. Answer: A

A is the correct answer because this is not the recommended approach toward advertising. It is a useful tool that can be used in the request seller responses process.

B, C, and **D** are incorrect because all of these are true statements about advertising as a tool in the request seller responses process.

138. Answer: C

C is the correct answer because approved change requests are an output of the integrated change control process. Remember, execution is all about implementation.

A, B, and **D** are incorrect because all these items are outputs of the direct and manage project execution process.

139. Answer: B

B is the correct answer because the manage project team process belongs to the project human resource management.

A, C, and **D** are incorrect because all these processes are part of project integration management.

140. Answer: B

B is the correct answer because you might need to negotiate with functional managers to acquire project team members.

A, C, and **D** are incorrect because negotiation is not one of the tools used in these processes.

141. Answer: C

C is the correct answer because administrative closure must be performed at the end of a project or each phase of a project.

A, B, and **D** are incorrect because these are false statements about administrative closure.

142. Answer: C

C is the correct answer because releasing resources is part of the close project process.

A and **B** are incorrect because there are no PMI processes named resource release and administrative closure. Administrative closure is a procedure that is an output of the close project process.

D is incorrect because resources are released by using the close project process.

143. Answer: A

A is the correct answer because a Pareto diagram is a tool used in the perform quality control process to rank errors based on the frequency of occurrences.

B and **C** are incorrect because a Pareto diagram is a tool used in the quality control process.

D is incorrect because auditing is a technique used in the QA process.

E is incorrect because inspection is another tool used in the quality control process.

144. Answer: B

B is the correct answer because the formula for cost variance is:

EV = BAC * (work completed / total work required)

which means

EV = $600,000 (10 miles / 30 miles) = $200,000
CV = EV – AC

which means

CV = $200,000 – $150,000 = $50, 000

A, C, and **D** are incorrect because if the correct formula is applied, these results will not be achieved.

145. Answer: A

A is the correct answer because a CPI value greater than 1 means the cost performance of the project is better than planned, and an SPI value of greater than 1 means the schedule performance of the project is better than planned.

B, C, and **D** are incorrect because a CPI value greater than 1 means the cost performance of the project is better than planned, and an SPI value of greater than 1 means the schedule performance of the project is better than planned.

146. Answer: D

D is the correct answer because the close project process is part of project integration management.

A and **B** are incorrect because the close project process is part of project integration management.

C is incorrect because monitoring and controlling is a process group, not a knowledge area.

147. Answer: B

B is the correct answer because implementation of recommended actions can be the output of the direct and manage project execution process.

A, C, and **D** are incorrect because all these items are the output of the close project process.

148. Answer: C

C is the correct answer because the contract closure procedure is the output of the close project process, not the input.

A, B, and **D** are incorrect because all these items are valid input to the close project process.

149.   Answer: B

B is the correct answer because the risk probability and impact matrix is a tool for the qualitative risk analysis.

A, C, and **D** are incorrect because all these items are included in the risk register.

150.   Answer: C

C is the correct answer because dynamic programming is a mathematical model, not a benefit measurement method.

A, B, D, and **E** are incorrect because these are the valid project selection methods included in the category of benefit measurement methods.

151.   Answer: A

B is the correct answer because a project can have positive as well as negative stake-holders.

A, C, and **D** are incorrect because these are true statements.

152.   Answer: C

C is the correct answer because change requests are approved or rejected by processing them through the integrated change control process.

A is incorrect because there is no PMI process named change approval.

B and **D** are incorrect because schedule control and quality control can generate recommendations for actions and requests for changes, but those actions and changes must be approved through the change control process.

153.   Answer: A and B

A and **B** are the correct answers because the initiating process group contains two processes: develop project charter and develop preliminary project scope statement.

C and **D** are incorrect because project management and the project schedule are developed in the planning stage of the project.

154.   Answer: B

B is the correct answer because a project manager is assigned to the project in the project charter, which is an output of the processes in the initiating process group.

A and **C** are incorrect because a project cannot start until the project charter is approved and the project charter names the project manager.

D is incorrect because there is no such process group called staffing.

155. Answer: C

C is the correct answer because risk was discovered during execution and was not identified during planning.

A is incorrect because testing is not a project management process.

B is incorrect because risk was discovered during execution and was not identified during planning.

D is incorrect because quantitative risk analysis is performed during the planning stage.

E is incorrect because executing is not a process; it is a process group.

156. Answer: D

D is the correct answer because it is a wrong statement about a program. A program is a set of related projects that can produce independent products for different customers.

A, B, and C are incorrect answers because these are the characteristics of a program.

157. Answer: D

D is the correct answer because changes are implemented by using the direct and manage project execution process.

A, B, and C are incorrect answers because all these items are output of the integrated change control process.

158. Answer: B

B is the correct answer because after you have planned the procurement by using the plan purchases and acquisitions process and possibly also the plan contracting process, the next process will be request seller responses.

A is incorrect because you have just finished the plan purchases and acquisitions process.

C is incorrect because the select sellers process is performed after request seller responses.

D is incorrect because there is no project management process named request bidders.

159. Answer: D

D is the correct answer because it is the project manager's responsibility to manage the project stakeholders' expectations and keep them on the same page about the project objectives.

A is incorrect because it is the project manager's responsibility to manage the project stakeholders' expectations.

B and C are incorrect because the differences about objectives (and conflicts among the team members) must be resolved. Different expectations from the project mean that the stakeholders are not on the same page about the project scope, and that can be damaging to the project.

160.   Answer: B

B is the correct answer because it deals with the problem head-on with the intention of solving it.

A, C, and **D** are incorrect because by choosing any one of these options, you are not dealing with the problem directly and effectively.

161.   Answer: B

B is the correct answer because the first thing you should do about a change request is study its effects and process it through the change control process.

A, C, and **D** are incorrect answers because the change first must go through the change control process.

162.   Answer: D

D is the correct answer because there is no such method as project-oriented programming used for project selection.

A, B, C, and **E** are incorrect because these are the valid project selection methods included in the category of mathematical models. Another method included in this model is dynamic programming.

163.   Answer: C

C is the correct answer because the code of conduct clearly states that any situation that can be looked upon as conflict of interest should be disclosed.

A, B, and **D** are incorrect because you are not being upfront and open.

164.   Answer: C

C is the correct answer because your job is to understand and resolve the conflicts, not to create them.

A, B, D, and **E** are incorrect because these are true statements.

165.   Answer: C and F

C and **F** are the correct answers because these are not part of the PMP Code of Professional Conduct.

A, B, D, and **E** are all incorrect because these activities are included in the PMP Code of Professional Conduct.

166. Answer: A and B

A and **B** are the correct answers because the project charter and the preliminary project scope statement are the two documents produced by the two processes in the initiating process group.

C is incorrect because there is no such document called the project initiation plan document.

D and **E** are incorrect because the project management plan and project schedule are produced in the planning stage of the project.

167. Answer: A

A is the correct answer because if in a foreign land you are asked to do something that is unethical and illegal, you are supposed to investigate whether it is illegal and unethical there as well.

B and **D** are incorrect because you don't know yet whether the sponsor is asking you to do something illegal.

C is incorrect because you think it is unethical and illegal, so you must investigate it.

168. Answer: A and B

A and **B** are the correct answers because the initiating process group contains two processes: develop project charter and develop preliminary project scope statement.

C and **D** are incorrect because project management and the project schedule are developed in the planning stage of the project.

169. Answer: C

C is the correct answer because if the project sponsor has cancelled the project, it's the end of the story, but you still need to close the project using the close project process.

A, B, and **D** are incorrect because these are not the appropriate actions to take.

170. Answer: A

A is the correct answer because the purpose of the change control is to manage the changes, not necessarily oppose them.

B, C, and **D** are incorrect because all these are valid purposes of the integrated change control process.

171. Answer: C

C is the correct answer because once you have a list of activities, you can sequence them.

A is incorrect because there are a number of processes that must be performed after preparing the list of activities and before scheduling the activities.

B is incorrect because you must have a schedule before you can control it.

D is incorrect because you must have a WBS before you can create a list of activities.

172. Answer: A

A is the correct answer because qualitative risk analysis is performed before quantitative risk analysis, and planning is performed before executing.

B is incorrect because qualitative risk analysis is performed before quantitative risk analysis.

C is incorrect because planning is performed before executing.

D is incorrect because you must identify and analyze risks before you can control them.

173. Answer: C

C is the correct answer because you cannot control a schedule unless you have a schedule; it's common sense. (Remember Thomas Paine?)

A, B, D, and **E** are incorrect answers because all these processes need to be performed before you can develop the project schedule.

174. Answer: C

C is the correct answer because the baseline should only be changed due to the approved changes in the factors that define the baseline.

A, B, and **D** are incorrect because these are no reasons to change the baseline.

175. Answer: B

B is the correct answer because project management involves performing processes belonging to knowledge areas, and you use your experience and skills to perform those processes.

A is incorrect because this is not the defining characteristic of project management.

C is incorrect because project management is a discipline that exists independent of functional managers.

D is incorrect because the size of the project is not a criterion for using project management. Each project needs to be managed for efficient execution.

Glossary

acceptance. A risk response technique that allows you to accept the low-impact risks or only take action contingent upon a condition being true. Acceptance also refers to the product acceptance by the customer at the completion of the project.

acceptance criteria. Criteria, such as performance requirements and essential conditions, that must be met before project deliverables can be accepted.

activity. A component of work that is scheduled and performed for a project. Also called a *schedule activity.*

activity attributes. The attributes of an activity, such as the predecessor activity, the successor activity, and the activity code. Activity attributes for each activity are included in the activity list.

activity code. The identification for the activity.

activity definition. The process of identifying the specific schedule activities that need to be performed to produce the project deliverables.

activity duration estimating. The process of estimating the time in work periods individually for each schedule activity required for its completion. A work period is a measurement of time when the work is in progress; it is measured in hours, days, or months depending upon the size of the activity.

activity duration. The time measured in calendar units between the start and finish of a schedule activity.

activity resource estimating. The process of estimating the types and amounts of resources that will be required to perform each schedule activity.

activity sequencing. The process of identifying and documenting the dependencies among schedule activities.

activity list. An output of the activity definition process that includes the activities to be scheduled and performed for the project.

actual cost (AC). The total cost actually incurred until a specific point on the timescale in performing the work for a project or a project activity.

administrative closure. Part of the project closure that includes obtaining final acceptance for the project deliverables, analyzing the project's success or failure, gathering lessons learned, archiving project information, and releasing project resources.

administrative closure procedure. A procedure, developed during the close project process, used to carry out and coordinate the activities needed for the administrative closure.

alternatives identification. A technique used to apply nonstandard approaches, such as brainstorming and lateral thinking, to perform project work.

analogous estimating. A technique that is used to estimate the duration of an activity based on the duration of a similar activity in a previous project.

arrow diagramming method (ADM). A technique used to draw a project schedule network diagram in which an arrow represents an activity and also points to the successor activity through a junction represented by a node (box).

assumption. A factor that you consider to be true without any proof or verification. Assumptions can appear in both the input and the output of various processes.

assumptions analysis. A technique used to examine the validity of an assumption and thereby identify the risk resulting from the inaccuracy, inconsistency, or incompleteness of each assumption.

asynchronous communication. A communication in which the two communicating entities do not have to be present on both ends of the communication line at the same time. E-mail is an example of asynchronous communication because when the sender of the e-mail pushes the send button, the intended recipient of the e-mail message does not have to be logged on to the e-mail server.

baseline. A reference plan for components, such as schedule, scope, and cost, against which performance deviations are measured. The reference plan can be the original or the modified plan.

benchmarking. Benchmarking is comparing practices, products, or services of a project with those of some reference projects for the purposes of learning, improvement, and creating the basis for measuring performance.

bottom-up estimating. A technique that estimates the requirements for pieces and then aggregates them to estimate the requirements for the whole component of work.

brainstorming. A creative technique generally used in a group environment to gather ideas as candidates for a solution to a problem or an issue without any immediate evaluation of these ideas. The evaluation and analysis of these ideas happens later.

budget at completion (BAC). The total budget authorized for performing the project work. This is the planned budget for the project, the cost that you originally estimated for the project.

change control system. A collection of formal documented procedures that specifies how the project deliverables and documents will be changed, controlled, and approved.

change request. A request for a change in some component of a project, such as adding a new feature to the project product.

close project. A process used to finalize all activities across all of the process groups to formally close the project. It's also used to establish the procedures for administrative and contract closures.

confidence level. A statistical term that refers to the certainty attached to an estimate and is often represented in percentage form, such as a 95% confidence level.

configuration management. Refers to controlling the characteristics of a product, a service, or a result of a project. It includes documenting the features of a product or a service, controlling and documenting changes to the features, and providing support for auditing the products for conformance to requirements.

constraint. A restriction (or a limitation) that can affect the performance of the project. Assumptions can appear in both the input and the output of various processes.

contingency. A future event or condition that is possible but cannot be predicted with certainty. In this case, an action will be contingent upon the condition—that is, the action will be executed only if the condition happens.

contingency reserve. The amount of funds, time, or both needed in addition to the estimates in order to meet the organization's and stakeholders' risk tolerances and thresholds.

contract. A mutually binding agreement between a buyer and a seller that obligates the seller to provide the specified product, service, or result and obligates the buyer to make the payment for it.

contract closure. The process used to complete and settle each contract, which includes resolving any open item and closing each contract applicable to the project.

contract closure procedure. A procedure developed during the close project process, used to carry out and coordinate the activities needed for the contract closure.

control account. A level in the WBS at which the WBS components can be planned to a limited detail.

corrective actions. Directions for executing the project work to bring expected project performance in conformance with the project management plan. This is an output item of the QA process.

cost baseline. The planned budget for the project over a time period, used as a basis against which to monitor, control, and measure the cost performance of the project. The cost performance is measured by comparing the actual cost to the planned cost over a time period.

cost performance index (CPI). A measure of cost efficiency of a project calculated by dividing earned value (EV) by actual cost (AC).

cost variance (CV). A measure of cost performance obtained by subtracting actual value (AV) from earned value (EV). A positive result indicates good performance, whereas a negative result indicates bad performance.

crashing. A project schedule compression technique used to decrease the project duration with minimum additional cost. A number of alternatives are analyzed, including the assignment of additional resources.

critical path. The longest path (sequence of activities) in a project schedule network diagram. Because it is the longest path, it determines the duration of the project.

critical path method (CPM). A schedule network analysis technique used to identify the schedule flexibility and the critical path of the project schedule network diagram.

decision tree analysis. A technique that uses a decision tree diagram to choose from different options available; each option is represented by a branch of the tree. EMV analysis is done along each branch, which helps to make a decision about which option to choose.

decomposition. A planning technique to subdivide the project scope, including deliverables, into smaller, manageable tasks called work packages.

defect. An imperfection or deficiency that keeps a component from meeting its requirements or specifications. A defect is caused by an error (problem) and can be repaired by fixing the error.

deliverable. A unique and verifiable product, a capability to provide a service, or a result that must be produced to complete a project or a process or phase of the project.

Delphi technique. An information-gathering technique used for experts to reach a consensus while sharing their ideas and preferences anonymously.

earned value (EV) or budgeted cost of work performed (BCWP). The value of the actually performed work expressed in terms of the approved budget for a project or a project activity for a given time period.

enterprise environmental factors. The environmental factors internal or external to the performing organization that can influence the project's success, such as the organization's culture, infrastructure, existing skill set, market conditions, and project management software. These are input to both the project charter and the preliminary project scope statement.

estimate at completion (EAC). The estimate from the current point in time of how much it will cost to complete the project or a project activity. The value of EAC is obtained by adding the value of ETC to AC.

estimate to complete (ETC). The expected cost, estimated from CPI, to complete the remaining work for the project or for a project activity.

expected monetary value (EMV) analysis. A statistical technique used to calculate the expected outcome when there are multiple possible outcome values with probabilities assigned to them.

experiment design. A statistical method that can be used to identify the factors that can influence a set of specific variables of a product or a process under development or in production.

fast tracking. A project schedule compression technique used to decrease the project duration by performing project phases or some schedule activities within a phase simultaneously, when they would normally be performed in sequence.

float time. The positive difference between the late start date and the early start date of a schedule activity.

initiating process group. A process group that contains two processes: develop project charter and develop preliminary project scope statement.

inspection. A technique to examine whether an activity, component, product, service, or result conforms to specific requirements.

knowledge area. A knowledge area in project management is defined by its knowledge requirements related to managing a specific aspect of a project, such as cost, by using a set of processes. PMI recognizes a total of nine knowledge areas, such as cost management and human resource management.

lag. A technique to modify a dependency relationship by delaying the successor activity. For example, a lag of five days in a finish-to-start relationship means the successor activity cannot start until five days after the predecessor activity has ended.

lateral thinking. Thinking outside the box, beyond the realm of your experience, to search for new solutions and methods, rather than only better uses of the current solutions and methods.

lead. A technique to modify a dependency relationship by accelerating the successor activity. For example, a lead of five days in a finish-to-start relationship means the successor activity can start up until five days before the finish date of the predecessor activity.

logical relationship. A dependency between two project schedule activities or between a schedule activity and a schedule milestone.

methodology. A system of procedures and techniques practiced in a discipline to accomplish a task. For example, risk management methodology is used in the discipline of project management to determine how risk management processes will be performed.

milestone. A significant point (or event) in the life of a project.

mitigation. The process of taking actions to reduce or prevent the impact of a disaster that is expected to occur.

model. A set of rules to describe how something works, which takes input and makes predictions as output.

Monte Carlo simulation. An analysis technique that randomly generates values for uncertain elements (that is, variables) and takes them as input into a model to generate output. In other words, it simulates a model by feeding randomly selected input values.

organization. A group of individuals organized to work for some purpose or mission.

organizational process assets. The assets that can be used to perform the project successfully, such as templates, guidelines, knowledge base, and policies and procedures.

parametric estimating. A quantitative technique used to calculate the activity duration when the productivity rate of the resource performing the activity is available.

perform quality assurance. A process used for applying the planned systematic quality activities to ensure that the project employs all the planned processes needed to meet all the project requirements.

performance measurement baseline. An approved integrated plan for the project specifying some parameters to be included in the performance measurements, such as scope, schedule, and cost. The performance of the project is measured against this baseline. Some technical and quality parameters can also become part of this baseline.

performing organization. The organization that is performing the project.

planning component. A WBS component at the bottom level of a branch of WBS hierarchy for which some planning can be performed.

planning package. A WBS component that is below the level of a control account and above the level of a work package.

precedence diagramming method (PDM). A technique used to construct a project schedule network diagram in which a node (a box) represents an activity and an arrow represents the dependency relationship.

preliminary project scope statement. The document that specifies the project scope during the initiation stage.

preventive actions. Directions to perform an activity that will reduce the probability of negative consequences associated with project risks. These preventive actions are recommended by the QA process during process analysis.

process. A set of interrelated activities performed to obtain a specified set of products, results, or services.

process analysis. A technique used to identify the needed improvements in a process by following the steps outlined in the process improvement plan.

procurement. Refers to obtaining (purchasing or renting) products, services, or results from outside the project team to complete the project.

procurement management. An execution of a set of processes used to obtain the products, services, or results from outside the project team to complete the project.

product scope. Features and functions that characterize a product, service, or result to be delivered by the project.

program. A set of related projects managed in a coordinated fashion to improve the overall efficiency and effectiveness.

program management. The centralized coordinated management of a specific program to achieve its strategic goals, objectives, and benefits.

program management office (PMO). Program management office (or project management office) refers to an entity in an organization that is responsible for providing centralized coordinated management for programs—that is, projects in the organization.

project. A work effort made over a finite period of time, with a start and a finish, to create a unique product, service, or result. A process consists of three elements: input, tools and techniques, and output.

project calendar. A calendar of working days or shifts used to establish when a schedule activity can be performed. A calendar typically specifies holidays and weekends when a schedule activity cannot be performed.

project charter. A document issued by the project initiator or the project sponsor that, when signed by an appropriate person in the performing organization, authorizes the project by naming the project manager and specifying the authority level of the project manager.

project interfaces. The formal and informal boundaries and relationships among team members, departments, organizations, or functions. An example might be how the development department and the QA department interact with each other while working on the same project.

project management. Application of knowledge, skills, and tools and techniques to project activities in order to meet project objectives. You do this by performing some processes at various stages of the project.

Project Management Information System (PMIS). An information system that consists of tools used to store, integrate, and retrieve the outputs of the project management processes. This can be used to support all stages of the project from initiating to closing.

project management methodology. A method that an organization uses to execute the project management plan for a project. This methodology is built on top of the standard project management processes discussed in this book.

project schedule. A schedule that consists of planned dates for performing schedule activities and meeting schedule milestones.

project schedule network diagram. A schematic display of logical relationships among the project schedule activities. The time flow in these diagrams is from left to right.

project scope. The work that must be performed (and only that work) to deliver products, services, or results with specified features that were promised by the project. The project scope draws the boundaries around the project: what is included and what is not.

project scope creep. Changes applied to the project scope without going through the approval process, such as the integrated change control process.

project scope statement. A document that defines the scope of a project by stating what needs to be accomplished by the project.

project stakeholder. An individual or an organization that is positively or negatively affected by the project.

qualitative risk analysis. A process used to prioritize risks by estimating the probability of their occurrence and their impact on the project.

quality. The degree to which the set of characteristics inherent to the product or services offered by the project meet the project requirements.

quality assurance. The application of the planned systematic quality activities.

quality audit. A structured and independent review to determine whether project activities comply with the policies, processes, and procedures of the project and the performing organization. It verifies the implementation of approved change requests, corrective actions, defect repairs, and preventive actions.

quality baseline. A criterion that specifies the quality objectives for the project and thereby makes the basis for measuring and reporting the quality performance.

quality management plan. A management plan that describes how the project management team will implement the quality policy of the performing organization for the specific project.

quality metrics. An operational criterion that defines in specific terms what something (such as a characteristic or a feature) is and how the quality control process measures it.

quality planning. The process of identifying the quality standards relevant to the project at hand and determining how to satisfy these standards.

quality policy. Overall intentions and high-level direction of an organization with respect to quality, established by the management at executive level.

quantitative risk analysis. A process used to perform the numerical analysis to estimate the effect of each identified risk on the overall project objectives and deliverables.

residual risk. A risk that remains after the risk response has been performed.

resource breakdown structure. The resource breakdown structure (RBS) is a hierarchical structure of resource types required to complete the schedule activities of a project.

risk. An uncertain event or condition that, if it occurs, has a positive or negative effect on meeting the project objectives.

risk breakdown structure (RBS). A hierarchical structure that breaks down the identified risk categories into subcategories. In developing this structure, you will end up identifying various areas and causes of potential risks.

risk identification. A process used to identify the risks for a given project and record their characteristics in a document called the *risk register*.

risk management plan. A document that describes how risk management will be structured and performed for the project at hand. It becomes part of the project management plan.

risk management planning. A process used to determine how to approach, plan, and execute risk management activities for a given project. This process produces the risk management plan.

risk register. A document that contains the results of risk analysis and risk response planning.

risk trigger. An alert that indicates a risk event has occurred or is about to occur.

role. A defined function that contains a set of responsibilities to be performed by a team member, such as a programmer or a tester.

rolling wave planning. A technique used to plan the project work at various levels of detail, depending upon the availability of information. Work to be performed in the near future is planned at the low level of the WBS, whereas work to be performed far into the future is planned at a relatively high level of the WBS.

schedule activity. A scheduled task (component of work) performed during the lifecycle of a project.

schedule baseline. A specific version of the project schedule developed from the schedule network analysis and the schedule model data. This is the approved version of the schedule with a start date and an end date, and it is used as a basis against which the project schedule performance is measured.

schedule development. The process of creating the project schedule by analyzing schedule activity sequences, schedule activity durations, resource requirements, and schedule constraints.

schedule milestone. A significant event in the project schedule, such as the completion of a major deliverable.

schedule network analysis. A technique used to generate a project schedule by identifying the early and late start and finish dates for the project.

schedule performance index (SPI). A measure of the schedule efficiency of a project calculated by dividing earned value (EV) by planned value (PV).

schedule revision. An update to the project schedule that includes changing the project start date, end date, or both.

scope baseline. The approved project scope, which includes the approved project scope statement, the WBS based on the approved project scope statement, and the corresponding WBS dictionary.

scope definition. The process used to develop the detailed project scope statement.

scope planning. The process of developing the project scope management plan.

secondary risk. A risk that arises as a result of implementing a risk response.

simulation. Any analytical method used to imitate a real-life system.

statement of work (SOW). A document that describes the products or services to be delivered by the project. It is an input to developing the project charter and the preliminary project scope statement.

strengths, weaknesses, opportunities, and threats (SWOT) analysis. A technique used to gather information for risk identification by examining a given project from the perspectives of its strengths, weaknesses, opportunities, and threats.

subprojects. Parts of the main projects that are independent enough that each can be performed by separate project teams.

triple constraints. Refers to cost, scope, and time: If one of these three changes, at least one of the other two must change.

variance. A measurable deviation in the value of a project variable, such as cost from a known baseline or expected value.

variance analysis. A technique used to assess the magnitude of variation in the value of a variable (such as cost from the baseline or expected value), determine the cause of the variance, and decide whether a corrective action is required.

virtual team. A team of members working on the same project with few or no face-to-face meetings. Various technologies, such as e-mail, video conferencing, and the World Wide Web, are used to facilitate communication among team members.

war room. A conference room used for project team meetings.

work breakdown structure (WBS). A deliverable-oriented hierarchical decomposition of the work that must be performed to accomplish the objectives and create the deliverables of the project.

work package. A deliverable or a task at the lowest level of each branch of the WBS.

workaround. A response to a negative risk that has occurred. A workaround is based on a quick solution and is not planned in advance of the risk occurrence event.

Index

A

acceptance
  on closing, 249
  of risk, 100
  scope statement including criteria, 58
**accommodation and conflict management,
  175–176**
activities, 114. *See also* **activity definition;
  activity duration estimating; activity
  lists; activity resource estimating;
  activity sequencing**
  attributes, 119
  definition, 11
  dependency determination and, 121–123
  predecessor/successor relationship between,
    121
  schedule control process and, 223
  team-building activities, 169–170
  and time management, 11–12
activity definition, 116–120
  output of, 119–120
  process, 116
  tools and techniques for, 117–119
**activity duration estimating, 127–131,
  128–129**
  input to, 128–130
  output of, 131
  process, 128
  tools and techniques for, 130–131
activity lists, 119
  and activity duration estimating, 128
  and activity resource estimating, 125

activity resource estimating
  input to, 125–126
  output of, 127
  process, 125
  tools and techniques for, 126
activity sequencing, 11, 120–124
  dependency determination in, 121–123
  network diagrams for, 122–124
  output of, 124
  process, 120
  tools and techniques for, 121–124
actual cost (AC), 227
actual cost of work performed (ACWP), 227
adjourning, 171
administrative closure, 245–246
  output of, 249
advertising, 189
agenda for team kickoff meeting, 170
alternative analysis
  in activity resource estimating, 126
  in scope definition, 56
analogous estimating, 130
approval requirements
  and integrated change control, 209
  scope statement including, 58
archiving files on closing, 249
**arrow diagramming method (ADM),
  122–124**
assumptions
  in charters, 39
  in preliminary project scope statement, 41
  in risk identification, 84
  in risk management planning, 79
  in scope statement, 57

R